ETHICS AND SPIRITUALITY

Readings in Moral Theology No. 17

D1599817

Previous volumes in this series

Readings in Moral Theology No. 1:
Moral Norms and Catholic Tradition (out of print)

Readings in Moral Theology No. 2:
The Distinctiveness of Christian Ethics (out of print)

Readings in Moral Theology No. 3:
The Magisterium and Morality (out of print)

Readings in Moral Theology No. 4:
The Use of Scripture in Moral Theology (out of print)

Readings in Moral Theology No. 5:
Official Catholic Social Teaching (out of print)

Readings in Moral Theology No. 6:
Dissent in the Church

Readings in Moral Theology No. 7:
Natural Law and Theology

Readings in Moral Theology No. 8:
Dialogue about Catholic Social Teaching (out of print)

Readings in Moral Theology No. 9:
Feminist Ethics and the Catholic Moral Tradition

Readings in Moral Theology No. 10:
John Paul II and Moral Theology

Readings in Moral Theology No. 11:
The Historical Development of Fundamental Moral Theology
in the United States

Readings in Moral Theology No. 12:
The Catholic Church, Morality and Politics

Readings in Moral Theology No. 13:
Change in Official Catholic Moral Teachings

Readings in Moral Theology No. 14:
Conscience

Readings in Moral Theology No. 15:
Marriage

Readings in Moral Theology No. 16:
Virtue

ETHICS AND SPIRITUALITY

Readings in Moral Theology No. 17

Edited by
Charles E. Curran
and
Lisa A. Fullam

PAULIST PRESS
New York • Mahwah, NJ

In memory of
Bernard Häring (1912–1998)
who pioneered the effort to bring
ethics and spirituality closer together.

The Scripture quotations contained herein are from the New Revised Standard Version: Catholic Edition, Copyright © 1989 and 1993, by the Division of Christian Education of the National Council of the Churches of Christ in the United States of America. Used by permission. All rights reserved.

See pages xi–xii for acknowledgments and permissions to reprint previously published material.

Cover design by Lynn Else

Library of Congress Cataloging-in-Publication Data
    Ethics and spirituality / edited by Charles E. Curran and Lisa A. Fullam.
        pages cm. — (Readings in moral theology ; No. 17)
    ISBN 978-0-8091-4873-8 (alk. paper) — ISBN 978-1-58768-362-6
    1. Christian ethics—Catholic authors. 2. Spirituality—Catholic Church. 3. Religion and ethics. I. Curran, Charles E., editor of compilation.
    BJ1249.E84 2014
    241`.042—dc23
                                                                        2014001300

ISBN 978-0-8091-4873-8 (paperback)
ISBN 978-1-58768-362-6 (e-book)

Published by Paulist Press Press
997 Macarthur Boulevard
Mahwah, New Jersey 07430

www.paulistpress.com

Printed and bound in the
United States of America

Contents

PART THREE: REFOCUSING ETHICAL TOPICS

Foreword

Ethics and Spirituality is volume 17 in the series *Readings in Moral Theology* from Paulist Press. Richard A. McCormick, SJ, and Charles E. Curran began editing this series in 1979. Lisa A. Fullam joins Curran as coeditor of this volume.

This series brings together previously published articles dealing with a common theme. Minimal editing has occasionally been done to adapt the articles for this volume. Three criteria ground the selection of essays. First, we attempt to cover enough of the salient aspects of the topic for readers to gain a fairly complete understanding of the more current literature. Second, as always in this series, we attempt to give a fair and objective picture of what is happening in Catholic moral theology by including a range of pertinent perspectives, including those of conservatives and liberals, senior and younger scholars, women and men. Third, we attempt to include the most significant voices on this issue, either by using their own work or by including more recent work influenced by those more foundational figures.

The call for the reintegration of spirituality with ethics arose fairly recently in Catholic moral theology. The beginning of the shift in moral theology from a rule-based system to a more holistic model of Christian discipleship arose with the turn to scripture and ascetical theology in the mid-twentieth century. This turn to discipleship may be seen in Fritz Tillman's *The Master Calls* (*Der Meister ruft*, 1937), in which the first principle he lists for moral theology is the following of Jesus. Bernard Häring's groundbreaking text *The Law of Christ*, first published in German in 1954, defined moral life as the imitation of Christ, with its motive being love, not merely law. Vatican II (where Häring served as a *peritus*) invited Catholics to reimagine morality in terms of a scripturally informed, spiritual, and practical engagement with the modern world, guided by the promptings of a well-formed conscience. The Council defined conscience not as a simple capacity or process of rationality, but as our "most secret core and sanctuary,...[where we are] with God,

vii

whose voice echoes in [our] depths" (*Gaudium et Spes*, 16). Häring's influence on moral theology may be felt throughout this volume.

As for spirituality (sometimes called spiritual theology), its emergence as a distinct academic discipline dates only to the later twentieth century. Walter Principe distinguishes three levels of spirituality: the real or existential level, the level of formulations of teachings about those existential realities (as in particular spiritual traditions like Franciscan or Ignatian spirituality), and the study by scholars of the first and second levels. The older tradition of spiritual theology (usually divided into ascetical and mystical theology) focuses on the practices of faith and the perfection of Christian life, and is generally limited to the first and second of Principe's levels.[1]

As a distinct academic discipline, spirituality engages all three of Principe's levels in a way that is deliberately interdisciplinary or multidisciplinary, transcultural, and multireligious. In its Christian form, study of spirituality may be in dialogue with such traditional theological disciplines as scripture and systematic theology, but it also tends to forge connections with psychology, sociology, aesthetics, literature, and other areas of academic interest. Spirituality emphasizes reflection on experience and so relies on a historical-contextual approach to its subject. As spirituality takes its place in the academy, in part by asserting its broad humanistic interdisciplinarity, and moral theology emerges from its fixation on sin to address broader questions of human formation and Christian discipleship, the need for the two disciplines to be in dialogue is clear.

This volume comprises three sections, each of which can be seen as a stage in the dialogue between ethics and spirituality. In each of the sections, the editors have had to select what we regard as representative; we invite readers to see this collection as an introduction to a literature, not a comprehensive collection. Further, there are developing discussions of spiritualities in various fields that may come to be seen as also touching on ethics. For example, there are nascent literatures of a spirituality of business, a spirituality of sports, and so on, any of which could be the subject of a volume of its own. But these tend to neglect the direct connection to ethical themes or questions that we sought in selecting these essays.

Part 1, "Reconnecting Ethics and Spirituality," traces the question of the nature of the two disciplines, their historical divergence, and the need, the challenges, and possible modalities for their rejoining. Mark O'Keefe traces the long view historical development of the disciplines and lays out five broad suggestions for the future. Norbert J. Rigali details the limitations of pre–Vatican II moral theology and notes the directions forward for renewed morals in the wake of the Council. Richard M. Gula provides a practical, pastoral definition of each discipline, and the late William C. Spohn surveys the important voices especially in ecospirituality and Christian pacifism, concluding that the project of uniting spirituality and ethics might be easier in more philosophical and universalistic ethical milieus. Concluding part 1, Curran shows how the conciliar call to holiness lived out in daily life requires a reexamination of how Catholics understand sanctity, holiness, and the role of priests in the Catholic community.

Part 2, "Reimagining the Tradition," shows how a more integrated ethics and spirituality reshape traditional concepts. James F. Keenan outlines ten points of confluence between Ignatian spirituality and virtue ethics. Enda McDonagh explores the "inner connections" between our response to the human other in moral life and to the ultimate Other in prayer. James Keating focuses on prayer in the work of Karl Rahner and the ways in which prayer liberates the one who prays to perceive moral truth more clearly. Donna L. Orsuto leads us to reconsider saints as exemplifying "what the moral life is....It finds its meaning in a loving relationship with Christ, a relationship which shapes one's actions." Concluding this section, Kenneth R. Himes looks at conscience: if we understand conscience in Vatican II terms, then the task of formation of conscience becomes an essentially spiritual one, a matter of formation rather than information.

Part 3, "Refocusing Ethical Topics," looks at ways in which particular ethical issues and categories are renewed by integrating spirituality. Walter J. Burghardt considers spirituality and justice: an engagement with justice in Scripture invites not just rational reflection but "fire in the belly," a matter of conversion shaped in community with God, people, and the earth. Mary Frohlich approaches ecological ethics as a spiritual matter, inviting us "to have the courage to ground our critical thinking in a deep contemplative consciousness" rooted in the life of the Earth. Colleen M. Griffith addresses bodiliness as the location of our spirituality against hierarchical dualisms of soul over body or understandings of bodiliness that are negative or (at best) ambiguous. Her purpose is to reimagine liturgy as an opportunity to delight in our bodily selves as God's gift. Ada María Isasi-Díaz looks at the concept of the common good. Beginning with an assertion that "spirituality and ethics are two sides of the same coin, different ways of looking at how we live, "she reminds us that in times of struggle, our ethical obligation to the common good is at the same time an invitation to rekindle our baptismal calling to holiness. Finally, Fullam unpacks the ways in which a virtue ethics of spiritual guidance leads to a greater appreciation for spirituality as an integral aspect of ministerial ethics.

The editors want to thank all the people whose assiduous work enabled us to produce this volume. First, we thank the authors whose work we have used, and the publications in which these essays first appeared. We are most grateful to Paulist Press for its willingness to sponsor and publish this series. Fr. Mark-David Janus, CSP, has been most encouraging in keeping this series going. Our editor, Nancy de Flon, has once again made us the beneficiaries of her efficient and helpful editing. We are also grateful to our editorial assistants who did much of the fine and labor-intensive work of copyediting and reformatting these essays. Ann Woods, doctoral student in Ethics and Social Theory at the Graduate Theological Union in Berkeley, CA, put her past editorial experience to good use in the service of this volume. Chris Dowdy, doctoral student at Southern Methodist University, has used his considerable computer skills to help prepare the manuscript for publication. Finally, we are grateful to Santa Clara University for a faculty grant supporting various editorial costs for this volume. Without this grant, this volume would have been greatly limited in scope.

Charles E. Curran and Lisa A. Fullam

Note

1. The terminology is still somewhat in flux. Bernard McGinn notes some thirty-five different definitions of *spirituality* and *spiritual theology*, the latter tending more to emphasize the connections of Christian spiritual life to dogmatic/systematic theology. Bernard McGinn, "The Letter and the Spirit: Spirituality as an Academic Discipline," in *Minding the Spirit: The Study of Christian Spirituality*, ed. Elizabeth A. Dreyer and Mark S. Burroughs (Baltimore: Johns Hopkins University Press, 2005), 29. Sandra Schneiders defines *spirituality* as "the experience of conscious involvement in the project of life-integration through self-transcendence toward the ultimate value one perceives," which for Christians is the triune God revealed in Jesus Christ. Sandra Schneiders, "The Study of Christian Spirituality: Contours and Dynamics of a Discipline," in *Minding the Spirit: The Study of Christian Spirituality*, 6.

Acknowledgments

We are most grateful to the following authors and publishers for permission to reprint the articles in this volume. Mark O'Keefe, *Becoming Good, Becoming Holy: On the Relationship of Christian Ethics and Spirituality* (New York: Paulist Press, 1995). © 1995 by Paulist Press. Reprinted with permission. Norbert Rigali, "On Theology of the Christian Life," in *Moral Theology: New Directions in Fundamental Issues: Festschrift for James P. Hanigan*, ed. James Keating (New York: Paulist Press, 2004), 3–23. © 2004 by Paulist Press. Reprinted with permission. Richard M. Gula, "Spirituality and Morality: What Are We Talking About?," in *The Call to Holiness: Embracing a Fully Christian Life* (New York: Paulist Press, 2003), 11–39. © 2003 by Paulist Press. Reprinted with permission. William C. Spohn, "Spirituality and Ethics: Exploring the Connections," *Theological Studies* 58 (1997): 109–23. © 1997 by Theological Studies. Reprinted with permission. Charles E. Curran, "How Vatican II Brought Spiritual Theology and Moral Theology Together," "Foreword" in William Shannon, *Silence on Fire: Prayer of Awareness* (New York: Crossroad, 2000), xi–xviii. © 2000 by Crossroad Publishing. Reprinted with permission. James F. Keenan, "Catholic Moral Theology, Ignatian Spirituality, and Virtue Ethics: Strange Bedfellows," in *The Way Supplement* 88 (Spring 1997): 36–45. ©1997 by The Way (*www.theway.org.uk*). Enda McDonagh, "Morality and Prayer," in *Doing the Truth* (Dublin: Gill & Macmillan, 1979), 40–56. © 1979 by Gill and Macmillan. Reprinted with permission. James Keating, "Prayer and Ethics in the Thought of Karl Rahner," *Studies in Spirituality* 7 (1997): 163–77. © 1997 by Peeters Publishers. Reprinted with permission of the author and publisher. Donna L. Orsuto, "The Saint as Moral Paradigm," in *Spirituality and Morality: Integrating Prayer and Action*, ed. Dennis Billy and Donna L. Orsuto (New York: Paulist Press, 1996), 127–39. © 1996 by Paulist Press. Reprinted with permission. Kenneth Himes, "The Formation of Conscience: The Sin of Sloth and the Significance of Spirituality," in *Spirituality and Moral Theology*, ed. James Keating (New York: Paulist

Press, 2000), 59–80. © 2000 by Paulist Press. Reprinted with permission. Walter J. Burghardt, "Spirituality and Justice," "A Spirituality for Justice," in *Handbook of Spirituality for Ministers*, vol. 2, ed. Robert Wicks (New York: Paulist Press, 2000) 527–45. © 2000 by Paulist Press. Reprinted with permission. Mary Frohlich, "Spirituality and Ecology," "Under the Sign of Jonah: Studying Spirituality in a Time of Ecosystemic Crisis," *Spiritus* 9 (Spring 2009): 27–45. © 2009 by The Johns Hopkins University Press. Reprinted with permission. Colleen M. Griffith, "Spirituality and the Body," in *Bodies of Worship: Explorations in Theory and Practice*, ed. Bruce T. Morrill (Collegeville, MN: Liturgical, 1999), 67–83. © 1999 by Liturgical Press. Reprinted with permission. Ada María Isasi-Díaz, "Spirituality and the Common Good," "To Be Fully Alive Is to Work for the Common Good," *Church & Society* 89 (September/October 1998): 11–18. © 1998. Reprinted courtesy of the Presbyterian Church (U.S.A.), copyright holder for *Church & Society* magazine. Digital copies of *Church & Society* articles may also be obtained through the journal's successor, *www.justice Unbound.org*, and the American Theological Library Association. Lisa Fullam, "Spirituality and Ministerial Ethics," "Ethics of Spiritual Guidance," in *Reflective Practice: Formation and Supervision in Ministry* 30 (2010): 83–96. © 2010 by *Reflective Practice: Formation and Supervision in Ministry*, an independent open access journal serving the disciplines engaged in forming and supervising future religious leaders. Reprinted with permission.

Part One

RECONNECTING
ETHICS AND SPIRITUALITY

1. Ethics and Spirituality: Past, Present, Future

Mark O'Keefe

This chapter first appeared in Mark O'Keefe, *Becoming Good, Becoming Holy: On the Relationship of Christian Ethics and Spirituality* (New York: Paulist, 1995).

Although we commonly distinguish between a Christian moral life and a Christian spiritual life, in the daily existence of Christian men and women these "lives" are, of course, one. There is no "moral life" separate from a "spiritual life." In the actual living of the Christian life, efforts to avoid sin, to grow in prayer, to make good moral decisions, and to grow in virtue are intimately intertwined. As lived experience shows and as the collective moral and spiritual wisdom of the Christian community has made clear, there can be no stable victory over serious sin in our lives without the assistance of grace encountered in prayer, both private and communal. Similarly, there can be no sustained growth in a habit and disposition of prayer without the overcoming of serious sin and a growth in good moral living.

Because of the interconnectedness of moral and spiritual striving in the daily experience of the Christian life, one might expect that the disciplines of Catholic moral theology and of Christian spirituality would also be closely interrelated. One might expect that, in their efforts to aid the growth of an authentic Christian existence, the two disciplines would be marked by mutual interchange. Such is not the case—at least not in a sustained and systematic way.

It is clear that moral theology and spirituality are distinct and separate disciplines with distinct objects of study and methodologies. There is no reason to suggest an attempt to return to some earlier unity of the two disciplines. In any case, anyone who attempts to keep up with the current literature in either discipline will quickly see that any attempt at such a reduction would be quite impossible. Still, it is important to recognize that the two disciplines are necessarily related in any authentic reflection on the lived experience of Christians and the traditional wisdom of those Christians who have advanced in the way of moral goodness and spiritual maturity.

This chapter suggests that the disciplines of moral theology and spirituality must ground their future development in explicit interaction with one another. Failure to attend to their relationship will cut them off from their own traditions and fail to provide the most authentic guidance to holistic growth in Christian living. The present study examines the historical relationship of the two disciplines up to their current state, in an effort to identify useful insights from the past and to suggest some ongoing challenges for the future. While certain insights of earlier periods might be profitably recovered in contemporary form, other past developments might better be avoided if contemporary moral theology and spirituality are to foster authentic growth in the one Christian life. The study will offer some modest suggestions for the ongoing development of both disciplines. The present chapter, then, should provide a context for the topics to be discussed in subsequent chapters.

A HISTORICAL OVERVIEW

Donal Dorr has suggested that a well-known verse from the prophet Micah (6:8) provides a basis for a balanced spirituality: "This is what the Lord asks of you, only this: that you act justly, that you love tenderly, that you walk humbly with your God."[1] In fact, the threefold directive seems to capture quite well the interconnection of moral and spiritual action—working to establish right relationships with God and with other persons, loving in action and from the heart, forming a spirit always open to God's promptings. Moreover, this interconnection seems entirely in line with the theme of covenant that marks so much of the Old

Testament. The covenant between God and Israel involves the commitment of the whole people to God in worship and in moral living. When
the prophets call the people back to covenant fidelity, it is a call both to
right worship and to right living.[2]

In the Synoptic Gospels, the call to discipleship involves a similar
challenge to an all-inclusive following after Jesus—even to the denial of
self after the pattern of the cross (Mark 8:34). For the true disciple of
Jesus there is no separation between prayer and action, between surren-
dering to the Father's will in prayer and in active service of one another.
After the model of Jesus, the disciple conforms his or her life to the radical demands of God's reign in every aspect of daily existence. Through
Christ, the disciple enters into a radically new relationship with God and
with God's coming reign—a newness to be reflected in the totality of the
disciple's life.

The Pauline literature likewise suggests both the challenge of a
total life-commitment to the Christian way of life and the absence of any
separation between moral and spiritual striving. For St. Paul, Christian
life is a "being" in Christ (1 Cor 1:30), a dying and rising with Christ
(Rom 6:2–11). Being baptized into Christ makes one a radically new
creation—with the implied but nonetheless clear expectation that *every*
aspect of the Christian's life will be transformed. The goal of Christian
striving would be a transformation in Christ which would allow every
Christian to say with St. Paul: "It is no longer I who live, but it is Christ
who lives in me" (Gal 2:20). From a Pauline perspective, then, there is
no conceivable separation between prayer/worship and moral striving.

The Johannine emphasis on the unity of love of God and of neighbor also suggests a unity of moral and spiritual striving. Anyone who
claims to love God but hates one's brother or sister is quite simply a liar
(1 John 4:20). One cannot claim, then, to have an authentically Christian
spiritual life—a loving relationship with the God who is love—without
a moral life grounded in love of brother and sister. One could never separate growth in loving prayer from the loving actions and relationships
of one's daily life.

Nourished by reflection on the Scriptures, and in the effort to
address the demands of Christian living, the theology of the patristic
period—and thus its spirituality—was utterly christocentric. Christ was
understood to be "the measure, the model, and the goal of the spiritual

life."[3] The whole of the believer's life was made possible by salvation in Christ, nurtured and rooted in the liturgy, and aimed at conformity and union with Christ. In this christocentric perspective—in line with the Synoptic emphasis on discipleship and the Pauline focus on "being" in Christ—there could be no separation between one's moral striving and one's life of prayer and worship.

From the patristic period comes the effort to identify and analyze stages or levels in the Christian life. Although various patristic and medieval theologians identified diverse numbers of stages—from two stages (Evagrius' distinction between the practical life and gnosis) to thirty such stages (St. John Climacus' degrees)—gradually the identification of these stages came to be identified as the Three Ways. The Ways could be identified as beginner, proficient, and perfect (following Origen and Evagrius Ponticus) or as purgative, illuminative, and unitive (following Pseudo-Dionysius). By the late medieval period these two sets of terms became virtually interchangeable. In any case, however many stages were identified or whatever names were given to them, two common elements appear in each of the designations: a sense of growth or progression in the Christian life and an essential connection between spiritual and moral growth in every authentic Christian life.

In St. Thomas' *Summa Theologiae*, we see the unity of the theological enterprise at its height, before its division into the specializations of dogmatic and moral theology (the latter including spiritual theology within its scope). What we today call moral theology and spirituality were elements of the wider theological synthesis exemplified by St. Thomas' *Summa*. The Christian life, moral and spiritual, was understood in the total context of the person's striving to attain the ultimate end, the beatific vision. In this synthesis, the moral life could no more be separated from striving for union with God than moral theology could be separated from its wider theological roots.

St. Thomas continues the threefold division of the Christian life into beginners, proficients, and the perfect with its connection between morality and spirituality (*ST* IIa–IIae, q.24, a.9; q.183, a.4). But the subtleties of the interrelation of moral and spiritual striving are further evident in the discussion of the virtues, acquired and infused, in which charity directed ultimately toward God becomes the "form" of the virtues (*ST* IIa–IIae, q.23, a.8). In this Thomistic context, the Christian moral life is the life of virtue formed by love and empowered and transformed by grace.

The development of moral theology as a separate discipline distinct from dogmatic theology began in the sixteenth and seventeenth centuries with the development of extended commentaries on the *Secunda pars* of the *Summa Theologiae*, such as those of Thomas de Vio (d. 1534), Francis de Vitoria (d. 1546), and Francis Suarez (d. 1617). The Counter Reformation period also saw the emergence of a new genre of manuals or textbooks of moral theology—the *Institutiones theologiae moralis*.[4] Some of the earliest of these manuals were those of the Spanish Jesuits, most notably John Azor (d. 1603). At about the same time, we see the appearance of great classics of spirituality in the writings of St. Ignatius, St. Teresa of Avila, and St. John of the Cross—spiritual classics which do not stem from classical speculative theology.[5]

The moral theology of the sixteenth and seventeenth centuries, however, manifested not merely a process of developing theological specialization but a bifurcation in the inherent relationship of the moral and spiritual dimensions of Christian living. Catholic moral theology, under the influence of the philosophy of nominalism, gradually became focused on acts, rules, and casuistry rather than the broader Thomistic emphasis on virtues in the context of a striving to attain the ultimate end. Discussion of virtue was reduced almost to providing an organizing structure for discussing the sinful acts that "opposed" particular virtues. Catholic moral theology—all the way up to the manuals of moral theology in use before the Second Vatican Council—remained tied to and more akin with emphases in canon law than to dogmatic theology and spirituality.

Moral theology was still aimed formally and remotely at "perfection" and the ultimate end, but usually only by way of introduction and as a prelude to the discussion of individual human actions aimed at discrete ends. In fact, moral theology seemed more aimed at natural human ends, cut off from the sense of the moral life as part of the Christian response to God. Moral theology came to concern itself largely with the avoidance of sin, and following the commandments for the ordinary Christian. Spiritual theology, on the other hand, as a branch of the moral theology still formally directed to the ultimate end, focused on the moral life beyond the commandments and with the life of prayer, largely for a special elite corps of Christians from among the priests and religious. For many, moral theology became the realm of precepts and commandments that obliged all Christians, while spiritual theology was the realm of counsels for those few called to a special holiness.

The seventeenth and eighteenth centuries saw the further distinction within spiritual theology between ascetical and mystical theology. Ascetical theology concentrated on advance in virtue and on the first stages of prayer up to infused forms of contemplation. It retained, then, the moral dimension of the Christian life as a necessary aspect of growth in Christian life and prayer. Although ascetical theology focused attention on infused rather than acquired virtues, it preserved many aspects of the unity of the moral and spiritual life—even while moral theology, of which it was formally a branch, was reduced to a minimalism cut off from the biblical and patristic emphasis on the Christian life as radically transformed in Christ. Beyond ascetical theology, mystical theology studied the further development of Christian life and prayer beyond what could be attained by human effort aided by the normal working of grace. Mystical theology focused on infused forms of prayer which involved the closest approach to the beatific vision that could be attained in the present existence.[6]

The Three Ways—purgative, illuminative, and unitive—continued to structure many manuals of ascetical and mystical theology. In this way, ascetical and mystical theology continued the traditional insight concerning the necessity for a concurrent moral and spiritual growth. The ability of spiritual theology to retain this insight is perhaps rooted in the ongoing *experience* of mystics who reported that authentic spiritual growth demanded a true moral growth. Nowhere is this more clearly exemplified than in *The Ascent of Mount Carmel* by St. John of the Cross—upon which generations of ascetical and mystical writers would base their own examinations of the spiritual life. Sadly, the work of the ascetical and mystical writers was intended for a spiritual elite and was not to be recommended for the average Christian.

At least since the separation of theology into its specializations of moral and dogmatic theology, then, the relationship of moral theology and spirituality involved the subordination of the latter to the former.[7] Drawing its principles from dogmatic theology, spirituality aimed at directing a few special Christians to attain the heights of the Christian quest, nominally the goal of a more minimalistic moral theology. Although Pierre Pourrat, the author of the first modern history of spirituality, maintained the superiority of spirituality over moral theology,[8] Sandra Schneiders has argued that Pourrat's claims of superiority merely elevated spirituality even further to the level of an esoteric discipline disconnected from the lives of ordinary Christians.[9]

It is really the explicit recognition of the universal call to holiness by the Second Vatican Council (*Lumen Gentium* 39–41) that has helped to break down and to overcome the dualism created by a two-tiered view of the Christian life—moral theology for the vast majority of average Christians, spirituality for an elite few. If every Christian life is aimed at union with God, then moral theology and spirituality should be interrelated perspectives on the development of the disciples' relationship with God. All Christians are called both to moral goodness and to authentic holiness.

THE CONTEMPORARY SITUATION

The contemporary renewal of both Catholic moral theology and Christian spirituality seems to hold a good deal of promise in reaffirming the interconnection between moral and spiritual striving. Still, while there have been some important efforts to demonstrate the connection between these two disciplines,[10] a great deal more work and attention lies ahead. The present state of each discipline manifests both the promise and the ongoing challenge.

As we pointed out in the introduction, the Second Vatican Council challenged moral theology to return to its theological and biblical roots and to reclaim its more transcendent goal:

Special care should be given to the perfecting of moral theology. Its scientific presentation should draw more fully on the teaching of Holy Scripture and should throw light upon the exalted vocation of the faithful in Christ and their obligation to bring forth charity for the life of the world. (*Optatam totius* 16)[11]

The response to this challenge has resulted in a contemporary moral theology more explicitly rooted in dogmatic theology and scripture, more personalist, more christocentric, more ecumenically aware, and more concerned with social dimensions of morality. Prodded a bit by the recent Protestant emphasis on virtue and character associated especially with the work of Stanley Hauerwas, Catholic moral theology has begun to return to its Thomistic emphasis on virtue and thus to root moral theology in the broader tasks of Christian living.[12] The Christian moral life is understood more explicitly in the context of the Christian community and in its liturgy and its formative narratives—the very context which nurtures the spiritual life.

Perhaps foremost in the modern renewal of contemporary moral theology has been the work of the German moral theologian Bernard Häring. Enda McDonagh has said of Häring's work:

> In the renewal of moral theology in which Father Häring's *The Law of Christ* proved such a seminal work, the artificial distinction between moral and ascetical theology and mystical theology was in principle overcome. The double standard of Christian living, symbolised by the precepts and counsels and to be realized by laity and religious, the less perfect and the perfect, gradually lost its significance.[13]

Häring's own work was fueled largely by the belief that there are two basic and inseparable forms of the human response to God's gratuitous self-offering: worship (both private and communal) and moral living.[14] The two responses cannot be separated in the lives of the individual Christian. Häring has devoted himself to the development of a faith-filled and prayer-nourished moral theology that has easily allowed him to cross over into numerous works on prayer, worship, and spirituality.

Many recent textbooks of fundamental moral theology make explicit reference to the important connection between moral theology and spirituality.[15] Still, the explicit effort to demonstrate the connection between the two dimensions of Christian existence and between the two disciplines is not extensive. Further, certain emphases in contemporary moral theology continue to mask or even impede our ability to see the connection between moral theology and spirituality. As McDonagh notes:

> Moral theology pays lip-service to its continuity with asceti-
> cal and mystical theology but in its literature and teaching
> continues to concern itself with the traditional moral areas,
> albeit in a new setting and with a new awareness of the pos-
> itive open-ended character of the moral call. This is partly
> due to the inertia of history and tradition.[16]

Although McDonagh's comment is now some fifteen years old, it
remains nonetheless largely accurate.

Contemporary Catholic moral theology continues to focus a great
deal of attention on specific moral issues and on the methodologies used
to address them. This important effort to address particular questions in
social, medical, and sexual ethics necessitates a discussion of methodologies—such as the contemporary controverted discussion of propor-
tionalism—for resolving these questions. This focus is certainly proper
to moral theology's essential purposes, but it does tend to keep the attention of Catholic moral theology on acts. As Protestant ethicist James
Gustafson has observed of contemporary Catholic ethics:

> My impression is that the traditional concentration of moral
> theology on acts is largely continued, and that those acts and
> their circumstances which have occupied attention for reli-
> gious reasons continue to receive dominant attention, e.g.,
> war, sexuality, contraception, abortion, euthanasia, suicide.
> Thomas Aquinas' "Treatise on Human Acts" seems always
> to be in the background.[17]

Within a focus on specific issues and methodologies, the discussion of
the relationship between moral theology and spirituality can seem sec-
ondary, abstract, or even ethereal. In fact, however, an understanding of
the relationship of ethics and spirituality provides the broad context
which makes sense of the actions of Christians. The point, obviously, is
not to neglect the important issues being discussed today; but, rather, to
focus attention on the broader context as well. It is certainly a task
proper to moral theology's essential purposes to help Christians to
understand their actions and their moral striving within the broader purposes of the Christian life itself.

Another emphasis of contemporary Catholic moral theology also seems to divert attention away from the relationship of ethics and spirituality. This is the ongoing—and, again, very important—discussion of the "distinctiveness of Christian ethics." The Catholic moral tradition has always been a "natural law" tradition, believing that human reason is a reliable source for the formulation of moral norms. This emphasis on reason has been the basis for allowing the Catholic tradition to enter into moral dialogue with "people of good will" who do not share Christian faith. Such dialogue is especially important in pluralistic, largely secular contemporary societies. But the very presupposition that reason is a reliable source for the attainment of moral truth raises the question of the "distinctiveness of Christian ethics": if moral truth is attainable by reason, in what way is Christian faith necessary for Christian ethics? Different moral theologians have answered this question differently.

The purpose in pointing to the "distinctiveness of Christian ethics" debate is not to enter into the important questions it raises. It is certainly not our purpose to deny a natural law foundation for moral norms nor to deny that norms are "in principle" available to people who do not share Christian faith. It does seem, however, that the effort to reaffirm the natural law, reason-based foundation of moral norms can divert attention from non-rational foundations of Christian ethics. Furthermore, the effort to affirm that moral norms are "in principle" available to those without explicit Christian faith can distract from the equally important questions of *how* explicit Christian faith—as lived and celebrated by ordinary Christians—does, in fact impact, form, and guide the Christian moral life. Finally, the vitally important task of dialogue on moral questions in a pluralistic society can divert attention from the essential *intra*-community task of helping committed Christians to make sense of their moral lives in light of their spiritual longing.

In short, while the contemporary, ongoing renewal of Catholic moral theology has largely reclaimed the discipline's theological and biblical foundations, the renewal has still not progressed to the point of manifesting the connection between moral and spiritual striving. It must be said, then, that Catholic moral theology is still cut off from the full dynamism of authentic Christian living. It does not yet fully reflect the actual lives of Christians who must pray in order to become truly good and who must become morally good in order to grow in prayer and in holiness.

For its part, contemporary Christian spirituality also seems to be in a state of fundamental reevaluation. It has clearly recognized and responded to the inadequacies of some aspects of pre–Vatican II spiritualities. John Heagle has suggested, for example, that pre–Vatican II spiritualities shared four problematic characteristics: (1) they were *theoretical* in their starting point—that is, largely deduced from doctrinal principles; (2) they were *elitist* in their assumptions—that is, directed only to certain priests and religious; (3) they were *other-worldly* in their perspectives— that is, suspicious and even hostile toward the present historical realities; and (4) they were *individualistic* in their practice—that is, detached from social concern and from an appreciation of the communal and liturgical dimensions of Christian life and spirituality.[18]

Contemporary literature in the academic discipline of spirituality suggests that there is, at present, a fundamental reevaluation of the appropriate terminology for and the definition of the discipline itself as well as a reevaluation of the scope and methods of the discipline.[19] The current preference by some authors for the term "spirituality," for example, to describe the discipline represents a disavowal of the term "spiritual theology," more traditional in Catholic circles. "Spirituality" seems to be more inclusive in its ability to incorporate *both* the religious experience of persons *and* the academic discipline which reflects on the experience. Further, "spirituality" seems better able to encompass the ecumenical and interreligious nature of the discipline and seems to distinguish it from the deductive approach of the earlier "spiritual theology" subordinated to dogmatic and moral theology.

Michael Downey has suggested that certain trends in contemporary spirituality are now identifiable, many of which seem to respond to some of the more problematic characteristics of pre–Vatican II spiritualities summarized by Heagle.[20] Among the ten trends identified by Downey, several hold immediate promise for fostering a more adequate relationship between spirituality and moral theology. Among these trends are: sustained attention to a more holistic understanding of spirituality; the effort to undercut any form of dualism which would excessively separate mundane life and activity from some "other-worldly" spiritual realm; the more interdisciplinary approach of spirituality; the conviction that prayer and action are two dimensions of the human person which must be held together; a greater awareness of the ecological impact of spiritualities; and the recognition of the need to retrieve the insights of the past. It would seem that these trends would naturally lead to a greater connection between the disciplines of moral theology and spirituality.

Beyond academic writings about spirituality, the popular literature of spirituality does not seem to manifest a great deal of attention to the relationship between moral and spiritual dimensions of Christian life — although, as Downey's trends suggest, there is a recognition that prayer and action cannot be separated. Contemporary ecological spiritualities[21] alluded to by Downey and discussions of spirituality and social justice[22] do suggest a unity between any authentic spirituality and the person's being in the world. By their very nature, of course, the developing liberation spiritualities presuppose that any authentic Christian spirituality is vitally connected with the sociopolitical dimensions of life.[23]

In sum, the contemporary, ongoing reevaluation and renewal of Christian spirituality as an academic discipline seems to hold great promise for a greater integration with moral theology. Still, it may be that contemporary spirituality must, at present, focus on its own internal questions before it can pursue this integration with moral theology more fully. At the same time, however, the continuing renewal of spirituality may be furthered by conscious attention to its foundational connection with moral theology.

SUGGESTIONS FOR THE FUTURE

Both Catholic moral theology and Christian spirituality continue their ongoing renewal and development as distinct theological disciplines. The purpose of the historical and contemporary sketch that occupied most of this chapter is not meant to suggest that they should somehow return to a simpler bygone era before they became distinct disciplines. It is obvious that each has its own legitimate and important focus.

This sketch has suggested, however, that the authentic further development of each discipline requires more than passing laudatory mention of the other. Both our moral and spiritual traditions and the continuing lived experience of Christians reveals that the Christian moral life is nurtured by a vibrant spiritual life and that authentic spiritual development cannot occur without a concurrent moral development. In order for each discipline to fulfill its ecclesial, pastoral purpose of nourishing and guiding Christian living, it will be necessary to pursue an explicit and ongoing dialogue between the disciplines and mutual incorporation of the insights of each. At least five broad suggestions seem to follow from the historical development and contemporary state of both disciplines.

First, Catholic moral theology must continue to reclaim the broader and even transcendent context provided by its relationship with spirituality. Moral theology cannot be restricted to norms and decision-making nor even to virtue and character. Moral theology serves the Christian life aimed at sharing together in the divine life of the Trinity— a life with our sisters and brothers in triune community. The Christian life is a radically new life in Christ, conformed to Christ, transformed in Christ. It is then a life animated by charity, empowered by the indwelling Spirit, aimed at sharing in triune love. The trinitarian focus of moral theology points to the important social dimension of both moral theology and spirituality. The authentic life of persons created in the image of a triune and personal God cannot ignore the needs and demands of other persons in the human community.

Second, contemporary moral theology must continue to orient to the Christian moral life as empowered by grace, made possible only by God's gracious presence and action in individual Christians, in the Christian community, and in the world. Moral theology must therefore recover what the tradition discussed as "infused virtue" (moral and theological), and charity as the "form" of the virtues and thus of the moral life—a love empowered by and ultimately directed toward God. It is only in this transcendent and grace-filled context that discussions of virtue, natural law, norms, acts, and decision-making can make sense as *Christian* ethics. Otherwise moral theology will continue the bifurcation of the moral life from the spiritual life and thus fail to provide authentic and holistic guidance to Christian men and women struggling to become both good and holy.

Third, for its part, contemporary spirituality cannot lose touch with the insights discussed in the traditional treatises on ascetical theology. The foundation of sustained spiritual growth in moral growth is a clear presupposition, not only of our own spiritual tradition but also of the mystical traditions of every major religion. Any authentic growth in prayer, contemplation, and mysticism requires overcoming sin and growth in moral goodness. Any spirituality that proposes a "quick road" to the heights of prayer (or even to an authentic, sustained life of prayer) without attention to moral conversion is both inauthentic to our tradition and alien to our experience. This requires that contemporary spirituality recover notions of purgation and asceticism that are authentically and appropriately world-affirming and creation-serving and that guide Christian women and men in the integration of all of their desires into their striving after God.

Fourth, the ongoing renewal of Christian spirituality seems well served by the contemporary discipline's attention to experience. The most fundamental human experience which is the focus of both spirituality and moral theology is the drive to authentic self-transcendence, in prayer and in action. As Schneiders reviews the current efforts to arrive at a common definition for "spirituality," she argues that "virtually everyone talking about spirituality these days is talking about self-transcendence which gives integrity and meaning to the whole of life and to life in its wholeness by situating and orienting the person within the horizon of ultimacy in some ongoing and transforming way." In this context, she defines Christian spirituality as "that particular actualization of the capacity for self-transcendence that is constituted by the substantial gift of the Holy Spirit establishing a life-giving relationship with God in Christ within the believing community."[24]

Both Christian spirituality and moral theology focus on and ultimately seek to serve the authentic self-transcendence in love which is at the heart of both true prayer and moral living. Such self-transcendence in prayer and in Christian living, modeled on the death and resurrection of Jesus, is the ongoing task of the Christian life as a whole. But this is but another way of saying that ongoing and continual conversion is the task of Christian living. It is perhaps the experience of conversion itself—both as a critical moment in the lives of many Christians but also the ongoing, continual conversion of Christians—that offers a most fruitful place to rediscover the unity of moral and spiritual striving.

Fifth, building on a foundation in experience, moral theology and spirituality might usefully develop a common language to discuss such realities as their foundational experiences, the authentic development of mature human and Christian living, and the supports and hindrances to that development. Moral theology and Christian spirituality do remain distinct disciplines with different objects and methods; still, they offer different perspectives on distinct aspects of the one Christian life. Thus, while each will necessarily develop its own distinctive vocabulary; they should speak a language which allows for clear and sustained interchange between the disciplines.

CONCLUSION

The contemporary recognition of the universal call to holiness must mean more than that the subject matter of the old manuals of ascetical and mystical theology is now for the laity. Surely it must mean that every Christian is called to moral goodness, rooted in an openness to the divine initiative and action through prayer and aimed at a share in the divine life itself. Every Christian, then, is called to a life grounded in conversion, rooted in community, empowered by grace, and aimed at communion with God and with others in God. All Christians are called to the life of ongoing self-transcendence in a continual conversion that seeks to manifest the unity of love of God and of neighbor. If contemporary Catholic moral theology and Christian spirituality are to help Christians to respond to this universal call to holiness, then they must attend to one another in an explicit and sustained way and they must speak a common language that challenges and guides people to become both good and holy.

Notes

1. Donal Dorr, *Spirituality and Justice* (Maryknoll, NY: Orbis, 1984), 8–18.

2. A helpful perspective on the moral implications of the Bible is provided in Thomas W. Ogeltree, *The Use of the Bible in Christian Ethics* (Philadelphia: Fortress, 1983). For a more detailed study of New Testament literature, see Rudolf Schnackenberg, *The Moral Teaching of the New Testament*, trans. J. Holland-Smith and W. J. O'Hara (New York: Seabury, 1973).

3. A helpful summary of patristic spirituality is provided by Boniface Ramsey, "The Spirituality of the Early Church: Patristic Sources," in *Spiritual Traditions for the Contemporary Church*, ed. Robin Maas and Gabriel O'Donnell (Nashville: Abingdon, 1990), 25–44. See also Boniface Ramsey, *Beginning to Read the Fathers* (New York: Paulist, 1985), 56–94.

4. Charles E. Curran, "The Historical Development of Moral Theology," in *Toward an American Catholic Moral Theology* (Notre Dame: University of Notre Dame Press, 1987), 3–6. For more extended histories of Catholic moral theology, see John Mahoney, *The Making of Moral Theology: A Study of the Roman Catholic Tradition* (Oxford: Clarendon Press, 1987); and John A. Gallagher, *Time Past, Time Future: An Historical Study of Catholic Moral Theology* (New York: Paulist, 1990).

5. Yves M. J. Congar, *A History of Theology*, trans. Hunter Guthrie (Garden City, NY: Doubleday, 1968), 166–70.

6. Some pre–Vatican II manuals of spiritual theology maintained a relative discontinuity between ascetical and mystical states; for example: Adolphe Tanquerey, *The Spiritual Life: A Treatise on Ascetical and Mystical Theology*, trans. Herman Branderis, 2nd rev. ed. (Westminster, MD: Newman, 1948). Other manuals maintained a greater continuity and thus, it seems, a greater sense of a universal Christian vocation to higher forms of prayer; for example: Reginald Garrigou-Lagrange, *The Three Ages of the Interior Life*, 2 vols., trans. T. Doyle (New York: Herder, 1948).

7. Jon Alexander makes the interesting observation that the first issue of the *Elenchus bibliographicus* of the *Ephemerides theologicae lovanienses* in 1924 placed the category "Theologica Ascetica et Mystica" as a subdivision of "Theologia Moralis." It was in 1951 that "Theologica Ascetica et Mystica" became a separate section. Jon Alexander, "What Do Recent Writers Mean by Spirituality?" *Spirituality Today* 32 (September 1980): 250–51.

8. Pierre Pourrat, *Christian Spirituality*, trans. W. H. Mitchell and S. P. Jacques (Westminster, MD: Newman, 1953–1955), I:v.

9. Sandra Schneiders, "Theology and Spirituality: Strangers, Rivals, or Partners?" *Horizons* 13 (Fall 1986): 263.

10. One of the earliest contemporary efforts was by the Protestant ethicist James Gustafson: "Spiritual Life and Moral Life," *Theology Digest* 17 (Winter 1971): 296–307. See also Sergio Bastianel, *Prayer in the Christian Moral Life*, trans. Bernard Hoose (St. Paul Publications, 1988); Michael K. Duffey, *Be Blessed in What You Do: The Unity of Christian Ethics and Spirituality* (New York: Paulist, 1988); William E. May, *The Unity of the Moral and Spiritual Life*, Synthesis series (Chicago: Franciscan Herald Press, 1979); and Enda McDonagh, "Morality and Prayer" and "Morality and Spirituality," in

Doing the Truth: The Quest for Moral Theology (Notre Dame: University of Notre Dame Press, 1979), 40–75.

11. No. 16, in *Vatican II: The Conciliar and Post Conciliar Documents*, ed. Austin Flannery (Collegeville, MN: Liturgical Press, 1975), 720.

12. See Romanus Cessario, *The Moral Virtues and Theological Ethics* (Notre Dame: University of Notre Dame Press, 1991).

13. McDonagh, "Morality and Prayer," 58.

14. While the discussion of the two forms of human responses to God can be found in Häring's recent work, it can be found more prominently in his doctoral dissertation, later published as his first book, *Das Heilige und das Gute*, in 1954.

15. See, for example, Richard M. Gula, *Reason Informed by Faith: Foundations of Catholic Morality* (New York: Paulist, 1989), 7–8; and Timothy E. O'Connell, *Principles for a Catholic Morality*, rev. ed. (San Francisco: Harper and Row, 1990), 254–55.

16. McDonagh, "Morality and Prayer," 59.

17. James Gustafson, "The Focus and Its Limitations: Reflection on Catholic Moral Theology," in *Moral Theology: Challenges for the Future*, ed. Charles E. Curran (New York: Paulist, 1990), 181. Gustafson goes on to reflect on the limitations of this narrow focus (181–89).

18. John Heagle, "A New Public Piety: Reflections on Spirituality," *Church* 1 (Fall 1985): 52–53.

19. See, for example, two important articles by Sandra Schneiders, "Theology and Spirituality"; and "Spirituality in the Academy," in *Modern Christian Spirituality*, ed. Bradley C. Hanson, American Academy of Religion Studies in Religion 62 (Atlanta: Scholars Press, 1990), 15–37. Articles by Ewert H. Cousins, Bradley C. Hanson, and Carlos M. N. Eire in the latter volume also provide helpful examinations of the present state of the discipline of Christian spirituality. See also Walter Principe, "Toward Defining Spirituality," *Studies in Religion/Sciences Religieuses* 12 (1983): 127–41.

20. Michael Downey, "Understanding Christian Spirituality: Dress Rehearsal for a Method," *Spirituality Today* (Autumn 1991): 273–77.

21. See, for example, Jay B. McDaniel, *Earth, Sky, Gods, and Mortals: Developing an Ecological Spirituality* (Mystic, CT: Twenty-Third Publications, 1990).

22. See, for example, two books by Donal Dorr: *Spirituality and Justice* (Maryknoll: Orbis, 1984) and *Integral Spirituality: Resources for Community, Peace, Justice and the Earth* (Maryknoll: Orbis, 1990).

23. There are already a significant number of works on liberation spirituality. See, for example, Gustavo Gutierrez, *We Drink from Our Own Wells: The Spiritual Journey of a People* (Maryknoll: Orbis, 1984); Jon Sobrino, *Spirituality*

of Liberation: Toward a Political Holiness (Maryknoll: Orbis, 1985); Segundo Galilea, *The Way of Living Faith: A Spirituality of Liberation* (San Francisco: Harper and Row, 1988); and Nestor Jaen, *Toward a Liberation Spirituality* (Chicago: Loyola University Press, 1991).

24. Schneiders, "Theology and Spirituality," 266.

2. On Theology of the Christian Life

Norbert J. Rigali

This chapter first appeared in *Moral Theology: New Directions in Fundamental Issues: Festschrift for James P. Hanigan*, ed. James Keating (New York: Paulist, 2004).

While promulgating guidelines for a renewal of theological studies in its decree on the formation of priests, the Second Vatican Council expressed, in an often-cited passage, particular concern about moral theology:

> Special attention needs to be given to the development of moral theology. Its scientific exposition should be more thoroughly nourished by scriptural teaching. It should show the nobility of the Christian vocation of the faithful, and their obligation to bring forth fruit in charity for the life of the world. ("Decree on Priestly Formation" 16)[1]

Reasons for finding preconciliar moral theology unsatisfactory are not hard to find. The discipline has been described as "all too often one-sidedly confession-oriented, magisterium-dominated, canon law-related, sin-centered, and seminary-controlled."[2]

INADEQUACIES OF PRECONCILIAR MORAL THEOLOGY

The peculiarities constituting this list, however, are neither all nor even the most important deficiencies of preconciliar moral theology. The list discloses aberrations of moral theology only in its relation to the church considered as ecclesiastical institution. When the discipline is viewed in relation to the church as Body of Christ or community of Christ's disciples, as servant or sacrament, other, weightier inadequacies, alluded to in the Council's directive for reform, come readily to light. In the detailed tables of contents and indices of a typical three-volume moral theology manual used in seminary instruction at the time, for example, one finds no mention at all of "Jesus" or "Christ."[3] One practitioner of the discipline even insisted that it is not really theology at all but moral philosophy.[4] Foremost on a complete list of questionable characteristics of preconciliar moral theology one might expect to find, then, "Jesus-estranged" and "Scripture-overlooking."

The Council assumed responsibility to call for the reform of moral theology as an ecclesial reality, a work from within the church, and to mandate its transformation from a Jesus-alienated discipline to a science rooted in Scripture and accordingly centered on Christ. Besides being an ecclesial reality, however, preconciliar moral theology was, like every other intellectual discipline, a cultural form, a linguistic creation in its specific social location of community, tradition, time, and place. Furthermore, also as a form of modern, Western European–United States culture, the received moral theology was problematic, for with other ethics of the modern age it shared the ahistorical, rationalist understanding of the moral life that finds classic expression in the work of Immanuel Kant.

The postconciliar challenge to the discipline, therefore, is not confined to the profound charge imposed upon it from within the church. Were one to expand the aforementioned list of pre–Vatican II moral theology shortcomings to include its inadequacies as a cultural form, one would have to invent another series of hyphenated-compound adjectives to describe respectively: (1) a tendency to reduce morality to decision making, and ethics to scientific reflection on decision making; (2) an ignoring of how character, virtue, vision, and narrative are constitutive of moral life; (3) a lack of attention to the ways in which community and tradition mold moral living; (4) an exaggerated sense of the individual as autonomous agent and a corresponding predisposition to individualism; (5) an overly simple view of the dynamic of personal freedom; and (6) a general failure to recognize the historicity of all things human or, in other words, a lack of historical consciousness.

If preconciliar moral theology shares with the rest of modern ethics the challenges of a postmodern age, however, the process of creating the needed replacement for preconciliar moral theology is nevertheless essentially different from the reform of all other studies of morality. In the case of moral theology, a sin-centered, canon law-related, seminary-dominated ethics must be replaced with a new ecclesial work, a science of life in Christ. Taking its point of departure from a classicist discipline in which discussion about Jesus is unnecessary in order to work toward creating a historical-minded study of life in Christ, the Council-mandated theological project clearly is not a process of merely retouching an already fundamentally sound, well-constructed theological discipline. True reform calls for much more radical change. While much work done by moral theologians since the Council has been rightly described as revisionist moral theology, revision is not an adequate model for what needs to be done. Transformation is necessary. There needs to be created a new kind of theology, a new theological discipline.[5] As a project of unmaking and remaking, reform, therefore, is a work of decades and demands the collaborative efforts of numerous members of the Catholic theological community together with the assistance of many others from various walks of life.

Theologians, moreover, should consider abandoning altogether the use of the term "moral theology" to designate their contemporary work, for it seems to be now more a hindrance than a help in identifying what they need to do today. Since "the manuals of moral theology… practically became identified with the whole discipline of moral theology during their existence from the late sixteenth century to the Second Vatican Council,"[6] it is inappropriate and a source of confusion today to apply the name used during its first more than three-and-a-half centuries for the ethics of the manuals to an emergent science differing from the earlier discipline in many essential ways. These essential differences will be detailed below. Should the suggestion to retire the name "moral theology" nevertheless seem extreme, however, it should be recalled that since the Council "dogmatic theology" and "ascetical theology" have been quietly consigned to the past.[7]

ESTABLISHING A FOOTHOLD

To become a science that, following the Council's directive, shows "the nobility of the Christian vocation of the faithful, and their obligation to bring forth fruit in charity for the life of the world" ("Decree on Priestly Formation" 16),[8] preconciliar moral theology clearly must be transformed into a theological study of the Christian life. This, then, is the point at which the transformed discipline must establish its foothold; for in both its method and its self-understanding moral theology was about something less than the Christian life.

With regard to its method, the preconciliar discipline was, as noted above, "sin-centered." More broadly described, its chief concern was with individual human *acts*, distinguishing sinful from lawful ones. The Christian life, however, is much more than the individual acts it encompasses.

With regard to its self-understanding, moral theology stood in counterpoint to ascetical-mystical (or ascetical) theology, each discipline dealing with a different part of Christian life:

> Moral Theology deals with the Commandments and the virtues insofar as they are obligatory, whilst Ascetical-mystical deals with Counsels and with the perfection of the Christian life beyond that which is of precept. Therefore Moral Theology differs from Ascetical-mystical Theology inasmuch as the latter "is not content to deal with the sins to be avoided, but goes beyond them to consider man's moral life as perfectible by the counsels to such a degree that he attains, through exalted virtue, the union of the created will with the Divine Will."[9]

Moral theology, accordingly, was "the theology for salvation," while ascetical theology was "the theology for perfection."[10]

Within this dichotomization of the Christian life between unequal classes of Christians, moral theology dealt with the lower class and ascetical-mystical theology with the higher class. When Vatican II called in 1965 for the reform of moral theology noted above, it had already, in the previous year, rejected this fragmentation of the Christian life on which the respective self-understanding of each discipline was based:

> The Lord Jesus, the divine Teacher and Model of all perfection, preached holiness of life to each and every one of His disciples, regardless of their situation: "you therefore are to be perfect, even as your heavenly Father is perfect."...[A]ll the faithful of Christ of whatever rank or status are called to the fullness of the Christian life and to the perfection of charity....All of Christ's followers, therefore, are invited and bound to pursue holiness and the perfect fulfillment of their proper state. ("Dogmatic Constitution on the Church" 40, 42)[11]

That the reformed discipline is a theology of Christian life means, then, that it is not a sin-oriented study of human acts; nor is it about a life of commandments and salvation as distinguished from a life of counsels and perfection. It is a study, rather, of the Christian life as this is understood in the teaching of the Second Vatican Council: a life of following Christ toward the perfect fulfillment of charity for the life of the world. It is what even before the Council, Bernard Häring, in a seminal work, was striving to make moral theology: "the doctrine of the imitation of Christ, as the life in, with, and through Christ."[12]

REDRAWING BOUNDARIES

Since subjects such as following Christ and Christian perfection, formerly relegated to ascetical-mystical theology, lie at the heart of the theology of Christian life, the change in self-understanding from preconciliar moral theology to the theology of Christian life presupposes an analogous change in self-understanding from preconciliar ascetical-mystical theology to its contemporary successor. The transformation of preconciliar moral theology entails, then, besides major changes in this discipline's self-understanding, method, and content, a redrawing of boundary lines for both itself and the former ascetical theology, as well as a redefining of the relation between the two fields. Moreover, now that the church has rejected the dichotomy of the Christian life on which their creation as two separate disciplines was based, one may not continue to assume that the relation between the two fields is an interrelation of two separate, autonomous sciences. It is, of course, not possible for a theology of the Christian life to prescind from spirituality.[13]

Other boundary markers of preconciliar moral theology, furthermore, have already had to be reset. As noted above, the discipline was "canon law-related." This adjectival term means, in an understated way, that the professor of the discipline and the moral theology manual author often held an advanced degree in canon law rather than in theology and that the discipline was excessively concerned with canon law,[14] even to the point of presenting as vital moral matters legalistic niceties.[15] Since the Council, however, the intrusions of moral theology into commentary on canon law have ceased.

The abandonment of the practice of moral theologians commenting on canon law, however, changes more than the role of the contemporary successor to the preconciliar moral theologian. It also points, with regard to the new discipline, to a need to define anew what is to count for it as ethical reflection and how ethical reflection is to be integrated with theology and the church.

WHAT COUNTS AS ETHICS?

What counted as the ethics in the preconciliar manuals? The moral theology manuals divided their subject into two parts: general and special moral theology, respectively. The first part studied principles of morality. Then seeking to distinguish sinful from lawful acts, special moral theology applied the principles to the Decalogue, to the commandments of the church, and to obligations seen as originating in the sacraments. This special moral theology was the practical knowledge about obligations arising from precepts and sacraments that counted as applied ethics and that constituted the moral theologian a general practitioner of ethics, which the confessor, in his own way, was also expected to be. Dividing its ethics into principles and specific matters to which the principles were applied, preconciliar moral theology proceeded in a deductive manner, and the individual moral theologian was responsible for the entire field. The moral theologian (a priest teaching in a seminary) and the confessor educated by him knew the principles and how to apply them to specific matters.

In the twenty-first-century world, however, general practitioners of ethics have been replaced, on the level of theology and philosophy, by ethical specialists. Today no individual scholar can reasonably be expected to have ethical expertise in more than a limited field of an unprecedentedly and ever-increasingly complex world. Work analogous to that of the former "general practice" of ethics by confessors is now the teaching of Christian morals on the level of catechesis and religious education in the church. It is the work of leading persons into a Christian moral tradition.

On the level of higher education today, however, as Albert Jonsen points out, "ethicists do something different than, but compatible with, the activities of philosophers and theologians. Ethicists invent arguments following the general patterns of reasoning proper to deliberation and persuasion in practical matters that were sketched by the classical rhetoricians."[16] The task of philosophers and theologians with regard to ethics, on the other hand, is to "present visions that reveal the depths of evil and the depths of the holy or of the good life" in the contemporary world. Theologians, for their part, "articulate that vision by the way in which they read the documents of their faith and interpret the experiences of the people, past and present, who have lived that faith."[17] The theologians' work, however, is not ethics.

> Ethics is at work in a quite different setting. It works where persons of decency and integrity attempt to understand how they can live humanly and humanely in a complex world of competing forces and enticements....[It works by] inventing arguments...that...will shed some light into the obscurity that besets the enterprises of decent but confused persons.[18]

Proceeding in a more inductive way and thus attending more closely than its predecessor to scripture, human experience, and history, the new discipline must see teaching about the Christian life as a complex work to be apportioned according to various competencies. No longer the task of an individual teacher, it is a communal Christian task. Through reflection on the documents of faith, on the lived faith of Christians, and on the "signs of the times," theologians give the church a theology of the Christian life, a Christian vision of the life of goodness or perfection and of the depths of evil that resist and subvert the reign of God in their time. In this work of theologians, the tasks of religious educators and of Christian ethicists, who may or may not be theologians themselves,[19] are rooted. Enlightened with the Christian vision of contemporary human life, religious educators hand on their Christian moral tradition, and Christian ethicists employ the creative, inductive method proper to their work to find answers to the numerous and enormously varied moral predicaments of contemporary life. A moral theology divided into general and special moral theology is now a thing of the past. The relevant distinction in today's Catholic intellectual life is among work done by theologians, ethicists, and religious educators, whose competencies are respectively theology of the Christian life, the various ethical specializations, and the teaching of the faith and morals of a Christian tradition.

HOW ETHICS IS INTEGRATED WITH THEOLOGY AND THE CHURCH

Christian ethics, then, is ethics inspired by and constructed upon a holistic theological vision, a vision of the vocation of the follower of Christ in a world marked by both the graces and the evils of its time or, in the Council's words, a vision of "the nobility of the Christian vocation of the faithful, and their obligation to bring forth fruit in charity for the life of the world" ("Decree on Priestly Formation" 16).[20] Through this relation to theology, Christian ethics is at the service of the church as the community of Christ's disciples and at the service of "the world," which this community is called to serve.

The relations of the ethics of the manuals to theology and to the church respectively, however, were very different from those just described. Understanding moral theology as the science of a system of obligations deriving from divine and ecclesiastical commandments and from the sacraments, and as a science to enable priests to exercise rightly the sacramental ministry of forgiveness of sins, the discipline was accordingly "confession-oriented, magisterium-dominated, canon law-related, sin-centered, and seminary-controlled." These characteristics, as already noted, describe moral theology in relation to the church as ecclesiastical institution. More specifically, they describe the discipline's relation to the church as the ecclesiastical institution authorized to absolve sins through the sacrament of penance. It is to the church as this ecclesiastical institution, rather than to theology, that the preconciliar discipline was directly related. This is to say, in other words, what amounts to the same thing: the theological view in which the ethics of the preconciliar discipline was grounded was not the Council's holistic theological vision of the Christian's vocation and obligation to service in charity for the life of the world; it was, to the contrary, an incomplete ecclesiology, in which the church is considered only as institution.

Since preconciliar moral theology was "Jesus-estranged" and "Scripture-bypassing," it was not possible, of course, for its ethics to be integrated with a holistic theological view; nor, for the same reason, could it be directly related to the church as the community of Christ's disciples. Its relations to theology and church respectively, accordingly, could be only very truncated ones. The moral theology textbook's claim, cited above, that moral theology is "not theology at all," was in fact for the most part true.

Neither directed to the priest-confessor nor designed to provide the knowledge needed to administer the sacrament of penance—which in an age of significantly less formal education among the general population was understood—the transformed discipline is directed immediately to the adult community of the faithful and is intended to help them to discern as disciples of Christ their respective paths of moral development and service in the world. In this "new era," as Bernard Häring taught, the purpose of the discipline is to help form persons "who will live their lives as discerning people and with the creativity and fidelity that characterizes those who believe in the living God."[21]

PERSONAL-SOCIAL ETHICS

There is yet another way in which the new discipline must differ radically from its predecessor. Preconciliar moral theology was a "personal ethics," as distinguished from what later in Catholic thought would emerge as "social ethics." Throughout most of the centuries-long history of the moral theology manuals, the Catholic intellectual tradition was without systematic ethical reflection on social matters. When such reflection eventually became part of the tradition, it did so not through the teaching and writings of moral theologians but through the papal social encyclicals.

Key in ethical considerations of social matters, the concept of social justice was missing altogether from the manuals. There justice was categorized into three types—commutative, legal, and distributive. Noting in his *The Law of Christ*, however, that "[a] fourth type of justice has been accepted in our [Catholic] moral teaching since the publication of the encyclical on the reconstruction of the social order (*Quadragesimo Anno*),"[22] in 1931, Häring expanded the traditional moral theology list by adding to it the category "social justice." The recent addition he explained as follows:

> Social justice is concerned with the common good and may be termed "justice of the common welfare" or "justice of the community."...It looks...above all, to those who are economically and politically weak, who, though they have nothing to give, still have natural rights....[It] places in sharp focus...those duties of justice which flow immediately from the social nature of man and also from the social purpose of the material goods of the earth.[23]

A theology of Christian life cannot be structured, of course, in the form of a "personal ethics," unmindful of social responsibilities. Both philosophically and theologically that ethical model is inadequate. On a philosophical plane, this individualist approach fails to recognize that "by his innermost nature man is a social being" ("Pastoral Constitution on the Church in the Modern World" 12).[24] Since the human being is by nature not only rational animal but also person-in-community, and since ethics must proceed from an understanding of the human being as such, there cannot be an autonomous ethics, Christian or other, of the individual separate from an autonomous ethics of individuals in society. This, of course, does not mean that different aspects of morality, such as biological, sexual, or environmental, cannot or should not be dealt with as distinct areas of ethics—which is, as noted above, precisely what contemporary Christian ethicists must do. It means, rather, that no ethics of a particular area of human life can be adequate unless it is grounded in a holistic vision of the human person, the identical vision that grounds also the ethics of every other area of human life. One and the same holistic Christian vision brings together the ethics of the many different areas of human living into the unity of Christian ethics. Christian ethics thus is the achievement not of an individual but of many Christians working together as members of the Christian community.

On the theological level, the preconciliar individualist model, "personal ethics," is incompatible with official church teaching about the Christian life. It is unable to show "the nobility of the Christian vocation of the faithful, and their obligation to bring forth charity for the life of the world." Nor can it undergird anything but the "merely individualistic morality" against which Vatican II warned: "Let everyone consider it his sacred obligation to count social necessities among the primary duties of modern man, and to pay heed to them" ("Pastoral Constitution on the Church in the Modern World" 30).[25] If the Council thus showed the inadequacy of a theological anthropology that does not envision the social responsibilities of Christians, indeed that does not emphasize the importance of such duties, the second worldwide synod of bishops, held shortly after the Council, explicitly linked creating justice in the world with proclaiming the Gospel: "Action on behalf of justice and participation in the transformation of the world fully appear to us as a constitutive dimension of the preaching of the Gospel."[26] Clearly, then, the individualistic, preconciliar model of ethics has been abandoned by the church.

THE END OF MORAL THEOLOGY

If the thesis that moral theology is not theology at all but moral philosophy was a logical conclusion and an inevitable outcome for the

Jesus-estranged, Scripture-bypassing, classicist discipline, it was also—although this was not its author's intention—a declaration that moral theology had come to an end. It was, in fact, however, not the first public signal to this effect. When this thesis emerged not long after the Council, there had already appeared, shortly before, another thesis from which this one followed as a corollary. The original thesis was that there is no specifically Christian morality. In other words, "human morality (natural law) and Christian morality are *materially* identical,"[27] and this material identicalness encompasses not only external action but also general motivation and intention.[28]

When these two theses appeared soon after the end of the Council in the revisionist moral theology of the period, the discipline had very recently ceased to be understood as a science oriented to seminarians preparing to administer the sacrament of penance, and it accordingly no longer intruded into commentary on canon law. Having relinquished, however, this relation to the church as the ecclesiastical institution authorized to absolve sin sacramentally, revisionist moral theology had become, paradoxically, even more problematic than preconciliar moral theology. Since this relation to the church *qua* ecclesiastical institution, rather than a comprehensive theological vision revealing the Christian's vocation of service for the life of the world, had been what heretofore grounded the ethics of moral theology, revisionist moral theology now lacked not only the necessary holistic theological vision for an ethic but also the earlier relation to the institutional church, which had until then substituted for a holistic theological vision. Moral theology, therefore, now appeared in an unprecedentedly secular light, and practitioners could conclude both that there is no specifically Christian morality, only natural law morality, and that moral theology is really only moral philosophy.

The theses that there is no specifically Christian morality and that moral theology is not really theology but moral philosophy, however, implied that moral theologians now needed to make a radical choice with regard to their work. One option for them was to become *de jure* moral philosophers. A second was to become commentators on official church documents about morality. A third option was that moral theologians could study the additional motivation that Christians can have when they make the same moral decisions that all people are obligated to make with motivation based on natural law. In any case, it was clear that there was no longer any need in the church for the autonomous discipline that moral theology had been since its inception at the end of the sixteenth century.

Besides the options for moral theologians just mentioned, nevertheless, there was another. Recognizing that what had been heretofore the discipline of moral theology was now, as both ecclesial reality and cultural form, a thing of the past, moral theologians could make a new beginning to create the holistic theological vision that would constitute a theology of Christian life. This is precisely what Bernard Häring undertook. Disagreeing with proponents of the thesis that there is no specifically Christian morality, he saw his task not as one of revising his earlier comprehensive *The Law of Christ* but of composing a new inclusive vision for a "new era," this time "a theology of responsibility essentially marked by liberty, fidelity and creativity."[29] If his previous *magnum opus* had laid foundations for a new discipline, his *Free and Faithful in Christ* was its introductory major exercise.

The subject of moral theology had always been, of course, Christian—indeed, Catholic—morality. When moral theologians began to ask about their discipline's subject—not what it is but whether it is and then responded negatively, the science clearly had run its course. The thesis that there is no specifically Christian morality marked the end of classicist moral theology, for the conceptualization of the very question that it purported to answer was itself derived from the classicist worldview and could not be fitted into contemporary, historical consciousness.

The question of whether there is a specifically Christian morality was not inquiring, of course, whether there is any morality at all. The question arose, rather, out of the assumption that there is a "human morality (natural law)" and asked whether there is also another morality, a specifically Christian one that adds to the former. The difference between the classicist understanding of morality assumed in this question and historical consciousness of morality is that the latter understands "human" or "natural law" morality as not a morality but, like human nature itself, an ahistorical "essence" abstracted from concrete realities, in this case from moralities. A morality, on the contrary, is a concrete dimension of a specific culture or subculture, a living (developing, declining, maintaining, or change-resisting) part of a community's ongoing tradition. A morality accordingly has to be, as Daniel Maguire pointedly put it, "Mahayana Cambodian Buddhist or early Trobriander, medieval French Catholic or Swiss nineteenth-century Calvinist"; for "[t]he mystery of the *humanum* does not reveal itself in a disincarnate, disencultured way."[30]

The fundamental question for a postclassicist theology of the Christian life, then, is not whether there is specifically Christian morality—or Mahayana Cambodian Buddhist or other moralities. It is, rather, a question framed by historical consciousness: What is the vocation of the Christian in today's world? From this question a second one flows: How are a Christian way of life and other ways of life interrelated?[31]

THE CONTEMPORARY TASK

The contemporary work of the theologian of the Christian life differs essentially from the work of the classicist moral theologian, as noted above, in every major respect: in its self-understanding, in its method, in its relationships to other fields of inquiry, in the demarcation of its boundary lines, in its goal, in the audience to whom it is directed, in its understanding of what counts as ethics, in its relating of ethics to theology, in its relation to the church, in its ethical model, in its understanding of the nature of the human person, and in its concept of the nature of morality itself.

The central and most important difference separating the new discipline from classicist moral theology, however, is that the new discipline's subject is unmistakably Christian: life in Christ. There is no question that the new discipline is theology; nor can it be confused with anything else. In it reason and faith are manifestly integrated, and the faith that it reflects is not simply Christian beliefs but faith in its fullest sense of a community's living commitment to God in Jesus Christ, present in the world in and through his church. This intertwining of reason and faith into a nascent discipline is found not only in the work of James Hanigan and Bernard Häring, but also in works such as Richard Gula's *Reason Informed by Faith*,[32] William Spohn's *Go and Do Likewise*,[33] and *Conscience and Prayer* by Dennis Billy and James Keating.[34] Central to the message of all these works is the truth that the very core of Christian morality is the Christian commitment to Christ in his church. Together the works show that the Council-mandated reform is well under way.

Notes

1. *Optatam Totius*, 1965, in *The Documents of Vatican II*, ed. Walter M. Abbott (New York: Guild Press, 1966), no. 16. It is significant that this directive, together with others for the reform of theology, appears in a document on priestly formation rather than in the Council's "Declaration on Christian Education" (*Gravissimum Educationis*, 1965) or its far-ranging "Pastoral Constitution on the Church in the Modern World" (*Gaudium et Spes*, 1965). Theology had long been a science for the clergy, and the recovery of it in a university curriculum for laity was at the time only beginning. Moreover, moral theology in a unique way discussed below was a seminary science.

2. Richard A. McCormick, "Moral Theology 1940–1989: An Overview," in *The Historical Development of Fundamental Moral Theology in the United States*, Readings in Moral Theology Ser. 11, ed. Charles E. Curran and Richard A. McCormick (Mahwah, NJ: Paulist Press, 1999), 47.

3. H. Noldin, A. Schmitt, and G. Heinzel, *Summa Theologiae Moralis*, 3 vols., 30th ed. (Innsbruck: Feliciani Rauch, 1952, 1954). See also B. H. Merkelbach, *Summa Theologiae Moralis*, 3 vols., 10th ed. (Bruges: Desclée de Brouwer, 1956); Henry Davis, *Moral and Pastoral Theology*, 4 vols., 6th ed. (London: Sheed and Ward, 1949); Heribert Jone, *Moral Theology*, trans. Urban Adelman (Westminster, MD: Newman Press,1956).

4. Timothy E. O'Connell, *Principles for a Catholic Morality* (New York: Seabury Press, 1978), 39–41. Produced shortly after the Council, this work is an updated revision of the first part of the typical three-volume preconciliar moral theology manual, whose initial volume, dealing with general (as distinguished from special) moral theology, was entitled "Principles."

> Christian ethics is human ethics, no more and no less....[It] knows nothing that all people do not know....It is a human task seeking human wisdom about the human conduct of human affairs....[I]n a certain sense, moral theology is not theology at all. It is moral philosophy....Thus, among all the potential criticisms which may be leveled against...this book, one must be rejected at the outset: He seems to be merely talking philosophy. Quite true! And quite intentional!

5. Shortly after Vatican II Josef Fuchs wrote: "As a matter of fact, no real tradition of the ideal moral theology contemplated by the Council exists

today. Some elements of it are to be found occasionally in certain types of moral theology which have appeared at various times in history." (*Human Values and Christian Morality* [Dublin: Gill and Macmillan, 1970], 50).

6. Charles E. Curran, *The Catholic Moral Tradition Today: A Synthesis* (Washington, DC: Georgetown University Press, 1999), 1.

7. In making his many contributions to the ongoing process of transforming moral theology into a new kind of Catholic theology, James Hanigan has undertaken some of the more difficult tasks. His *Homosexuality: The Test Case for Christian Ethics* gives the church an in-depth theological study of one of the more vexing ethical questions in contemporary Christian life (Mahwah, NJ: Paulist Press, 1988). His *As I Have Loved You: The Challenge of Christian Ethics* provides what few other theologians have attempted to give the church: a study of Christian morality that can be used by undergraduates, indeed a textbook focused on the love of Christ (Mahwah, NJ: Paulist Press, 1986). In the spirit of striving for the reform for which he has worked, these present reflections on the study of the Christian life are respectfully dedicated to Professor James Hanigan.

8. In *The Documents of Vatican II.*

9. Joseph de Guibert, *The Theology of the Spiritual Life*, trans. Paul Barrett (New York: Sheed and Ward, 1953), 6. The quotation within the cited text is from D. Schram, eighteenth-century author of *Institutiones Theologiae Mysticae.*

10. Alban Goodier, *An Introduction to the Study of Ascetical and Mystical Theology* (Milwaukee: Bruce, 1946), 5.

11. *Lumen Gentium*, 1964, in *The Documents of Vatican II*, 66–72.

12. *The Law of Christ: Moral Theology for Priests and Laity*, trans. Edwin G. Kaiser, vol. 1 (Cork: Mercier Press, 1963; German 5th ed., 1959), 61. Comprising also two other volumes, this work is a foundation for the reformed discipline. Even its entitlement signals a new day, the title revealing the discipline's Christ-centeredness and the subtitle suggesting a theology for the whole church in place of a sin-oriented study for ministers of the sacrament of penance. Not long after the German version of this work had made its first appearance, Häring, now a *peritus* at the Second Vatican Council, suggested and composed what became the conciliar directive, quoted above, for the reform of moral theology (Bernard Häring, *My Witness for the Church*, trans. Leonard Swidler [Mahwah, NJ: Paulist Press, 1992], 60).

13. See Dennis Billy and Donna Orsuto, eds., *Spirituality and Morality: Integrating Prayer and Action* (Mahwah, NJ: Paulist Press, 1996); James Keating, ed., *Spirituality and Moral Theology: Essays from a Pastoral Perspective* (Mahwah, NJ: Paulist Press, 2000); James Keating, "A Mystical Moral Theology," *New Blackfriars* 83, no. 976 (June 2002): 264–78; Mark

O'Keefe, *Becoming Good, Becoming Holy: On the Relationship of Christian Ethics and Spirituality* (Mahwah, NJ: Paulist Press, 1995).

14. The subtitle of Merkelbach's widely studied *Summa Theologiae Moralis*, mentioned above, is *Ad Mentem D. Thomae et ad Normam Iuris Novi* (According to the mind of St. Thomas and to the morm of the new law)—the new law being the 1917 *Code of Canon Law*.

15. A not untypical example: Explaining that valid matter for baptism is "natural water," a moral theology manual presents three detailed lists. There are "certainly valid matter" and "certainly invalid matter," as well as this third category: "Doubtful matter is thin soup, weak beer, coffee, tea, water from dissolved salt, sap from vines and other plants, rose water and similar liquids extracted from vegetative matter" (Jone, *Moral Theology,* 321).

16. Albert R. Jonsen, "The Ethicist as Improvisationist," in *Christian Ethics: Problems and Prospects*, ed. Lisa Sowle Cahill and James F. Childress (Cleveland: Pilgrim Press, 1996), 232.

17. Ibid., 233.

18. Ibid., 233–4.

19. Ibid., 232.

20. In *The Documents of Vatican II*.

21. *Free and Faithful in Christ: Moral Theology for Clergy and Laity*, 3 vols. (New York: Seabury Press, 1978–1981), 1:4.

22. *The Law of Christ*, 1:518.

23. Ibid., 518–20.

24. In *The Documents of Vatican II*, 211.

25. Ibid., 228–9.

26. Catholic Church, Synod of Bishops, *Justice in the World* (Vatican City: Vatican Press, 1971), 6.

27. Richard A. McCormick, "Notes on Moral Theology," *Theological Studies* 32 (1971): 74.

28. Charles E. Curran, "Is There a Distinctively Christian Social Ethic?" in *Metropolis: Christian Presence and Responsibility*, ed. Philip D. Morris (Notre Dame, IN: Fides Publishers, 1970), 114.

29. *Free and Faithful in Christ*, 1:4. Proponents of the thesis that there is no specifically Christian morality, in Häring's judgment, "come from that tradition of manuals which presented a rather static code morality or an ethics of principles and norms which could be well controlled. Although reacting against the controller, they continue to look just for norms regarding the common element in decisions" (23).

30. "Catholic Ethics with an American Accent," *in America in Theological Perspective*, ed. Thomas M. McFadden (New York: Seabury Press, 1976), 15.

31. See Norbert J. Rigali, "Christian Morality and Universal Morality: The One and the Many," *Louvain Studies* 19 (1994): 18–33.

32. Mahwah, NJ: Paulist Press, 1989.

33. New York: Continuum, 1999.

34. Subtitled *The Spirit of Catholic Moral Theology* (Collegeville, MN: Liturgical Press, 2001).

3. Spirituality and Morality: What Are We Talking About?

Richard M. Gula

This chapter first appeared in Richard M. Gula, *The Call to Holiness: Embracing a Fully Christian Life* (New York: Paulist, 2003).

The terms *spirituality* and *morality* resist easy definition. No universal agreement exists about their meaning, and the boundaries of their relationship are difficult to determine. Yet any attempt to bring spirituality and morality into creative relationship with one another requires that we settle on some features that help us to name the range of interest of each and to distinguish one area of concern from the other. This chapter tries to do that.

SPIRITUALITY

Spirituality has become a buzzword. It is used in religious circles for sure, just as one might expect. But it also appears frequently and unexpectedly in the corporate world in discussions about renewing organizations that are falling apart, or "losing their soul." It is also used to describe New Age practices, Twelve Step programs, holistic living, therapeutic strategies, and social reform movements. Spirituality is also used to refer to practices for developing the interior life, such as prayer, retreats, and spiritual direction. Spirituality indeed covers a wide range of interests.

Although definitions of *spirituality* are elusive, we use the term all the time as though its meaning were obvious. What do you associate with "spirituality," or what do you think of when you name someone as "spiritual," or when you want to improve your "spiritual life"? Just what are we talking about when we talk about spirituality? Compare your connotations with the ones represented in the following models.

From the time he was thirteen, the "Pillar Saint," Simeon Stylites (390–459), devoted his life to prayer, fasting, and other austerities, including physical punishment of his body, in ways that even exceeded the monastic practices of his time. In fact, he left the monastery to seek stricter austerity and seclusion by living on a small platform on top of a pillar (thus the nickname, "Pillar Saint"). As a solitary ascetic, he adopted body-denying disciplines in order to curb his passions so that he could be totally open to God. He fasted completely every Lent for twenty-six years. He believed that continual prayer, fasting, humiliation, and patient suffering were the road to eternal happiness and that the solitary life was the best opportunity to practice the virtues.[1] Simeon Stylites reflects one expression of the ascetical model of spirituality, and an extreme version at that. His asceticism conjures images of monastic celibates, wan and emaciated with eyes gazing heavenward. This way is optional. It is for those few who have a particular bent for it, since it demands striving for perfection through rigorous ascetical practices exceeding the scope and intensity of ordinary believers.

While Simeon's self-denial may be extreme, self-denial is a characteristic feature of this approach to spirituality. In its best form, ascetical self-denial fosters a simplicity of life, a concentration on God, and growth in love. We only need to think of how Francis of Assisi has fascinated so many and attracted such a following over the centuries with his way of integrating ascetical simplicity with generous service.

On the debit side, the ascetical model of spirituality risks opposing matter and spirit, with the spiritual realm being considered a separate sphere of life that is on a higher, and thus more important, plane than the material world. The material world of the body, passions, and emotions is regarded as something base, dispensable, and the source of evil temptations. The real self that must be saved is separate from the body and all that it experiences. In such a view, the body, and all material things, must be disciplined, kept under control, and even punished, for the sake of attaining a higher state of life and achieving the spiritual end of "saving the soul."

Another approach to spirituality that stands out in striking contrast to the ascetical austerities that separate matter and spirit is the incarnational spirituality of Zorba the Greek, that memorable character of Nikos Kazantzakis's life-affirming novel by the same title.[2] Whether working in a mine, confronting monks, or making love, Zorba's life is rich with all the joys and sorrows that life brings. He is madly in love with life, exuberant, and ready to dance at the sound of a downbeat. He knows what to do with a good bottle of wine, and how to pray and play as the occasion warrants. Zorba's spirituality is not about some other kind of life standing over against this one, but it is about all that belongs to being human. It represents a thirst for wholeness without taking on self-imposed punishments. While Zorba's spirituality is attractive for the way it engages the whole person in all of life's experiences, it can be self-absorbed, deceptive of one's need for conversion, and misleading about how ascetical disciplines of self-denial can be a positive means for growing in love and wholeness and not obstacles to it.

Sally Mae represents yet another approach to spirituality that fits roughly into the contemplative tradition. I first met her in the parish in 1970. She is a wife and a stay-at-home mom of two daughters. Everyone in the parish knew her as the "contemplative" one. Her version of the contemplative approach to spirituality consisted largely of devotional practices. Each morning, she would silently slide into the back pew for Mass, and then always stay afterward to complete her holy hour. During Lent she added the Stations of the Cross to her morning ritual. Whenever the parish held any special devotional services, penance services, parish missions, or weekend retreats, Sally Mae was there with her rosary, her holy hour book, a packet of holy cards of saints with prayers on the back, and a well-worn devotional book of prayers and readings.

The contemplative approach to spirituality has the great advantage of holding before us the goal of spiritual striving—union with God. Its danger is escaping from the world and human concerns. Thomas Merton comes to mind as one who lived as a contemplative but with an intense sensitivity for the deepest yearnings of life. He taught us that contemplative spirituality that is deaf to the cries of humanity is like an incomplete sentence. It risks reducing spirituality to a myopic "me and God" exercise of saving one's soul without including the lives of those who suffer.

If escapism is the danger of a contemplative approach to spirituality, then activism is the danger of the spirituality that makes works of charity and justice its core. While the contemplative risks losing touch with the world, the social activist risks losing touch with God. Take Billy Joe, for example. He was raised Catholic and came of age in the sixties when the church opened its windows on the world and the civil rights and antiwar movements were seizing the American conscience. He became deeply involved in movements to achieve racial integration, to improve wages and working conditions for farm workers, and to bring about peace in Vietnam. His passion for justice outdistanced his spiritual practices. In time, he gave up being a practicing Catholic but never lost his fascination with the writings of Dorothy Day and Thomas Merton. He remains committed to social reform and is actively involved in trying to help the homeless. But what Billy Joe is missing is what Dorothy Day and Thomas Merton witnessed—namely, the dynamic of turning outward in solidarity with all that yearns for fulfillment cannot be detached from the dynamic of prayer moving inward to remain rooted in God.

Each of these models—the ascetical, the incarnational, the contemplative, and the social activist—complements the other. Each can be an effective springboard to virtue, as the lives of the saints through the ages have shown. Another approach to spirituality tries to integrate the best features of these models in such a way that it cannot be characterized as any one of these approaches. This is what Mary Jane witnesses. She is a wife and the soccer mom of three boys. She regularly attends the 11:00 a.m. Sunday Mass. I met her when she was chairing the social action committee of the parish. Professionally, Mary Jane is the director of human resources for an electronics firm located in the parish. Other parishioners who work in the same firm say that they do not want a day to go by without having a chance to see Mary Jane. She is a calm oasis in the midst of frenetic activity. A few moments with her energy, attitude, humor, and attentiveness brighten one's day. Some would like to say that she is a very "holy" person, but they don't want that notion to be mistaken for sanctimony. Mary Jane is certainly not like that. When I asked what makes them think that she is holy, they answered that they feel "holy" in her presence. They touch a deeper center in themselves because she relates to them from a center of peace in herself. When I asked Mary Jane how she was able to manage so many responsibilities with such grace and yet to be present to people in such an effective way, she said that it is her "quiet time" each day that gets her focused and helps her to be present to whatever comes her way. She starts her day knowing to whom she belongs and to what she is committed. Her identity is secure.

For Mary Jane, spirituality connects to the "something more" or to the "depth dimension" of human experience. This is what some refer to as the "inner meaning" of life, or the "deeper reasons" that motivate a person. We can touch into the depth dimension of life, for example, in those times when we are moved by a sunset or music, or when we are shocked by the devastations of war or other acts of violence, or when we are touched by random acts of uncommon kindness by people who expect no reward, or when we are struck by an unconditional offer of forgiveness, or when we are inspired by the courageous endurance of serious illness or the calm acceptance of death, or when we are moved by a parent nurturing a child. Experiences such as these connect us to a level of reality that is greater than the present moment and to a deeper mystery than meets the eye. A spiritual practice such as Mary Jane's contemplative prayer helps us to attend to this depth dimension of our life and to recognize our basic beliefs, root values, and fundamental outlook on life. Those who live out of their center manifest their spirituality in a style of life characterized by an attentive presence to what is going on, by a nondefensive posture in the face of criticism, by peace of mind when facing situations of great ambiguity, and by a sense of hope that goodness will prevail even in the face of evil, tragedy, or death.

These are only a few approaches to spirituality. What else would you add? I have caricatured these models a bit to sharpen the point. Remember, the aim here is to try to come to some understanding of what we are talking about when we talk about spirituality. There is no one way to express one's spirituality, and there is no single, universally agreed-upon meaning of spirituality or, more specifically, "Christian spirituality." In the Appendix of the opening chapter, "Christian Spirituality," in their book by the same name, Lawrence Cunningham and Keith Egan list twenty-three different definitions of spirituality and/or Christian spirituality.[3] It seems that everyone who writes about spirituality has his or her own definition for this dimension of life. At present, there is not, and perhaps there cannot be, an exhaustive and all-embracing definition of spirituality. But what we assume to be included in spirituality will influence how we see its relationship to morality. So we need some working definition.

To put it simply, spirituality expresses a way of life animated by the longings of a restless human spirit. Or, to be more formal about it, *spirituality designates a way of living that strives to integrate our diverse experiences into a meaningful whole by connecting all of life to what we believe gives ultimate meaning and value to our lives*.[4]

What gives ultimate value answers our deepest desire, our most urgent longing—to find meaning. This desire for meaning is the most easily recognized form of spiritual hunger. Without meaning, our life wanders aimlessly and our self-worth erodes. Meaning in life comes from the sum of the loves in our life. There's no other source. Only when we live with love do we truly live. Love makes our hearts rail against meaninglessness. Spirituality is ultimately about how we connect with what counts most for us in living.

No one has the luxury of choosing whether they want to have a spirituality or not. Everyone has one. It is not just for those who seem to have a particular bent for it. We all live with some sense of meaning, though we differ on just what it is and where to find it. Some find it in religion, others in the stars, and still others in a commitment to peace and justice, to protecting the environment, or to saving the whales. Wherever it is that we find meaning, spirituality follows as the way we make sense out of what is happening to us and around us so that we do not become undone. The opposite of having a spirituality is to lose one's soul, to live without love, to be disconnected and unglued, to drop out and to wander aimlessly.

Whether we want it to or not, our spirituality shows itself in and through everything that we do and all the relationships that make up our lives. We recognize our spirituality from the outside in. Indices of our spirituality, for example, are such behaviors as whether we sleep at night or toss and turn, whether we have to rely on tranquilizers to get us through the day or not, whether we live in harmony with our bodies or out of touch with them, whether we are loving or bitter, whether we are giving ourselves over to God and the poor or to drug-induced highs and the fast track. Spirituality is the center of our lives, and it is capable of "bubbling up" everywhere. It lies behind our outlook on life and gets expressed in our ways of coping with life. It is also a powerful force influencing our evaluation of the possible courses of action we can take so as to live with meaning and integrity. This partly explains how some disagreements in ethics are, at root, often matters of spirituality. The disagreements over how to respond to removing life support from a person in a coma are less about differences in methods of decision making and more about differences about what counts most in life. Since spirituality also shows itself in the style of life through which we express our basic attitudes, convictions, and emotions, no aspect of our lives escapes the influence of our spirituality. It is like the seasoning that flavors the sauce. It expresses who we are and what we genuinely believe, for spirituality is where we ultimately integrate the diverse experiences of our life into a meaningful whole.

Understood in this way, spirituality characterizes both those who believe in God and those who do not. There is nothing particularly religious about it. A secular humanist could endorse it. So what makes spirituality religious, or, more specifically, Christian? Christian spirituality is that specific form of religious spirituality that presupposes belief in a personal, loving God, revealed in Jesus through the Holy Spirit in the community of the church. Christian spirituality is life in God's Spirit. It is possible because God has taken the initiative in loving us and continues to be at work in us. Christian spirituality began with God giving us the Holy Spirit through the resurrection of Jesus with the intent of transforming every dimension of our life through the same Holy Spirit—our work, our leisure, our civic duties and home life, our health and well-being. At the basis of Christian spirituality, then, is a personal experience of God as our ultimate value, reaching out to us in love through the Holy Spirit and inviting us and leading us to the fullness of life in communion with divine love. In brief, then, Christian spirituality is about our living through faith in relationship with God's Spirit.

While spirituality includes our response to God, it begins with God loving us first, preeminently in Jesus but also in and through all the people and events of our lives. In every experience we are already involved with God and drawn to God. With God as our starting point, we see all things in God and respond to God in and through all things.

As a response, spirituality entails a morality, a way of life, a life lived with a certain spirit—in the case of the Christian spiritual life, a life lived in the spirit of Jesus.

The discipline that studies the experience of God and the various traditions, ways of life, and practices that have emerged to express our response to God is also called "spirituality." Spiritualities (plural) are the distinctively different set of beliefs, stories, and practices people have developed to stay in touch with the spiritual dimension of their lives.

Sandra Schneiders has suggested that we could simplify the discussion of what Christian spirituality is about by agreeing that the referent of the term *spirituality* is "Christian religious experience."[5] As "Christian," it is affected by all of our theological convictions that shape our framework of meaning, such as our convictions about God, Jesus, and the human person, as well as how these get expressed in worship and in our lifestyle. Our spirituality changes as we nourish our theological convictions through spiritual and moral practices, such as prayer, worship, and social service, and try to integrate new perceptions and convictions into the whole context of our life. Moreover, as Christian, spirituality is a way of discipleship involving a personal relationship with Jesus under the power of the Holy Spirit working in and through the community of believers to bring about a world marked by justice and peace. In this sense, Christian spirituality is not fully understood as a person's subjective dispositions, nor is it sustained entirely on one's own. Holiness is a cooperative adventure. Thus, we can expect Christian spirituality to come with the notice we often find on boxes of Christmas toys—"Some Assembly Required." Christian spirituality is ultimately communitarian. Without some involvement in a community of faith, we can too easily make spirituality the working out of a private agenda rather than a way of discipleship. Christian spirituality requires stable, enduring relationships with a community of faith that shares common practices and stable convictions about who we are and who God is in Jesus and through the Spirit. The community's discernment can keep us honest about whether we are becoming who we profess to be as disciples of Jesus.

As "religious," Christian spirituality has both intellectual and affective dimensions. These are nurtured and expressed in the ways that we address God in prayer and ritual. The religious dimension takes us beyond an intellectual acknowledgment that God is self-giving love to an affective appreciation that God loves me. Moreover, the religious aspect of Christian spirituality must hold in balance a sense of transcendence and immanence. An overemphasis on the transcendent, as we saw with Simeon Stylites and Sally Mae, reduces spirituality to one's relationship with God and can lead to ignoring one's daily tasks and social relationships for the sake of a deeper interior life. An overemphasis on immanence, as we saw with Zorba and Billy Joe, can reduce spirituality to some form of self-absorbing therapy or social action. Christian spirituality as religious must remain rooted in the world while accepting that there is more than meets the eye, as it does for Francis of Assisi, Dorothy Day, Thomas Merton, and Mary Jane.

As "experience," Christian spirituality cannot be limited to moments of prayer or the interior movements aroused in prayer. It must encompass whatever enters into the actual living of our lives—daily events and tasks, family and social relationships, hopes and fears, work and play, health and illness, birth and death. Christian spirituality refers primarily not to having extraordinary experiences but to how we handle ordinary, day-to-day experiences. When we take the experiential dimension seriously, there can be no disjunction between the spiritual and the human. They work together in such a way that the spiritual is expressed in and through the human. In this way, our spirituality is shaped by our response to what comes our way in the course of living day by day. The widespread interest in spiritual direction can be explained, in part, by a growing appreciation that we can understand what is happening in our relationship with God to the extent that we understand what is happening in our experiences. The reason we can speak of different kinds of Christian spirituality (lay, marital, clerical, monastic, feminist, African American, and others) is that different experiences are the context for meeting God and responding to God.

In summary, then, when we talk about spirituality, we mean how we will relate to what we believe gives ultimate meaning and value to our everyday lives. Spirituality polishes the lens whereby we see more clearly in order to walk more rightly according to the vision of life that our ultimate value gives us. Christian spirituality integrates life around the personal experience that God, our ultimate value, values us. Jesus is our model and the inspiration of what life can look like when we entrust our lives to God and take to heart that God loves us.

MORALITY

If the spiritual dimension of being human pertains to seeing all things in relation to what we believe gives ultimate value, the moral dimension, by contrast, pertains to our effort to flourish as persons and communities in response to our ultimate value. The terms of reference for morality are the *person* expressing one's self in *action*. Morality engages our capacity both to make someone of ourselves and to determine the kind of actions we ought to perform. In a nutshell, morality is about what we should do because of who we are. Or, to be more formal about it, *morality is about acquiring those virtues and doing those actions that enhance the full flourishing of human life in community and in harmony with the environment*. Morality asks, "Who should I be?" and "What should I do?" so that we can live together in peace and harmony with one another and with our environment.

Understood in this way, morality has no particularly religious aspect, and "ethics" is the common way of referring to the disciplined way of thinking about who is a good person and what are right and wrong actions. When God is included as a necessary and fixed point of reference, then morality takes on a religious dimension, and moral theology, or theological ethics, is the way to name its disciplined study.

Of morality's two terms of reference—person and action—more often than not, people associate morality with actions. Moral quandaries fit well into many people's notion of what morality is all about—solving problems in such a way that we "do the right thing." If we restrict the meaning of morality to problems and right actions, we focus merely on how we should treat others and on the rules or principles that should guide and justify our conduct. Do I have a moral obligation to treat a terminal patient? What is my duty to my aging parents? Am I morally bound to pay all my taxes? Do I have a moral obligation to fulfill my promise? The focus of morality, then, becomes problems to solve and the strategies we use (principles or consequences) to determine the actions that will solve the problems. Such an understanding reflects a legal model for morality.

One of the great limitations of the legal model is that it turns the moral life into a series of "cases" requiring decisions. That is to say, we do not think of ourselves as living the moral life except when we are solving problems by following rational procedures. Living morally becomes a matter of determining the right thing to do by appealing to some abstract, universal principle, as though we were permitted to make some disinterested judgment from a neutral standpoint. In such a view, all those components of character, such as our convictions, intentions, perspective, emotions, commitments, cultural and religious background, past history, or future plans, seem to have nothing to do with the way we ought to act now.

In many ways, it is quite understandable that so many people think about morality as occasionalistic, analogous to law, and oriented toward solving a problem. Certainly, we need commonly accepted rules if we are going to ensure harmonious relations among diverse people. Moreover, in the Catholic tradition, centuries of maintaining a functional relationship between moral theology and the sacrament of penance has instilled the legal model of the moral life in the Catholic consciousness. Haunting questions, like "What do I have to do?" "Is it allowed?" and "How far can I go?" echoed in our consciences. Unfortunately, the necessary role of law in correcting our inconstancy and instructing our ignorance has given way to a legal mentality that sees everything in legal terms—God is the supreme lawgiver, living morally is governed by laws, obedience to authority is our principal virtue, loyalty is measured by obedience, and we live in order to receive a reward (heaven) or to avoid punishment (hell).

The legal mentality gives the impression that morality is episodic and primarily about actions governed by rules that someone else has imposed on us for the sake of controlling our behavior. But moral imperatives (the "must" and "ought") do not come in the first instance from some rule externally imposed. The *ought* in "I ought to!" comes from the nature of being human in relationship. The demand to be good and to do what is right arises from being in the presence of another. We tell the truth because of our commitment to the other person; we care about them and do not want to deceive them. In this sense, we experience the other as an invitation to come out of ourselves and relate in ways that will enable everyone to flourish in their humanity. Rules or laws (*Be truthful*, *Do not lie*) emerge later as expressions of what experience has shown are reliable ways to protect the dignity of persons, to give stability to social relationships, and to live in harmony with the environment. So morality is not to be thought of as being just about actions (doing the right thing) but primarily about persons (being good). The more adequate understanding of the moral life is not mere obedience to law but fidelity to life-giving personal relationships.

When we begin with relationships rather than the law, we can better appreciate how morality is fundamentally social. Morality expresses our responsibility for the relationships that constitute our lives so that there is no split between the person and society. Since the very identity of the individual is conceived in terms of his or her relationships, "private morality" is a contradiction in terms. To be a moral person means that we are searching for ways to live together that will enable everyone to flourish. After all, our lives are constituted by relationships and by our response to those relationships. That we must relate to others is inevitable. How we respond to them is a matter of character and choice.

A relational-responsibility oriented morality[6] is born in the heart. It begins with a sensitive awareness of the worth of another. Not to sense the moral call that the preciousness of another makes in our presence is to have an underdeveloped heart. To lack such empathy is to be morally paralyzed. No wonder those who have been emotionally traumatized lack any feeling of responsibility toward others. They get closed in upon themselves. Not until we are able to experience the other as distinct from ourselves and worthy of our careful attention will we be able to act upon values that protect and promote the well-being not only of that one other but of all living things. Moral living, then, expresses our sensitivity to what this perception of preciousness requires of us so that we can contribute to the full flourishing of persons and community in harmony with the environment.

Thus far there is nothing specifically religious or Christian about this description of the moral dimension of being human. It can be said of anyone. No reasonable atheist could object to it. What makes it religious and Christian is our belief that the One to whom we are ultimately responding in and through all of the relationships of our life is God, revealed in Jesus as the love we ultimately desire. So whether we experience God, how we experience God, and what beliefs we hold about God will have a pervasive, though not exclusive, effect on the sort of person we are and on what we do. For Christian believers, morality expresses the experience that we have of knowing and being loved by God. In this sense, the moral life is like worship. It is a response to the experience of God, and so it is spiritual in its roots.

For the Christian, then, morality cannot but be closely related to spirituality, to experiences of God, and to beliefs about God. The Christian cannot do justice to his or her moral experience and moral worldview without seeing all things as being related to God in some way as the source and goal of it all. Christian morality has a desired and anticipated end—union with God. In fact, God is the horizon against which the believer sees and values all things. As a result, the morality of those whose imagination is influenced by the experience of God and the beliefs of the Judeo-Christian tradition about God has a distinctively spiritual-theological element to it. The very purpose of the moral life is to live in the Spirit of God in imitation of Christ.

Moreover, morality for the religious believer is not authorized merely by social convention, or merely by the desire for self-fulfillment, or merely by the requirements of general rules of conduct that reason demands. Though all of these are legitimate ways to authorize morality, they are not sufficient from a theological point of view. From a theological point of view, God authorizes and requires morality. As a result, moral responsibilities are not merely to oneself or to other persons, nor are they only to the demands of rationality. They are, rather, responsibilities to God. The moral call to be good and to do what is right that arises from our encounter with the other is always a call from God (cf. Matt 25). So everyday relationships and mundane acts are not separate from our spirituality and moral life but are very much a part of them. They are, theologically speaking, acts of worship. That is, they participate in responding to God's purpose for life as revealed in Jesus and kept alive in the Spirit.

"God loves you!" is at the core of Christian revelation. Believing that God loves us is perhaps our most difficult act of faith. Yet, it is our first step in moral living. It is not what we do but rather what God first does on our behalf (grace) that is the bedrock upon which we can build a moral life. God's love for us is an invitation to love God in return by imitating God's love revealed in Jesus. Our responding to God is possible in the first place because God has taken the initiative to love us through acting in creation, preeminently in Jesus, but most immediately through all the people and events of our lives.

One of the ways that we can interpret the scene of Jesus' baptism as recorded in the Synoptic Gospels is that through it Jesus experienced an incredible affirmation of being loved by God: "You are my Son, the Beloved; with you I am well pleased" (Luke 3:22; Mark 1:11; Matt 3:17). Because Jesus was able to take this assertion to heart, he was able to make his life what he did. He never lost touch with his truth; he knew whose he was, so he lived under the blessing of his Father. Unfortunately, not all of us can claim the same for ourselves. But if we allowed ourselves to be affected by God's love for us, then we too could live confidently under God's blessing and love God in return. As with growth in any true love, as we come to know what is important to the beloved, we seek to love what the beloved loves. This is so not only in human love but in our love for God as well.[7]

So, the first major feature of the Christian moral life is that it is grounded religiously (in an experience of God) and is expressed as worship (a response to God). The ultimate purpose of the Christian moral life is to love God and be forever in union with God. The moral mandate to love God is enshrined in the first of the Ten Commandments and it is summarized in the first part of the Great Commandment: "You shall love the Lord your God with all your heart, and with all your soul, and with all your mind" (Matt 22:37). We show that we love God when we pray as well as when we cooperate with God by caring for what God cares about. In taking time for prayer, we make a conscious, intentional effort to direct our awareness to God. When we pray, we attend to loving God more directly than when we are loving our neighbor. Edward Vacek has insightfully distinguished loving God and loving neighbor in such a way that each is related to the other but one is not identified with the other: "We should love God directly, we should love our neighbor as an overflow of our love for God, and we should love God in and through loving our neighbor."[8] Thus, the other part of the Great Commandment is inseparably linked to loving God but is not identical with it: "You shall love your neighbor as yourself" (Matt 22:39).

Putting the two parts of the Great Commandment together, then, makes the moral life spiritual at its source and the spiritual life moral in its manifestations. That is, the love of neighbor and self are ultimately grounded in our love for God. We have expressed this liturgically in the ancient prayer to the Spirit: "Come Holy Spirit, fill the hearts of your faithful. And kindle in them the fire of your love." This process of loving God and caring about what God cares about presumes an active prayer life, nurtured by Scripture, supported by the community's common prayer, and tested within a community of discernment. Those whose moral life is born out of the experience of God's love and that is nurtured by spiritual practices can and ought to be able to discern what God is enabling and requiring them to be and to do.

How do we know what God's love for us is calling us to be and to do right now? Where do we look to find God? We look right into the heart of those places where we are living our lives, especially the relationships that make up our lives. James Keenan has argued that we are relational in three ways: generally, specifically, and uniquely. Each demands a cardinal virtue in response. As a relational being in general, we need justice; our specific relationships call us to fidelity; the unique relationship we have with ourselves calls us to self-care. Living in response to God requires the prudential discernment of what constitutes the just, faithful, and self-caring way of life we ought to follow.[9] So morality is best understood not as a set of laws imposed from without, but as a dynamic expression of virtue responding to the experience of being loved by God. Character and virtue are where morality and spirituality converge.

In the process of becoming virtuous, morality is more concerned with what is happening to the person performing actions than with the actions the person performs. William Spohn has it exactly right when he reflects on the relation of character and decisions:

> Most of the "work" of the moral life happens before we get to the moments of decision. The quality of our lives between decisions will determine what we see, how we are affected, how truthfully we examine our options, and consequently what we decide. The quality of our lives will determine our ability to discern.[10]

Spohn has captured here an insight that goes back to Aristotle: we are what we do habitually.[11] The moral quality of our lives does not lie in the occasional, dramatic decisions that we sometimes have to make, but in the character that we have formed by living from day to day doing things over and over again. This daily living creates a certain degree of moral momentum in the habits that express our character. For example, we wouldn't expect a liar suddenly to tell the truth, a slanderer to break forth into paeans of praise, or a domineering and controlling boss to have a fit of collaboration. How we behave in a crucial moment is born out of the habits we form from the way we behave in the day-to-day course of our lives. So, if we want to make a virtuous decision in hard times, then we need to develop the habit of virtue in daily affairs. The moral life goes on continually. We don't switch it on and off with the occasional moral choice.

Character gives us moral continuity. It is our tendency to feel, think, and act with a certain degree of consistency and so gives stability and an abiding quality to our lives. Our character, or moral identity, involves our sense of direction established over time and continues to be demonstrated through the pattern of actions we perform, the vision we have of life, the convictions or beliefs we live by, the intentions we seek to fulfill, the dispositions that ready us to act as well as the affections and motivations that move us to do what we believe to be right. Character explains not merely why we act in a certain way now but why we can be counted on to act that way in the future. With considerable momentum that does not go into reverse easily, character has a kind of stability. Since we generally stay "in character," people can detect patterns to our actions. Likewise, atypical behavior is suspect because it is so "uncharacteristic."

This focus on character and virtue (those dispositions of heart and mind to act in a certain way) takes seriously that who we are affects what we do, and what we do affects who we become. This is the very lesson Forrest Gump's mother taught him early on in life when she said, "Stupid is as stupid does." If we do something well, we become better; if we do it poorly, we become worse. If we drive like a maniac, chances are we will become one. If we treat our friends with respect, chances are we will become respectful and treat even strangers respectfully in turn. But if we treat friends in a condescending manner, then we will likely become arrogant and patronizing and so treat others in a condescending manner as well. The way we act now will affect how we act later. If we want to be a better person, then, we need to recognize and to take the opportunities we have to do better. That is to say, if we want to be more loving, peaceful, gentle, sincere, and friendly, then we have to act in those ways when we have the chance. Our choices and actions will either deepen our already existing habits and so strengthen our character, or will create new habits and so modify our character. Our character, while stable, is not fixed in stone. We are all works in progress. No one is finished. Conversion is always possible, whereby one's perception of the world, one's convictions or intentions will be changed, and one's character refashioned.

In contrast to the act-centered approach to morality that asks, "What is the right thing to do?," a morality focused on character and virtue asks, "From what inner place are you doing it?" In answering this question, morality meets spirituality. While actions are important in either approach to morality, the character of a person is crucial to the morality of the action focused on virtue, for character is the source of perspective in judging what to do and of the steadiness of intention for doing it.

Being formed in virtue makes us morally fit to meet our daily responsibilities. With virtue, we acquire sensitivity to values that we have internalized and so acquire a readiness to act in a certain way because of who we are. Virtue gives us a cognitive advantage to know what is right and an emotional predisposition to do it. Virtues influence how we assess what is going on. Cognitively, we speak of virtuous people as having a "nose" or a "special sense" for what is right. The morally good person knows the right thing to do, not so much through refined moral analysis or dependence on external rules, but by feeling of resonance or harmony between one's own being and the act to be done. Emotionally, virtuous people will want to do what is right and avoid what is wrong because virtues make them affectively committed to certain values. The virtuous person, for example, who has developed a habit of being sensitive to others has an interior compass pointing to what fits a person in need and then acts on it somewhat spontaneously. Rules may point to such an action as right, but rules are not the first recourse for the virtuous. Well-established habits are. Character, in a sense, chooses for them.

In sum, morality asks, "What should we do because of who we are?" For Christians, our character and choices ought to be a dynamic expression of the experience of being loved by God and sustained by God through our commitment to Christ, the full revelation of God. Moral living is moving conscientiously toward the goal of union with God by living in the Spirit of God revealed in Jesus. The challenge for us is to give concrete expression to what being faithful to God in the imitation of Christ would look like in our contemporary circumstances. As the incarnational principle tells us, only through the human will we come to know what God is enabling and requiring us to be and to do. Morality, then, must take seriously critical reflection on the experience of human relationships as the source for discerning what is required of us.

SPIRITUALITY AND MORALITY

Given what has just been described as the spiritual and moral dimensions of human life, we can see a little more clearly where the points of convergence might be. A long time ago, spirituality and morality went their separate ways. Chapter 1 gave an account of this divorce in greater detail. It showed that one of the reasons for the separation was that morality became too preoccupied with actions and left concern for the person to spirituality. But that is all changing now. It is time that we put back together what belongs together. Spirituality's drive toward integrating the whole of one's life around what gives ultimate value and morality's emphasis on the centrality of personal character and virtue offer a point of convergence for spirituality and morality.

By way of conclusion to this chapter, I want to give a brief glimpse of this convergence by retrieving some of the key notions that express what we mean by spirituality and morality. The basic unity of Christian spirituality and morality is related to their common starting point and goal—the experience of God and union with God. Whether we experience God and how we experience God will have a great influence on the content and quality of our spirituality and moral life. Christian spirituality is centered on the experience of God's loving us in Christ and through the Spirit in the church. Spiritual practices, such as vocal prayers, meditating on Scripture, and rituals of worship like the Eucharist, can nurture a way of life centered on God's love for us and our love for God.

Christian morality is rooted in the experience of God's love (spirituality) and expresses our response to the love of God for us in moral practices of virtue, such as honoring the self through appropriate self-care, helping our neighbor in need, working for justice, or protecting the environment. The sort of person we ought to be and how we ought to behave in the world as a result of our experience of God remain the central concern of morality. The fully human response to the love of God is revealed in Jesus. In the moral life, we follow Jesus as disciples alive in his spirit. Our encounter with Jesus through the spiritual practice of meditating on his words and deeds as recorded in the Gospels, for example, can have a formative influence on our moral life. The key question, then, for relating spirituality and morality, is this: Who should we be and how should we live if we believe that God loves us and that we love God?

Spirituality can never be separated from morality as some external aid that helps us be good. Spirituality, with its array of practices, nourishes the moral life at its very roots by deepening our awareness of being loved and by energizing our commitment to living in a way that makes this love a real, transforming presence in the world. Spirituality is the wellspring of the moral life. That is to say that morality arises from, rather than generates, spirituality. The moral journey begins in that spiritual space where we accept God's love for us and awaken to responsibility for promoting the well-being of persons and the community in harmony with the environment. In this way, morality reveals one's spirituality. In other words, how we live reveals who we are, what we genuinely value, and how we are integrating life experiences around what gives ultimate value. To reduce spirituality to the interior life apart from its public expression is to fall back on some kind of dualism. But we do not respond to God by some disembodied, internal word of acceptance or refusal. We respond with all dimensions of our self. Spirituality's drive toward integration and morality's response to God includes all aspects of life and pervades the whole of a person's identity—one's convictions, feelings, perspective, motivations, attitudes, and behavior. There is no area untouched by spirituality.

While we might want to distinguish the respective interests of spirituality and morality by focusing spirituality on our relationship to God and morality on who to be and how to behave in the world, we ought not to separate them so much that we lose their mutual influence on one another. In fact, spirituality so pervades morality that differences between moral judgments and lifestyles can often be explained by different spiritualities. We may hold to the same principles, use the same method of argument, do the same moral practices, but we can ultimately differ because we have different outlooks on life, different assumptions about what befits human well-being, different priorities of value, different depths of passion and zeal for common values, and a different vision of what life is ultimately all about. These are basically differences in spirituality that influence our morality. Morality can influence spirituality, too. Our involvement in working for justice, for example, can awaken us to examine our inner motivations and source of our commitment to justice in the first place, and it can send us back to engage spiritual practices that focus us on the deeper dimensions that unite us to one another and that lead us to our ultimate dependence on a source of life and love greater than us.

This brief preview of the relation of spirituality and morality suggests that they function in a critical-dialogical relationship. This means that they shape and reshape one another. While spirituality gives rise to morality, morality in turn reacts upon spirituality to correct or to confirm its direction. A sign of an authentic spirituality is the kind of life it engenders. As the biblical criterion would have it, "You will know them by their fruits" (Matt 7:20). Morality is the public face of one's spirituality, for morality is the place where we express our experience of God and our response to God. Without spirituality, morality gets cut off from its roots in the experience of God and so loses its character as a personal response to being loved by God, or being graced. Then it easily gets reduced to abiding by laws and to solving moral problems. Likewise, without morality, spirituality can spin off into ethereal ideas that never become real. Then the criticisms of spirituality as being about some other life in some other world would be true. But spirituality permeates all aspects of morality. It is the atmosphere within which we form and express our virtue.

Recent developments in moral theology give us the context and concepts for understanding this relationship more clearly. We have for too long kept spirituality separate from morality. It is time to put back together what belongs together.

Notes

1. See the account of his life in "St. Simeon the Stylite," *Butler's Lives of the Saints*, vol. 1, ed. Herbert Thurston and Donald Attwater (New York: P. J. Kenedy & Sons, 1956), 34–37.

2. Nikos Kazantzakis, *Zorba the Greek*, trans. Carl Wildman (New York: Simon and Schuster, 1952).

3. Lawrence S. Cunningham and Keith J. Egan, *Christian Spirituality: Themes from the Tradition* (New York: Paulist Press, 1996), 22–28.

4. This description of spirituality is highly influenced by the work of Sandra Schneiders and her appeal to a broadly based approach to spirituality. See especially, "Theology and Spirituality: Strangers, Rivals, or Partners?" *Horizons* 13 (Fall 1986): 266; and "Spirituality and the Academy," *Theological Studies* 50 (December 1989): 684.

5. Schneiders, "Theology and Spirituality," 267.

6. The relational-responsibility model of morality is often associated with H. Richard Niebuhr, *The Responsible Self* (New York: Harper & Row, 1963); Bernard Häring, *Free and Faithful in Christ: Moral Theology for Clergy and Laity*, vol. 1, *General Moral Theology* (New York: Seabury Press, 1978); and Charles E. Curran, *The Catholic Moral Tradition Today: A Synthesis* (Washington, DC: Georgetown University Press, 1999).

7. For a well-developed argument on the love of God at the foundations of the moral life, see Edward C. Vacek, *Love, Human and Divine: The Heart of Christian Ethics* (Washington, DC: Georgetown University Press, 1994).

8. Edward C. Vacek, "Love for God: Is It Obligatory?" *Annual of the Society of Christian Ethics* (1996): 220.

9. For Keenan's argument, see his "Proposing Cardinal Virtues," *Theological Studies* 56 (December 1995): 709–29.

10. William C. Spohn, *Go and Do Likewise: Jesus and Ethics* (New York: Continuum, 1999), 157.

11. On habituation as critical practice in Aristotle, see Nancy Sherman, *The Fabric of Character: Aristotle's Theory of Virtue* (Oxford: Clarendon Press, 1989), 176–83.

4. Spirituality and Ethics: Exploring the Connections

William C. Spohn

This chapter first appeared in *Theological Studies* 58 (1997).

There are promising and problematic connections between ethics and the emerging phenomena of spirituality. Any definitive resolution of this relationship would be premature because the discipline of spirituality is still defining itself. The variety of spiritualities is enormous, ranging from New Age practices to feminist political writings and Twelve Step programs.

On the positive side, certain forms of spirituality can augment those ethical systems that have achieved intellectual rigor at the cost of ignoring the wellsprings of motivation necessary to live morally. In addition, practical considerations from spirituality may open up ethical debates that have become hardened in academic and ecclesiastical circles.[1] On the negative side, some forms of spirituality appear resistant to any form of normative reflection, whether it be ethical, religious, or theological. Personal intuition and pragmatic results supply their own warrants for the validity of certain practices. This private assurance parallels the current preference for personal spirituality over institutional religion.[2] One hears people assert, "I'm not a religious person, but I am very spiritual." This may mean that they have found resources for inner strength in practices that are not burdened by the doctrinal and historical baggage of institutional religion. Or it may mean that their practices make no reference to God or any comparable ground of meaning. One wonders how such people are able to assess their spiritual experience without the intellectual and moral criteria that have been honed in religious communities.[3]

Michael Downey discerns two recurrent themes in the multiple varieties of spirituality: "First, and most importantly, there is an awareness that there are levels of reality not immediately apparent....Second, there is a quest for personal integration in the face of forces of fragmentation and depersonalization."[4] Since this quest is usually directed to the highest value in the individual's belief system, spirituality has direct reference to morality, though not necessarily to God.

"Spirituality" was mostly a Roman Catholic term until the late nineteenth century.[5] Although it originally referred to living according to the Spirit of Jesus in response to God, the term "gradually came to mean that life as the special concern of 'souls seeking perfection' rather than as the common experience of all Christians."[6] This elitist description has been rejected in the past two decades in favor of more inclusive definitions. Bernard McGinn proposed a working definition of spirituality that has guided the editors and contributors of a major series in the field:

> Christian spirituality is the lived experience of Christian belief in both its general and more specialized forms....It is possible to distinguish spirituality from doctrine in that it concentrates not on faith itself, but on the reaction that faith arouses in religious consciousness and practice. It can likewise be distinguished from Christian ethics in that it treats not all human actions in their relation to God, but those acts in which the relation to God is immediate and explicit.[7]

The recent widespread interest in spirituality in American Protestant circles may be attributed to an increased interest in more personal forms of religion, to ecumenical interaction, and to popular retrieval of Reformation piety described by Charles Taylor as "the affirmation of ordinary life."[8] Although initially suspected by some as a reappearance of anti-intellectual pietism, spirituality has begun to appear as a regular component of Protestant seminary curricula and in widely read texts by Protestant theologians.[9]

TERMS OF DISCUSSION

First, a provisional stipulation about terminology. Let me distinguish morality from ethics and, in parallel fashion, spirituality as lived experience from spirituality as academic reflection. "Morality" refers to "first-order" descriptive accounts of the lived experience of human values and obligations. It is a rich "fabric of sensibilities—perceptions, beliefs and practices."[10] "Ethics" refers to the "second-order" reflection that probes their rational supports and systematic interconnections. Bernard McGinn makes an analogous distinction about two orders of discourse in spirituality.[11]

"Lived spirituality," analogous to morality, refers to the practice of transformative, affective, practical, and holistic disciplines that seek to connect the person with reality's deepest meanings. It is concerned not primarily with isolated experiences such as visions or insights, but with a way of life that consciously seeks to live in tune with ultimate or comprehensive realities. "Reflective spirituality," analogous to ethics, stands for the second-order interpretation and communication of this dimension of experience as experience. It employs theological, historical-contextual, artistic, anthropological, and hermeneutical methods to analyze the lived experience.[12]

Morality and lived spirituality overlap inasmuch as devotional practices often seek to inculcate virtues and pursue moral values to their ultimate depths. However, morality and lived spirituality cannot be identified, because spirituality often addresses regions of experience that seem "off the scale" of ordinary morality. At one end of the spectrum, radically evil threats to meaning such as the scandal of the Holocaust and ecological devastation have generated contemporary spiritualities; so too have the witness of heroic sanctity and mystical union with the Good at the other extreme.[13] In addition, morality does not emphasize personal transformation and holistic integration to the degree which most forms of lived spirituality do.

Many versions of lived spirituality are more pedagogical than ordinary morality. They inculcate a way of life by practices of study, meditation, and compassion that develop certain intellectual, moral, and religious capacities.[14] With the help of a guide or director, these practices help the person break with an unauthentic way of existence in order to embrace a more authentic level, usually through contact with a more radical level of reality.[15] The spiritual disciplines then provide a structure for deepening and expanding the initial conversion.[16]

Ethics and reflective spirituality may examine the same phenomena but on different grounds. The virtue of compassion and practices of justice may be justified normatively by philosophical ethics or by theological and metaphysical warrants. Since disciplined reflection on spiritual experience should be normative as well as historical, reflective spirituality remains incomplete without reference to ethics. Spirituality, however, is not merely the application of principles derived from religious morality and belief, as in the older Catholic definition of "ascetical and mystical theology" that served as practical adjuncts to "dogmatic theology."[17]

Problems arise when a lived spirituality is cut off from an adequate reflective spirituality, that is, from traditions and communities that could provide normative theological and ethical categories. In their absence, spiritual practices are often justified by appeal to unexamined cultural commonplaces or narcissistic good feelings that are ripe for self-deception. In addition, contact with the sacred can be employed as an instrument to advance a particular ideology and social program. (Compare the "spiritual tourism" of New Age movements that offer odd medleys of practices divorced from the convictions and traditions that grounded them: Buddhist chanting, Native American vision quests and sweat lodges, tantric yoga, astrology, ersatz witchcraft rituals, and the like.)

Other problems arise in the relation of lived spirituality to ethics. Some practitioners want spiritual practices to "do the work" of ethical reflection by immediately and intuitively grounding their preferred way of life. Conversely, some ethicists consider the practices of spirituality to be sectarian because they are not accountable to public criteria of truth and meaning.[18] The relation between reflective spirituality and ethics is more promising, since the former can expand the scope of ethics beyond a strictly formal or impartialist account, while ethics can encourage the study of spirituality to move beyond historical, psychological, and sociological description to normative reflection. Many discussions of lived spirituality quickly shift into more reflective modes, because the experiential components of lived spirituality are primarily accessible to nonpractitioners through those more formal presentations. While most of the authors discussed here argue on a second-order level of discourse, their reflections consciously arise from personal engagement.[19]

In recent writings, one finds still more comprehensive uses of the term "spirituality" in relation to morality. Daniel Maguire cites "a sense of the sheer giftedness and sanctity of life....From this primal awe, moral oughts are born; and from this primal reverence, religion emanates. The moral response pronounces the gift good; the religious response goes on to proclaim it holy."[20] Peter J. Paris describes the core of African peoples' religion and morality in these terms: "The 'spirituality' of a people refers to the imaginative and integrative power that constitutes the principal frame of meaning for individual and collective experiences."[21] The distinctive interconnection of spirit, history, and nature leads in African peoples' spirituality to the basic "moral obligation to build a community in harmony with all the various powers in the cosmos."[22] These broader usages retain aspects of lived and reflective spirituality since they point to aspects of experience that are empowering, holistic, practical, affective, religious, and integrative.

SPIRITUALITY AND ETHICS OF CHARACTER

Perception, motivation, and identity are three regions of moral experience where the concerns and practices of spirituality are supplementing, if not supplanting, formal ethical approaches. Moral philosophers who are reviving Aristotelian ethics and others interested in the implications of psychology for the moral life (often associated under the rubric "ethics of character") are beginning to pay attention to these dimensions of moral experience.[23] Kantian, utilitarian, and contractarian approaches, however, tend to move from lived experience to morality and ethics by a rigorous process of pruning away the influences of emotion, particular relationships, and preferences that emanate from specific life plans or religious traditions. Spirituality poses a greater challenge to these universalist and impartialist forms of ethics.

Perception

What we value depends on what we pay attention to and how we pay attention to it. We make choices in the world that we notice, and what we notice is shaped by the metaphors and habits of the heart that we bring to experience. These resources for attentiveness may be derived from spirituality or from morality and ethics. Prior to thinking clearly about injustice one needs to recognize situations as morally problematic and also notice salient features in them that can lead to change. Evil conditions persist more frequently by reason of apathy and moral obtuseness than by conscious collusion. New moral categories like sexism and racism make us less obtuse to forms of injustice that had previously been taken for granted.[24] Philosophers and social critics fashion new moral categories, but how does one acquire the virtues that foster moral discernment and clarity?

Belden C. Lane turns to the desert to learn moral attentiveness and indifference.[25] He posits "the surly, discourteous piety of the desert fathers and mothers" as the antidote to the egoistic, undemanding niceness of much American spirituality. Stimulated by the endless onslaught of consumer culture, we are "plagued by a highly diffused attention" and "give ourselves to everything lightly. In saying yes to everything, we attend to nothing."[26] The desert teaches that attentiveness comes out of familiarity with emptiness. "Indifference" is the "slowly-learned attitude of abandonment that comes from prolonged desert experience."[27] Attachment to God made the detachment of the desert monks possible. "Indifference serves as a corrective lens, indicating what does and doesn't deserve attention."[28] An AIDS ward or shelters for the abused and addicted are today's deserts, places where the hard discipline of self-emptying takes place through solidarity with the suffering.

Iris Murdoch, the prolific novelist and occasional philosopher, writes about the importance of moral attention from a spirituality that is nontheistic.[29] She has for some time urged that ordinary moral vision is egocentric and needs transformation by getting connected with a transcendent source of beauty and goodness, some version of Plato's Form of the Good.[30] Unfortunately, she did not mention any practical means to effect this transformation. Recently she has discovered spiritual practices to train moral perceptiveness. Contemplative prayer, even without reference to God, can help purify human desires. Attachment to a transcendent goodness and beauty detaches us from sentimental distortion of the other, thereby freeing us to appreciate the other as it is. "But there is also a natural way of mysticism, as indicated by St. Paul, which involves a deepened and purified apprehension of our surroundings."[31]

Zen meditation provides the forms of spiritual practice for this natural mysticism. Through practices that empty the mind, Zen engenders the typically Buddhist respect and love of all things by training the person to empty the self by focusing on small details of ordinary life and nature.[32] Admittedly, such practices do not guarantee moral improvement: "One may not be sure that those who observe stones and snails lovingly will also thus observe human beings, but such observation is a *way*, an act of respect for individuals, which is itself a virtue, and an image of virtue."[33] Murdoch believes that with the collapse of traditional religion new forms of spiritual practice must be discovered to connect morality with its mystical background. "We can make our own rites and images, we can preserve the concept of holiness."[34]

At the level of perception, the practices of spirituality do not threaten ethics, but they can correct the abstract and universal emphases of some philosophies that neglect the particular contours of actual persons and unique situations.

Motivation

Spirituality corrects impartialist moral philosophies in a second way by attending to virtues and vices, the defining elements of character. Religion has often been more aware of the connection between vision and virtue, as Murdoch points out: "The most evident bridge between morality and religion is the idea of virtue," which calls us to a goodness that goes beyond fulfilling our duties.[35] Spiritual practices aim to inculcate specific habits of the heart that will serve to guide conduct. Dispositions like justice and compassion establish an embedded network of values that functions normatively in at least two ways.[36] It screens out contrary courses of action and sets the context for evaluating particular deeds. Proposed actions that harmonize with the set of dispositions will be discerned as appropriate, while those that clash with it are discerned as unfitting.[37] In practical discernment, the set of dispositions exercises a normative function often neglected by philosophers and theologians who concentrate on rules and principles as the only normative elements in morality.[38]

Many contemporary spiritualities shy away from explicit moral norms and principles. They often rely on a set of dispositions that are expected to characterize the practitioner and function normatively in decision and action. It is not clear that any set of dispositions can do all the work of ethics. Although dispositions are scenarios of action for those who follow a particular spiritual path, it is not clear that they can provide the explicit normative criteria that are needed to justify action to those outside that spirituality. Let me cite two instances of spiritualities that present a normative *Gestalt* of dispositions in place of rules and principles:

1. Gustavo Gutiérrez does not outline a theory of justice or apply the norms of just-war theory to the problem of revolution. Instead he describes a pattern of familiar gospel dispositions that have been reshaped by the Latin American struggle for liberation: conversion as a requirement for solidarity, gratuitousness as the atmosphere for effective action, joy as the victory over suffering, spiritual childhood, radical dependence on God as the requirement for commitment to the poor, and community born out of solitude.[39] The encounter with God that occurs in identifying with the poor in Christian faith ought to evoke these particular virtues; it establishes a path along which these dispositions are the roadmarkers. Like every major Christian spirituality, this path is shaped by the gospel story and specific sociohistorical challenges: "the concrete forms of the following of Jesus are connected with the great historical movements of an age."[40]

   This spirituality of liberation is grounded in self-conscious reflection, which includes critical interpretations of Scripture, theology, sociohistorical conditions, philosophy, and other traditional spiritualities with which it shares common patterns of Christian discipleship such as those reflected in the writings of John of the Cross.[41]

2. Elisabeth Schüssler Fiorenza also presents a normative pattern of dispositions behind her proposals for an emancipatory feminist biblical hermeneutics. Although her work is concerned more with critical method than with explicating a spiritual experience, she mentions features common to other spiritualities: conversion, struggle against entrenched evil, the discovery of the divine presence in the struggle, practices of imagination and celebration.[42]

Schüssler Fiorenza, however, stands in sharp contrast to Gutiérrez when it comes to dispositional content and justification. Scripture, she argues, cannot set any normative pattern of dispositions for feminism because it is thoroughly contaminated by androcentric interpretation and inscribed patterns of domination. Every authority is subject to the authority of experience expressed in contemporary feminist praxis. One aim controls the reading of Scripture: to determine "whether and how Scripture can become an enabling, motivating resource and empowering authority in women's struggle for justice, liberation, and solidarity."[43]

The normative set of dispositions is grounded in contemporary democratic and egalitarian convictions rather than in theology, tradition, or philosophical ethics. A "spirituality of vision and imagination" grounded in the logic of democracy "requires passionate involvement, respect, and recognition of the other, desire for justice, recognition of needs, zest for life, the capacity to relate to others, and especially the vision of a different community of equals."[44] Richard B. Hays expresses serious reservations about Schüssler Fiorenza's project: "The danger is that her approach might ultimately undermine the authority of the New Testament so thoroughly that its liberating power would also be lost, as the church finds its identity increasingly shaped by the ideals of liberal democracy and the apparent dictates of contemporary experience."[45] Unlike Gutiérrez, this spirituality of liberation seems immune to criticism from Scripture or tradition. The experience of struggle against patriarchy judges the Bible, doctrinal and moral theology; but can anything judge the movement? Schüssler Fiorenza's work may indicate what happens when the lived spirituality of a movement lacks an adequate theoretical justification.

Other spiritualities ground their strategies and practices in psychology as well as in ethical and religious warrants. James D. Whitehead and Evelyn Eaton Whitehead analyze the negative emotions of anger, shame, and guilt and suggest practical ways to transform them in creative directions.[46] Wilkie Au and Noreen Cannon use Scripture and Jungian psychology to address contemporary issues from workaholism to individuation.[47]

Identity

Ethics and spirituality make identity a central concern. Both assume that action flows from the specific identity of the person, the constellation of habits, commitments, and emotions that we call character. Since we tend to discern the moral appropriateness of actions in relation to our "sense of self," the question of identity assumes priority in moral reflection. Who we think we are and who we want to become, our *identity*, comes to a considerable extent from *identification*, namely, the persons, causes, and values with which we identify. Spirituality usually adds a transformative urgency to the question of identity. When the self overidentifies with external goods like success, power, and pleasure, it is bound to be unauthentic. Spiritualities insist on conversion and dedication to worthwhile sources of meaning in order to forge a genuine identity.

In her recent historical survey *Love Your Enemies*, Lisa Sowle Cahill finds that the issue of identity lies behind the tension between Christian pacifism and just-war theories.[48] Pacifists from Erasmus, the Anabaptists, and the Quakers to Dorothy Day and Thomas Merton have had a sense of urgency about the reign of God that had led them to reject worldly ways in order to identify with the ways of Jesus witnessed in the New Testament.[49] That urgency does not always derive from belief in an imminent return of Jesus. Instead, it arises from a sense of identification with the neighbor and with Christ: "they are cognizant…of his life as putting them within reach in the present of a new life for us, out of which flows conduct often indicated in the language of demand, but actually constituting a spontaneous and characteristic mode of being for those united to Christ."[50] The joy and steadfast witness of Quakers and Anabaptists in the midst of suffering are unintelligible without this sense of identification with the suffering Jesus who is also the risen and present Lord.

Advocates of just-war theory, on the other hand, usually miss the lived spirituality that drives Christian pacifism because they interpret it through the lens of ethics. Christian pacifism, however, cannot be understood to be a strategy deduced from a general conviction of the value of human life. Nor is it concerned with detailing exceptions to a general moral prohibition against violence. Rather, Christian pacifism "seems to arise before the point at which just war thinking begins. It asks first of all not about the exceptional case, but about the quality of a communal life based in Christ and in the kingdom of God, a life that turns out to make violence incomprehensible."[51]

Christian pacifism is originally a lived spirituality whose second-order discourse may perhaps be better understood as a reflective spirituality than an ethics. This second-order discourse has an ethical dimension that is translated into certain moral practices and prohibitions. Pacifism's moral stance rests on an intuition that violence is incompatible with Christian identity. That intuition cannot always be expressed in terms that will be persuasive to others, even fellow Christians, who do not share that same spirituality. This failure will almost certainly occur if the critic insists that the discussion be carried on in the language of strategy and political prudence or if one rules out religious warrants as "sectarian" or insufficiently "public."[52] When ethical discourse strips Christian pacifism of its particularity, it renders it unintelligible. When pacifists couch their witness too narrowly, however, they court misunderstanding from those who do not share their spirituality. Although spirituality cannot do the work of ethics, ethicists ought not to dismiss spirituality as necessarily premoral or sectarian.

The question of identity also lies at the heart of the discussion about the environmental crisis.[53] Do we conceive of nature anthropocentrically or as a complex system of which humanity is one part among many? Should our moral community extend beyond humanity to other sentient and nonsentient beings? Environmental devastation is increasingly seen not only as immoral but also as a violation of the sacred. Buddhist forms of ecospirituality are invoked to resacralize nature.

Practices of meditation contribute to a reinterpretation of personal identity: "By accepting and yielding to…groundlessness I can discover that *I have always been grounded* not as a self-contained being but as *one manifestation of a web of relationships which encompasses everything*."[54] This identification with the whole shapes an ecospirituality that inculcates the virtues of interdependence and universal compassion.[55]

John D'Arcy May calls for a critical correlation of Buddhist and Christian resources to ground an interreligious ecological ethic. Today's "consumerist" ethic ("I want it all, and I want it now") can be checked by a more ascetic ethic ("I want it, but I don't need it"). Spiritual practices of the world's religious traditions, however, propose a "contemplative" ethic whose motto would be "I don't want it, because I love it." If I espouse this stance, possessing or exploiting the desired object "would seem like a betrayal of myself and my world."[56] Western Buddhists have pioneered a more activist ecological ethic of care, but they have had difficulty integrating it into a Western appreciation of rights and justice. May argues that the two traditions are not incompatible, and that "deep ecology requires a deep ecumenism," which can integrate an ethics of justice with an ethics of cosmic care.[57]

The question remains, however, whether the theoretical foundations of Buddhism will be adequate to ground a social morality. A Western Buddhist critic faults his coreligionists for being "committed to ethically unproblematic issues—like rainforests, whales, primal peoples, animal rights, even human rights and world peace—and to all forms of service, rather than involving themselves with the militant wretched of the Earth (especially those close to home), and with the structural violence of our social system."[58] Christian commentators voice similar concerns, fearing that the Buddhist principles of interconnectedness and "mutually conditioned co-origination" may lead to a "depersonalizing of ethics, thus undermining the concept of responsibility with its intrinsically social dimension."[59] "The widening circle of ethical concerns must not skip over human beings, but move through them."[60] However much we identify with nature and the earth, the fact remains that the costs of ecocide are borne mostly by the poor and people of color. The convergence between certain Buddhist and Christian practices at the level of lived spirituality may be undermined by incompatible ethical and ontological suppositions at the more theoretical level.

CONCLUSION

In ecospirituality and Christian pacifism a cause integrates the self and locates it in a comprehensive framework of meaning. Certain actions are morally proscribed because they would betray the sense of self which has been fashioned by spiritual convictions and practices. Moral philosophy does not seem capable of creating personal identity. Philosophical ethics may have to be content to set certain outer limits of action that will inevitably remain rather formal. Ethics must look to specific traditions and movements to fill in the outline with narratives, symbols, and practices that constitute a more or less coherent way of life. Reflective spirituality should be one of these supplementary sources for ethics. It may also be true that every ethics rests on some particular tradition that implicitly contains a life narrative that gives content to virtue terms and gives priority to some common human values over others.

The authors cited here connect spirituality and ethics in relatively irenic approaches because, with some exceptions, they are compatible with philosophical ethics and universalist forms of theological ethics. In the ideal sense, spiritualities get their practitioners in touch with meaning that is humane and constructive of human community. Indeed, some would reserve the name "spirituality" to these constructive practices and movements.

An examination of spiritualities that reject ethics would be the topic for another study. Moral perception, motivation, and identity can be enhanced by most of the forms of spirituality that I have examined. Some are religious; some are primarily moral but presume an undogmatic religious background. The least dogmatic of the authors, Iris Murdoch, makes a good case that at base morality, religion, and mysticism overlap. Spiritualities that arise from an experience of great trauma, like the Holocaust, ecocide, or the oppression of women and the poor, may be more susceptible to using spirituality ideologically. The sacred is enlisted as an ally to remedy social conditions of evil. However, if the sacred is primarily used as an instrument rather than appreciated in its own right, legitimate suspicions arise. Some movement spiritualities are more willing to be accountable to other visions and voices than to those coming from their own ranks. Insofar as they are not accountable to other voices, they run the risk of being insular and ideological, because they will inculcate some of the very oppressive and exclusionary traits that their writings denounce.

Notes

1. See John P. Burgess, "Does Scripture Matter? Scripture as Ethical Norm in a Time of Ecclesial Crisis," an unpublished paper delivered at the Society for Christian Ethics convention at Albuquerque, January 7, 1996. Christian ethicists' customary neglect of the moral import of loving God is ably redressed in Edward Collins Vacek, SJ, *Love, Human and Divine: The Heart of Christian Ethics* (Washington, DC: Georgetown University, 1994).

2. See Wade Clark Roof, *A Generation of Seekers: The Spiritual Journeys of the Baby Boom Generation* (San Francisco: HarperSanFransico, 1993), esp. the bibliography, at 269–85.

3. Michael Downey comments that both the institutional dimension of religion and critical reflection "are sorely neglected in so many developments of spirituality today which tend to be overly subjective to the detriment of more objective and external consideration, as well as preoccupied with pragmatic result....The results, as so many currents in contemporary spirituality manifest, is a highly individualized, indeed privatized approach to the sacred, devoid of any clear sense of belonging to a community, and a lack of a clear sense of critical social responsibility which any authentic awareness of the sacred demands" (*Understanding Christian Spirituality* [New York: Paulist, 1996], 25). This volume is the best available overview of contemporary Christian spirituality.

4. Ibid., 14.

5. For a historical treatment, see Mark O'Keefe, OSB, *Becoming Good, Becoming Holy: On the Relationship of Christian Ethics and Spirituality* (New York: Paulist, 1995); see also the various articles in *The New Dictionary of Catholic Spirituality*, ed. Michael Downey (Collegeville, MN: Liturgical Press, 1993).

6. Joann Wolski Conn, "Spirituality," in *The New Dictionary of Theology*, ed. Joseph A. Komonchak, Mary Collins, and Dermot A. Lane (Collegeville, MN: Liturgical Press, 1991), 972.

7. Bernard McGinn, John Meyendorff, and Jean Leclercq, *Christian Spirituality: Origins to the Twelfth Century* (New York: Crossroad, 1985), xv–xvi. I do not insist that the relation between moral acts and God considered by spirituality must be "immediate and explicit," since this would give the impression that spirituality is concerned only with commands of God or direct inspirations, mystical discernments, etc. Sandra M. Schneiders uses personalist

vocabulary to define spirituality as religious self-transcendence that provides integrity and meaning to life by situating the person within the horizon of ultimacy ("Theology and Spirituality: Strangers, Rivals, or Partners?" *Horizons* 13 [1986]: 253–74). For more historical treatments, see Louis Bouyer, Jean Leclercq, and François Vandenbroucke, *A History of Christian Spirituality*, 3 vols. (New York: Seabury, 1977). Gustavo Gutiérrez describes liberation theology as a spirituality of the poor of Latin America; like every spirituality, it is "a distinctive way of being Christian" (*We Drink from Our Own Wells: The Spiritual Journey of a People* [Maryknoll, NY: Orbis, 1984], 37).

8. "The affirmation of ordinary life finds its origins in Judeo-Christian spirituality, and the particular impetus it receives in the modern era comes first of all from the Reformation" (Charles Taylor, *Sources of the Self: The Making of the Modern Identity* [Cambridge, MA: Harvard University, 1989], 215). The collapse of the mediating role of church and clergy led to an appreciation for the sanctity of work, marriage and family, and lay life in general. This led to an intensification of religious practice and a new stress on the individual. Catholicism is witnessing a similar development since the Second Vatican Council.

9. Marcus J. Borg writes that he began to understand Jesus when he "began to see Jesus as one whose spirituality—his experiential awareness of Spirit—was foundational for his life" (*Meeting Jesus Again for the First Time: The Historical Jesus and the Heart of Contemporary Faith* [San Francisco: HarperSanFrancisco, 1994], 15). Jesus was a "Spirit person," that is, one who has "a strong sense of there being more to reality than the tangible world of our ordinary experience" and one who is also a mediator of the sacred to others (ibid., 32). See also Dorothee Sölle, *The Window of Vulnerability: A Political Spirituality* (Minneapolis: Fortress, 1990). For womanist expressions of spirituality, see Emilie M. Townes, *In a Blaze of Glory: Womanist Spirituality as Social Witness* (Nashville: Abingdon, 1995); and *A Troubling in My Soul: Womanist Perspectives on Evil and Suffering*, ed. Emilie M. Townes (Maryknoll, NY: Orbis, 1993).

10. Wayne A. Meeks, *The Origins of Christian Morality: The First Two Centuries* (New Haven: Yale University, 1993), ix; see also his definition of ethics as second-order discourse (ibid., 4).

11. Bernard McGinn, "The Letter and the Spirit: Spirituality as an Academic Discipline," *Christian Spirituality Bulletin* 1, no. 2 (1993): 4. See also Henry David Aiken, "Levels of Moral Discourse," in *Reason and Conduct: New Bearings in Moral Philosophy* (New York: Knopf, 1962), 65–87.

12. Sandra M. Schneiders assesses the various strengths and weaknesses of these methods; see her "Spirituality as an Academic Discipline: Reflections from Experience," *Christian Spirituality Bulletin* 1, no. 12 (1993): 10–15, and "A

Hermeneutical Approach to the Study of Christian Spirituality," *Christian Spirituality Bulletin* 2, no. 11 (1994): 9–14. Joann Wolski Conn notes "the advantages of spirituality's method of staying close to experience in all explanations and testing past assumptions against one's critical reflection upon experience" ("Spirituality," in Komonchak et al., *The New Dictionary of Theology*, 985).

13. See Bernard McGinn, *Anti-Christ: Two Thousand Years of the Human Fascination with Evil* (San Francisco: HarperSanFrancisco, 1994); Roger S. Gottlieb, "Ethics and Trauma: Levinas, Feminism, and Deep Ecology," *Cross Currents* 44 (1994): 222–39; Donna L. Orsuto, "The Saint as Moral Paradigm," in *Spirituality and Morality: Integrating Prayer and Action*, ed. Dennis J. Billy, CSSR, and Donna Lynn Orsuto (New York: Paulist, 1996), 127–40. Some forms of virtue ethics not affiliated with religious traditions have a somewhat broader but still limited range. Liberal virtue theorists such as Judith N. Shklar allow for a gamut running from cruelty to fairness and tolerance (*Ordinary Vices* [Cambridge, MA: Belknap, 1984]), but that range seems a bit pallid next to many spiritualities. On the difficulties of conceptualizing sanctity in a strictly philosophical framework, see Susan Wolf, "Moral Saints," *Journal of Philosophy* 79 (1982): 419–39, and the reply by Robert Merrihew Adams, "Saints," *Journal of Philosophy* 81 (1984): 392–401.

14. See Richard J. Foster, *Celebration of Discipline: The Path to Spiritual Growth*, rev. ed. (San Francisco: Harper Collins, 1988). Foster, a Quaker, describes the gradual transformation from a life of self-interest and fear to one that welcomes God's abundance. This transformation is God's work in which the person cooperates by committed practice of traditional spiritual disciplines. Foster describes four "inward disciplines" (meditation, prayer, fasting, and study), four "outward disciplines" (simplicity, solitude, submission, and service), and finally four "corporate disciplines" (confession, worship, guidance, and celebration).

15. Spiritual directors have ensured accountability since the desert monks of Egypt; see Lawrence S. Cunningham, "Cassian's Hero and Discernment: Some Reflections," in *Finding God in All Things: Essays in Honor of Michael J. Buckley, S.J.*, ed. Michael J. Himes and Stephen J. Pope (New York; Crossroad, 1996), 231–43.

16. See, e.g., the various articles in *The Westminster Dictionary of Christian Spirituality*, ed. Gordon S. Wakefield (Philadelphia: Westminster, 1983); and *The Islamic Spirituality: Foundations*, ed. Seyyed Hussein Nasr (New York: Crossroad, 1987).

17. See Downey, *Understanding Christian Spirituality*, 117–9.

18. See Amelie Oksenberg Rorty, "Moral Imperialism vs. Moral Conflict: Conflicting Aims of Education," in *Can Virtue Be Taught?*, ed. Barbara Darling-Smith (Notre Dame: University of Notre Dame, 1993), 33–51.

19. Spirituality is still in the process of being defined as an academic discipline. See Walter H. Principe, "Toward Defining Spirituality," *Studies in Religion/Sciences religieuses* 12 (1983): 139, and "Christian Spirituality," in Downey, *The New Dictionary of Catholic Spirituality*, 931–38; Wakefield, *The Westminster Dictionary of Christian Spirituality*, v; Joann Wolski Conn, ed., *Women's Spirituality: Resources for Christian Development* (New York: Paulist, 1986), introduction; Jon Sobrino, *Spirituality of Liberation: Toward Political Holiness* (Maryknoll, NY: Orbis, 1988), 13–45; Sandra M. Schneiders, "Spirituality in the Academy," *Theological Studies* 50 (1989): 676–97.

20. Daniel C. Maguire, *The Moral Core of Judaism and Christianity: Reclaiming the Revolution* (Minneapolis: Fortress, 1993), 41.

21. Peter J. Paris, *The Spirituality of African Peoples: The Search for a Common Moral Discourse* (Minneapolis: Fortress, 1995), 22.

22. Ibid., 35.

23. See Martha C. Nussbaum, *Love's Knowledge: Essays on Philosophy and Literature* (New York: Oxford University, 1990), 54–105; Owen Flanagan, *Varieties of Moral Personality: Ethics and Psychological Realism* (Cambridge, MA: Harvard University, 1991); William C. Spohn, "Passions and Principles," *Theological Studies* 52 (1991): 69–87.

24. Lawrence A. Blum questions one new moral commonplace: the assumption that women operate under an ethic of care and relationships while men operate under an ethic of principles and rationality does not stand up empirically or philosophically (*Moral Perception and Particularity* [Cambridge, UK: Cambridge University, 1994], 183–267). See also Kathryn Tanner, "The Care That Does Justice: Recent Writings in Feminist Ethics and Theology," *Journal of Religious Ethics* 24 (1996): 171–91.

25. Belden C. Lane, "Desert Attentiveness, Desert Indifference: Countercultural Spirituality in the Desert Fathers and Mothers," *Cross Currents* 44 (1994): 193–206.

26. Ibid., 197.

27. Ibid., 195.

28. Ibid., 200; see Richard A. McCormick, SJ, who uses the same metaphor for a moral theology attuned to spirituality (*Corrective Vision: Explorations in Moral Theology* [Kansas City, MO: Sheed and Ward, 1994]).

29. For another nontheistic spirituality, see Vaclav Havel, *Living in Truth*, ed. Jan Vladislav (Boston: Faber and Faber, 1990). Geraldine Finn takes exception to Havel and other "spiritual" readings of the fall of Communism in her "The Politics of Spirituality: The Spirituality of Politics," *Listening* 27 (1992): 119–32.

30. See Iris Murdoch, *The Sovereignty of Good* (New York: Schocken, 1971).

31. Murdoch cites Phil 4:8 in her *Metaphysics as a Guide to Morals* (London: Viking Penguin, 1992), 301.

32. Ibid., 245.

33. Ibid., 244.

34. Ibid., 249.

35. Ibid., 481.

36. Culture redefines virtues and vices according to quite distinctive paradigms and religious warrants; see Bernard T. Adeney, *Strange Virtues: Ethics in a Multicultural World* (Downers Grove, IL: InterVarsity, 1995).

37. On discernment in Jesuit spirituality, see David Lonsdale, SJ, *Listening to the Music of the Spirit: The Art of Discernment* (Notre Dame: Ave Maria, 1993); Philip Sheldrake, SJ, *Befriending Our Desires* (Notre Dame: Ave Maria, 1994); Herbert Alphonso, SJ, "Docility to the Spirit: Discerning the Extraordinary in the Ordinary," in *Spirituality and Morality*, 112–26.

38. See G. Simon Harak, SJ, *Virtuous Passions: The Formation of Christian Character* (New York: Paulist, 1993).

39. Gutiérrez, *We Drink*, 91–135. Jon Sobrino endorses this work of Gutiérrez as the finest expression of Latin American liberation spirituality (*Spirituality of Liberation*, 50–79); see also Jon Sobrino, *The Principle of Mercy: Taking the Crucified People from the Cross* (Maryknoll, NY: Orbis, 1994).

40. Ibid., 27.

41. See ibid., 87. In more recent writings Gutiérrez has mined another classic journey of purgation and solitude struggling toward God; see his *On Job: God-Talk and the Suffering of the Innocent* (Maryknoll, NY: Orbis, 1992).

42. See Elisabeth Schüssler Fiorenza, *But She Said: Feminist Practices of Biblical Interpretation* (Boston: Beacon, 1992), 89, 115, 156, 176.

43. Elisabeth Schüssler Fiorenza, *Bread Not Stone: The Challenge of Feminist Biblical Interpretation* (Boston: Beacon, 1984), 60.

44. Schüssler Fiorenza, *But She Said*, 157. The logic of democracy defines a moralized version of the reign of God. The *basileia* is "G-d's intended world" that occurs whenever Jesus or any of his followers tells stories "about the uninvited who are invited or about the least who will be first....In sum, the well-being and happiness of everyone is the central vision of the *basileia* movement" (ibid., 215–6).

45. Richard B. Hays, *The Moral Vision of the New Testament: A Contemporary Introduction to New Testament Ethics* (San Francisco: HarperSanFrancisco, 1996), 282. Similar questions about Schüssler Fiorenza's book *Jesus: Miriam's Child, Sophia's Prophet* (New York: Continuum, 1994) are raised by Pheme Perkins in *America*, May 13, 1995, 26–27.

46. James D. Whitehead and Evelyn Eaton Whitehead, *Shadows of the Heart: A Spirituality of the Negative Emotions* (New York: Crossroad, 1995).

47. Wilkie Au and Noreen Cannon, *Urgings of the Heart: A Spirituality of Integration* (New York: Paulist, 1995).

48. Lisa Sowle Cahill, *Love Your Enemies: Discipleship, Pacifism, and Just War Theory* (Minneapolis: Fortress, 1994).

49. Ibid., 151.

50. Ibid., 176.

51. Ibid., 229.

52. Stanley Hauerwas's arguments for Christian pacifism exemplify Cahill's thesis since they are conversion-based rather than rule-based. They arise out of identification with the path of the gospel Jesus. As such, neither the reasoning nor the depth of motivation that drives his prohibition of violence are likely to be fully grasped by those whose identity is not centered on this story and person (Stanley M. Hauerwas, *The Peaceable Kingdom: A Primer in Christian Ethics* [Notre Dame: University of Notre Dame, 1983], 145). See also James M. Gustafson, "The Sectarian Temptation: Reflections on Theology, the Church, and the University," *Catholic Theological Society of America, Proceedings* 40 (1985): 83–94, and Hauerwas's reply in *Christian Existence Today: Essays on Church, World and Living in Between* (Durham: Labyrinth, 1988), 1–21.

53. See Christopher Manes, *Green Rage: Radical Environmentalism and the Unmaking of Civilization* (Boston: Little, Brown, 1990); *Reweaving the World: The Emergence of Ecofeminism* (San Francisco: Sierra Club, 1990); Ian Ball, Margaret Goodall, Clare Palmer and John Reader, eds., *The Earth Beneath: A Critical Guide to Green Theology* (London: SPCK, 1992); Charles Cummings, *Eco-Spirituality: Toward a Reverent Life* (New York: Paulist, 1991); John F. Haught, *The Promise of Nature: Ecology and Cosmic Purpose* (New York: Paulist, 1993); Richard N. Fragomeni and John T. Pawlikowski, eds., *The Ecological Challenge: Ethical, Liturgical and Spiritual Responses* (Collegeville, MN: Liturgical Press, 1994); Michael Schramm and Udo Zelinka, eds., *Um des Menschen Willens: Moralität und Spiritualität*, (Würzburg: Echter, 1994); George E. Tinker, "Spirituality, Native American Personhood, Sovereignty and Solidarity," *Ecumenical Review* 44 (1992): 312–24; John Bolt, "The Greening of Spirituality: A Review Article," *Calvin Theological Journal* 30 (1995): 194–211.

54. David Loy, "Avoiding the Void: The Lack of Self in Psychotherapy and Buddhism," *Journal of Transpersonal Psychology* 24 (1992): 176, cited in Corrado Pensa, "A Buddhist View of Eco-Spirituality: Interdependence, Emptiness and Compassion," in *Eco-spirituality: Perspectives from World Religions*, ed. Augustine Thottakara, CMI, Spirituality Series No. 5 (Rome: Center for Indian and Inter-Religious Studies, 1995), 80–96, at 89.

55. James Gustafson points out that nature is characterized by conflict as

much as by harmony (*A Sense of the Divine: The Natural Environment from a Theocentric Perspective* [Philadelphia: Pilgrim, 1994]).

56. John D'Arcy May, "'Rights of the Earth' and 'Care for the Earth': Two Paradigms for a Buddhist-Christian Ecological Ethic," *Horizons* 21 (1994): 56; see also Kenneth Kraft, "The Greening of Buddhist Practice," *Cross Currents* 44 (1994): 163–79.

57. Ibid., 61.

58. Ken Jones, "Getting Out of Our Own Light," in *Dharma Gaia: A Harvest of Essays in Buddhism and Ecology*, ed. Allan Hunt Badiner (Berkeley, CA: Parallax, 1990), 188.

59. May, "Rights of the Earth," 58.

60. Gottlieb, "Ethics and Trauma," 238.

5. How Vatican II Brought Spirituality and Moral Theology Together

Charles E. Curran

This chapter first appeared as "Foreword" in William H. Shannon, *Silence on Fire: Prayer of Awareness* (New York: Crossroad, 2000).

Vatican Council II (1962–65) brought about many significant changes in Catholic life and understanding, but clearly its teaching on spirituality should be one of the most significant contributions for the daily life of the people of God. Unfortunately this understanding of spirituality has not been effectively communicated within the church. William A. Shannon in his book *Silence on Fire* helps people to practically live out the theory of spirituality proposed at Vatican II. This chapter will consider the Vatican II approach to spirituality that Shannon so ably translates into practice.

Vatican II's teaching on spirituality has two fundamental assertions — the call of all Christians to holiness and perfection and the fact that the answer to this call to holiness comes in and through our life in the world.

UNIVERSAL CALL TO HOLINESS

Chapter five of the "Constitution on the Church" is entitled "The Universal Call to Holiness." The document clearly asserts that all Christians in whatsoever state or way of life are called to the fullness of the Christian life and to the perfection of charity. The holiness of the people of God clearly shows forth in the lives of so many saints in the church. This chapter cites a number of Scriptural passages that make this point. Matthew 5:48 concludes the fifth chapter of his Gospel with the admonition that all are to be perfect even as the heavenly Father is perfect. Our sanctification is the will of God (1 Thess 4:3, Eph 1:4). We are to live as becomes saints (Eph 5:3); to live as God's chosen ones holy and beloved (Col 3:12); to possess the fruits of the Holy Spirit unto holiness (Gal 5:22, Rom 6:22).

Unfortunately this strong teaching of Vatican II has not become widely accepted and lived within contemporary Catholicism. Three concepts carried over from a pre–Vatican II approach have influenced the general failure to recognize the call of all Christians to holiness—a poor notion of the saints, an older understanding of Christian perfection limited to those who leave the world to follow the Gospel, and a concept of priesthood as mediator between God and the laity in the church.

The Saints

The word *saints* in the New Testament has different uses referring to angels, pious Jews who have already left this world, or Christians who died in midst of persecution. However, the primary usage of "the saints" found over sixty times in the New Testament refers to the members of the Christian community—the community of the disciples of Jesus. The letters of Paul well illustrate such an approach especially in their opening greetings and often in their conclusions. The First Letter of Peter is addressed to those who are to be made holy by the Spirit (1:2). The letter goes on to cite two famous passages from the Hebrew Bible dealing with holiness: Be holy for I am holy (Lev 19:2) and you are a chosen race, a royal priesthood, a consecrated nation (Isa 43:20–21).

However, today the average Catholic would be quick to deny that she is a saint. When Robert Livingston, a Louisiana Congressperson, was running for Speaker of the House, he recognized some personal failings but explained that he was running for the Speakership of the House of Representatives and not for sainthood. When I read that in the press, I knew that Robert Livingston was a Roman Catholic. What he said there has become a commonplace among Catholics. I am not a saint.

Behind such a remark lies the honest recognition of our own limitations and sinfulness. But still the question naturally arises: Why do Catholics even today deny that they are called to be saints despite the teachings of Vatican II and of the New Testament?

Elizabeth A. Johnson, in her justly acclaimed book *Friends of God and Prophets: A Feminist Theological Reading of the Communion of Saints*, explains why Catholics have lost the New Testament understanding of the saints as the members of the community of the disciples of Jesus. For most Catholics, saints refer to people who have gone before us in a spirit of great sanctity and now act as intermediaries between God and us. As saints they are now close to God, and there they can intercede with God on our behalf. The understanding of the saints as very holy people, much different from ourselves, who have gone before us and intercede for us before the throne of God plays a prominent role in Catholic self-understanding and in the piety of many people. The process of the canonization of saints and the veneration of saints in the Roman Catholic tradition strengthens such an understanding of the meaning and role of saints.

But what happened? How and why did the church forget or lose the New Testament understanding of saints as the people of God, the members of the church? Elizabeth Johnson points out how the original understanding of the saints as the people of God in this world expanded to include also those who had gone before us in death. However, in the beginning those who had gone before us were understood on the basis of a companionship model as an inspiration and encouragement to us but basically equal with us. However, in the early centuries a hierarchical and patriarchal model developed and became predominant. The saints in heaven went from being primarily in communion with us as witnesses in a partnership of hope to become intercessors on our behalf in a patriarchal structure of power and mediation. As a result the church lost the idea that all of us are saints who are called to holiness. In the light of the limited but very popular understanding of holiness as associated with the canonized saints who intercede for us before the throne of God, many Catholics today fail to realize that all the baptized are saints who are called to holiness.

Holiness Associated with Leaving the World

Just as a pre–Vatican II theology understood the saints as outside and above the people of God, the same theology identified the holy people as those who left the world and went into religious life. Religious heard the call of Christ to be perfect, left the world, and took the three vows of poverty, chastity, and obedience. Catholics who continued to live in the world thought of themselves as second-class citizens who did not receive a call to holiness but tried to live in accord with the Ten Commandments and the natural law but not the evangelical counsels. Leaving the world and taking the three religious vows made one holy.

However, even Thomas Aquinas had trouble with this understanding of the vows. For Aquinas all Christians have the same end or goal for their spiritual life—charity that involves loving union with God and neighbor. The three evangelical vows do not change or affect the basic end of charity that is the same for all Christians. The vows concern only the means to the end and these three religious vows aim at overcoming obstacles that might prevent our growth in the love of God and neighbor. Poverty deals with the obstacle coming from an inordinate love of material goods; chastity with an inordinate love of bodily pleasures; obedience with an inordinate love of the spiritual self. The vows thus deal only with the means to the end and have only the negative function of removing possible obstacles in the way of charity. Unfortunately, both theoretically and practically the vows became ends in themselves rather than means to serve the love of God and neighbor. Thus people who took these vows were better than those who did not take them.

But many theologians today have a different understanding. Vatican II calls for Scripture to play a central role in Catholic spirituality, liturgy, theology, and life. The gospel call to conversion and change of heart challenges all believers. All are called to be perfect, as our gracious God is perfect. The challenge of the Gospel addresses all Christians.

Many contemporary theologians now recognize the primacy of the baptismal commitment. The baptismal commitment to discipleship and following Jesus involves a call to holiness for all Christians and striving for an ever-greater love of God and love of neighbor. All other vows do not add anything to this fundamental vow but specify how the individual Christian lives out the baptismal vow. Thus the marriage vows or the religious vows add nothing to the baptismal vow which is the same for all but merely specify how the individual Christian lives out the baptismal commitment. This baptismal commitment involves the call to holiness.

Priests as Mediators between God and Her People

Even today most Catholics look upon the priest as called to a greater holiness than lay people. Such a perspective comes from seeing the priest not as a member of the community of the people of God but rather as the mediator between God and the people. The priest stands outside and above the community of the people of God.

The French school of spirituality in the seventeenth century provided the basis for such an understanding of the priest as a mediator between God and the people. The priest was "another Christ" called to bring God to men (*sic*) and men to God. I learned this concept of priesthood in the pre–Vatican II seminary. Unfortunately such an understanding still predominates for most Catholics today.

However, a Vatican II theology again puts primary emphasis on the community of the disciples of Jesus, the people of God. The priest is not outside and above the community but performs a function within the community. The "Constitution of the Church" of Vatican II recognizes the primacy of the church as the people of God with the hierarchical and priestly offices exercising functions within the community.

The pre–Vatican II theory and practice of the Eucharist well illustrate the role of the priest as the mediator between God and the community. The priest turned his back to the people, prayed silently in Latin, and consecrated the body and blood of Jesus so that the people in the pews could adore Jesus and then receive communion from the priest. Recall how people knelt at the communion rail to receive communion on their tongue. At the conclusion of the mass the people knelt again to receive the priest's blessing.

Changes in the theology of the Eucharist in the post–Vatican II church illustrate the centrality of the community of the people of God with the priest exercising a special function within the community. The older approach called the priest the celebrant because he alone brought

Christ to others. Now the priest is the presider of the assembly and the whole community celebrates. The role of the people of God in the liturgy involves active participation and celebration not just passive acceptance of what the priest provides for them.

Again, the postures associated with the Eucharist well illustrate the newer approach. The priest presides as a part of the community and facing it. The presider prays in the name of the community and out loud. At communion people stand, receive communion in the hand, and communicate themselves. The community no longer kneels for the final blessing. Many newer churches put primary emphasis both on the altar table and the community, and some in accordance with the best of the theological tradition have no kneelers. The community stands for the Eucharistic prayer.

The primary purpose of the Eucharist is not the transformation of the bread and wine into the body and blood of Christ but rather through this important change the transformation of the community, the mystical body of Christ. Through Christ, with Christ, and in Christ in the unity of the Holy Spirit, the total community gives praise and thanks to God, the gracious parent for her many gifts and receives the transforming love of God so that their lives might be changed as they go forth from the Eucharist.

Vatican II clearly taught the universal call of all Christians to holiness and sanctity. But this teaching has not taken hold in the Catholic community because of poor understandings of sanctity, holiness, and the role of priests in the community.

HOLINESS IN THE WORLD

The second assertion in the teaching of Vatican II about spirituality emphasizes that the call to holiness is lived out in the midst of our daily life in this world. The "Pastoral Constitution on the Church in the Modern World" develops this idea. According to this document one of the great errors of our time is the dichotomy between the faith that many profess and the practice of their daily lives (43).

The pre–Vatican II approach recognized significant distinctions or dualities—supernatural-natural, Gospel-natural law, religious-lay, and divinization-humanization. In fairness these distinctions or dualities did not constitute total dichotomies but existed in a hierarchical ordering with the first element in the duality being more important than the second.

The supernatural-natural duality constitutes the most basic reality that helps to explain the others. The natural order involves our temporal existence and life in the world. The supernatural involves our spiritual life—relationship with God through grace. The natural law governs life in the natural or temporal sphere of this world. The natural law maintains that human reason reflecting on what God has made can determine how God wants us to act in this world. The Gospel or grace does not directly affect life in the world. Those who want to be perfect leave the world to follow the evangelical counsels. The church has two missions—divinization and humanization. On the supernatural level the church offers God's gracious love and life in word and sacrament to God's people—the mission of divinization. On the natural level or the temporal sphere of this world, the church and its members work with all others for a greater humanization of life in temporal society. The humanizing mission of the church is important for two reasons. First, conditions in the temporal or natural order have some influence on the supernatural order. Second, God has a plan for human existence in this world that all should follow.

The Vatican II approach did away with these dualities. Jesus, faith, and the Gospel must affect who we are and what we do in all aspects of our life. The supernatural-natural distinction should not exist. There is no aspect of human existence that is not affected by faith and the Gospel. Grace touches the family, the neighborhood, the workplace, recreation, politics, and all aspects of human existence. There is no such thing as the merely natural order.

"Justice in the World," the document coming from the 1971 Synod of Bishops makes the point very clearly: "Action on behalf of justice and participation in the transformation of the world fully appear to us as a constitutive dimension of the preaching of the Gospel, or, in other words, of the church's mission for the redemption of the human race and its liberation from every oppressive situation." Thus, the Gospel affects daily life, and there is only one mission of the church that involves the preaching of the Gospel and the church's mission for the redemption of the human race. Christians living in the world are called to holiness.

WILLIAM H. SHANNON'S CONTRIBUTION

In *Silence on Fire*, William H. Shannon makes two important contributions to this Vatican II spirituality. First, he insists on the call to holiness in the midst of our daily life in this world. Our author coins a marvelous metaphor to describe the older approach—spiritual apartheid. Spiritual apartheid separates our spiritual life from our life with family, friends, work, play, and the broader social and political life of the world. In developing a spirituality for holiness in the world, the book follows the approach of Thomas Merton, the well-known Trappist monk. However, Merton was not a monk who left the world behind in order to find God only in the monastery. Merton continued to have an important interest in and great concern for what happened in the world and in daily life precisely because he believed that the living God is truly present in the world.

Shannon's book clearly and lucidly explains the basis for a spirituality of holiness in the world. The living God is already present in all things. Too often we think of God as an object. There are many objects in our world, but for believers God is the biggest and the most important object of them all. However, God as object is different from and apart from all the other objects in our lives. But God is not an object. God is a subject—the ground of being who is present in all reality. We cannot separate God from all that is because the gracious God has already chosen to be present there. This understanding of God's presence in all reality stands behind the beautiful opening prayer of the Twentieth Sunday in Ordinary Time (B) "Oh God...may we love you in all things and above all things." Such is the prayer of the Christian striving for holiness in the world.

Shannon's second and even more important contribution involves the practical order. Once Catholics learn and accept the Vatican II approach that the call to holiness is addressed to all Christians in our daily lives, an even greater problem arises. Vatican II itself gives us no help in answering the most important and existential question of how we live out this spirituality. However, *Silence of Fire* puts flesh and blood on the bare bones of the Vatican II skeleton. The prayer of awareness serves as the basis for such a spirituality. This joyful awareness of God by its very nature also involves an awareness of all other people and things precisely because the living God has chosen to be present there. Shannon here develops an approach to prayer that is quite different from the popular notion of prayer as our talking with God through our words. The prayer of awareness is primarily wordless prayer.

But the problem here is obvious. How do you use words to explain wordless prayer? Here Shannon the teacher takes over. The author was a college teacher of theology for forty years. William Shannon is not only a wonderful guide for the spiritual life but also an excellent pedagogue. The book deftly explains the theory and practice of the prayer of awareness that serves as the basis for a life of Christian holiness in the world.

Vatican II by its insistence that all of the baptized are called to holiness lived out in the daily life of the world has thus insisted on the close relationship between moral theology and spirituality. In this perspective prayer is not a withdrawal from the world to be alone with God. William H. Shannon in *Silence on Fire* develops in detail the prayer of awareness based on God's presence in all reality.

Part Two

REIMAGINING THE TRADITION

6. Catholic Moral Theology, Ignatian Spirituality, and Virtue Ethics: Strange Bedfellows

James F. Keenan

This chapter first appeared in *The Way Supplement* 88 (Spring 1997).

Contemporary moral theology has led us from an occupation with specific kinds of particular wrong actions (lying, killing, inappropriate sexual conduct, etc.) to a much broader reflection on the entirety of the person standing before God. To realize this change, many moral theologians have begun reexamining the virtues.[1] There they have been able to address questions about the type of persons we ought to become and the virtuous practices that we ought to engage in order to realize that moral vision.

Moral theologians have also recognized the importance of the claims of Norbert Rigali who has argued for the need to integrate the vision of the moral life into a living spirituality.[2] Such a spirituality could both root the moral virtues in a relationship with God and neighbor and provide a vision of the type of Christian and the type of church we ought to become. In a word, the moral life could be a virtuous response to a spirituality that animates us both individually and communally.

Yet, as easy as it may seem to be to develop a virtue ethics out of Ignatian spirituality, we must recognize that for the greater part of its history, Catholic moral theology has been interested in neither spirituality nor the virtues, but rather predominantly in particular kinds of spe-

cific wrong actions. This nearly inherent tendency cannot be underesti-
mated: indeed, already there are voices summoning moralists back to
actions and away from the virtues and spirituality.

I begin this essay by presenting the contributions of three English
Jesuits who convey both the possibility and the extraordinary challenge
that lies before us in developing a virtue ethics out of Ignatian spirituality. Then, I argue that virtue ethics is rather congruent with the aims of
Ignatian spirituality and can serve as a worthy vehicle for expressing a
morality stemming from such a spirituality.

JOHN MAHONEY'S ARGUMENT: MORAL THEOLOGY'S OBSESSION WITH SIN AND ITS NEED FOR SPIRITUALITY

In *The Making of Moral Theology*, Jesuit ethicist John Mahoney
demonstrates convincingly that the roots of moral theology are found in
the practice of confessing sins.[3] To guide the confessor in determining
the nature of sin and its suitable penance, "penitentials" were repro-
duced throughout Europe from the sixth to twelfth century.[4] In these
penitentials, the general classifications of moral conduct were described
in terms of particular external actions: the lie, the act of theft, the blas-
phemous word, the adultery, and so on. From these books, moral theology developed its primary interest in sin and identified sin as these
particular external acts that corresponded to one of the seven deadly
sins. Moral theology during these many centuries showed no sense of
idealism or vision; it showed no concern for Christian identity nor for
spirituality; and there is no developed concept of discipleship. Judgment
day alone was its central preoccupation, where persons' deeds in lieu of
their hearts were scrutinized.

The growth of religious orders and their work of evangelization of
the emerging towns was a hallmark of the thirteenth century. This period
emphasized not the decay but the possible growth of the Christian.
Ironically this movement was in part circumvented by the Fourth
Lateran Council (1215), when Pope Innocent III imposed the Easter
duty, making the turn to penance no longer a matter of spiritual election
but ecclesiastical law. Henry Lea called this "the most important legisla-
tive act in the history of the Church."[5]

For the next three centuries, then, two types of moral instructions developed: the great *Summae theologiae* of high Scholastics and the confessional manuals which were effectively sophisticated penitentials. Clearly, Thomas Aquinas' *Summa* represents the greatest achievement from this time. There he presented three parts, each representing a movement: God's movement toward us, our movement toward God, the two movements in the incarnation of Jesus Christ, both human and divine. Thomas directs the reader in pursuit of the end, which is union with God and is achieved through charity; he provides the virtues, the cardinal ones for the moral life and the theological ones for the spiritual life (together, the seven virtues embody the end for all Christians); and he presents intentionality and not external deeds as the proper concern for determining moral living. Though other Scholastics share Thomas' concern with interiority, the virtues and the integrated anthropological vision, by the fourteenth century moral reflection begins again to focus not on who we are or who we ought to become, but on what we did wrong. While Thomas held that "all moral matter comes down to the virtues,"[6] those with a less integrated view of the person preferred simply to look at the confessional manuals that stretch from Innocent's edict until the Reformation.

Recent studies have shown that the moral reasoning of the sixteenth and seventeenth century was highly innovative in meeting the needs of the Europeans who through the explorations of the New World and trade with the East could no longer accept the older moral methods of the past. To answer those new and urgent needs, a new moral method rose quickly that looked not to existing principles but rather to cases. That new method of looking at cases was known as casuistry.[7] Regardless of the new method, the content of moral theology was the same: to determine which actions were forbidden and which ones permitted. Moreover, from the eighteenth through the twentieth century that imaginative casuistry evolved into the rather unimaginative manuals of theology, which were textbooks, again, for confessors.

A survey of the history of moral theology, then, shows that with few exceptions, moral theology has been nearly exclusively concerned with sins, that is, with particular actions determined to be wrong. Mahoney is right, then, to make the claim that he does: the roots of theology are in its obsession with sin as external actions, but Mahoney also insists that, excepting Thomas, moral theologians have never done what they were always called to do: to recognize morality as a response to the Spirit's movements in our lives.[8]

THOMAS SLATER'S ARGUMENT: SEPARATE MORALITY AND SPIRITUALITY

If an English Jesuit is the clearest writer criticizing the sin legacy of morality and the strongest champion of morality's need to be rooted in a spirituality, it is another English Jesuit who is Mahoney's historical nemesis. At the beginning of this century the first moral manual in English appeared, written by Thomas Slater. In his famous preface he describes the manuals of moral theology as:

> Technical works intended to help the confessor and the parish priest in the discharge of their duties. They are as technical as the text-books of the lawyer and the doctor. They are not intended for edification, nor do they hold up a high ideal of Christian perfection for the imitation of the faithful. They deal with what is of obligation under pain of sin; they are books of moral pathology.

After discussing the "very abundant" literature of ascetical theology, he added,

> moral theology proposes to itself the much humbler but still necessary task of defining what is right and what wrong in all the practical relations of the Christian life....The first step on the right road of conduct is to avoid evil.[9]

Thirty years later another English Jesuit, Henry Davis, wrote: "It is precisely about the law that Moral Theology is concerned. It is not a mirror of perfection, showing man the way of perfection."[10]

Moral theology then has been simply about sin and its avoidance. Moral theology has not concerned itself with the positive task of growing as a disciple of Christ. Slater helps explain, then, why virtue language, outside of Thomistic theology, is so rare in moral theology: it was not interested in the development of the person; that task was left to those in ascetical or spiritual theology.

ROBERT PERSONS' ACHIEVEMENT: A FOUNDATIONAL WORK OF IGNATIAN SPIRITUALITY THAT LED TO A MORAL THEOLOGY

Ironically one of the rare instances of developing a morality out of a spirituality via the virtues was achieved in England by the early moderate Puritans, using Ignatian spirituality. That tale, worth telling, gives us a clue of what we can do for the future.

Early British Puritan practical divinity developed out of the Roman Catholic devotional works of Christian perfection or spirituality.[11] Among these works was the Jesuit Robert Persons' *The First Booke of the Christian Exercise*. No contemporary work of devotion compared to it, "the most popular book of devotion among both Catholics and Protestants in Elizabethan and Jacobean England."[12] The first edition appeared just after Persons' escape from England at the time of arrest in 1582. Two years later, the Puritan Edmund Bunny "protestantized" that edition and then a subsequent one. By 1640, the original Catholic edition went through more than seven editions; the Puritan versions went through more than forty-five editions!

More remarkable than the fact that a Puritan pirated a Jesuit writing is the fact that Bunny's editing of the text was rather slight. More than 90 percent of the Jesuit text remains intact in the Puritan text.[13] From this text, subsequent Puritans built a morality. Having examined the self and found the need for resolution, the next generation of Puritans asked questions about discerning the certitude of salvation; about the way of being vigilant of temptation; about the need for developing a proper household and for ordering one's life through practices, and so on. These later texts began with introverted self-examinations but proceeded to build the person up from within, using the virtues to guide the reader into becoming a more ardent Christian.[14]

While Puritans were innovative with these spiritual texts, Roman Catholics continued to distinguish works of morality (casuistic manuals about sinful deeds) from spiritual manuals. For instance, besides doing his major devotional opus, Persons wrote his own small casuistic manual with Dr. William Allen.[15] Catholic moral theology resisted any sustained attempts at developing out of a spirituality an ethics of character.

The Puritans were interested in Persons' spiritual text because it impressed on them the deep need to examine oneself before God. Through a series of meditative reflections, Persons approached the reader with the insights of the First Week of *The Spiritual Exercises*. Prompting them to tread through the marshy untrampled terrain of their own deplorably unexamined life of sin, Persons guided the reader gently but repeatedly by the controlling insight of the First Principle and Foundation.

Basically the work considers sin's violent affront to God; the exercitant's affective awakening to the offence; the tangible appreciation of the harm that sin brings to the exercitant; the realization that though the exercitant merits eternal damnation, God has kept the exercitant until this point from death and just judgment; and, finally, the appreciation of what Christ has done through his death for the sake of the exercitant. It is a contemplation on the state of one's soul, an invitation to experience one's own condition and to see therein the appalling state of one's sinfulness. This is not a sinfulness of specific actions catalogued in casuistic manuals; on the contrary, it locates the tragedy of sin in the profoundly distorted relationship between a loving, merciful but just God and a wickedly obtuse reader. This sinfulness is rooted in one separated from Christ because of inconsideration.

The self-examination here is different from any in the Catholic works seen earlier. Unlike those works that start with wrong actions and recede into the agent's intentionality, Persons' point of departure is always the reader; he bypasses ever starting with an external action or its causal intention. Persons turns not to the effects of sin, but more profoundly toward its root: the negligent, unthinking ungrateful heart.

A SOLUTION: BUILDING A VIRTUE ETHICS
OUT OF IGNATIAN SPIRITUALITY

If Persons could develop a major work of spiritual devotion out of the *Exercises*, we can develop a virtue ethics out of the insights of the

Exercises. To begin this project, I offer ten foundational points which illustrate similarity between Ignatian spirituality and a virtue ethics.

The Priority of the Spiritual

Because Ignatian spirituality so stresses the initiative of God as prior to the individual's response, then a virtue ethics in this context is always subsequent to God's movement. The Puritans recognized this: they developed a virtue ethics from Ignatian spirituality, not vice versa.

Instances of the opposite movement would be where a moral principle shapes a spirituality, for example, the Pro-Life movement, Pax Christi, Bread for the World. In Ignatian spirituality, God shapes the participants and they in turn seek virtues to express their response. In this way, both the spirituality and the moral agenda have extraordinary breadth and are not restricted by a particular principle.

Morality as a Response

Throughout the *Exercises*, there are two striking movements: on the one hand, the exercitant is constantly seeing God's movement toward him or her, supporting her; on the other hand the exercitant is constantly being prompted to offer his or her whole self, whether in the offering of the meditation on the Kingdom[16] or the *Suscipe* in the final contemplations.[17]

Since the offering is one's self, an ethics of character rather than an ethics of principles governing particular actions suitably embodies that response. As the exercitant offers him- or herself, they offer the possibility of being more in the image of Christ who saves them.

Deep Interiority

As we saw above, the Puritans were attracted to Persons' Ignatian writings because of their deep interiority. In developing a moral theology they did not turn to principles which govern actions, but virtues which perfect dispositions. As a morality responding to a spirituality, the former emerged from the depths of the latter.

The Uniqueness of the Individual

Though the Puritans may not have grasped this insight (after all they only appropriated from the First Week of the *Exercises*), Ignatian spirituality has always appreciated the uniqueness of the individual. The exercitant is always urged to deepen their unique relationship with the Lord by seeing that Jesus Christ has done "all this for me." For this reason, Ignatius warns the director never to get between the exercitant and the Lord but rather to "permit the Creator to deal directly with the creature, and the creature directly with his Creator and Lord."[18]

The orientation to safeguard an individual's prayer complemented the Jesuit defense of the individual conscience, where the individual person heard their own distinctive call and worked out their relationship with the Lord.[19]

Likewise, the virtues perfect an individual's dispositions uniquely. For this reason, we think of the virtues as tailor-made. Each person tries to find the mean appropriate for a particular person's dispositions. The mean of virtue is, then, the mean as it relates to the specific agent.[20] As Thomas put it, the virtues are second nature.

The Need for Self-Examination

Persons rightly proposed the practice of self-examination as a central component in the *Exercises*. For instance, we hear the triple question right in the very first colloquy of the First Week: "What have I done for Christ?" "What am I doing for Christ?" "What ought I do for Christ?"[21]

In his important work *After Virtue*, Alasdair Macintyre says that there are three central questions to virtue ethics: "Who am I?" "Who ought I to become?" "What steps ought I take to become that person?"[22] Macintyre's questions move from self-examination to an expression of goals to finally a discernment of means to achieve those goals. His questions are similar to the triple question of the exercitant, for in those questions the person sees who they are and who they are called to be as a disciple of Christ. Knowing what she or he ought to do for Christ is effectively to prepare her or himself for the tasks that lie ahead.

An Ongoing Task

The self-examination is not simply a once-for-all event. On the contrary, inasmuch as we are each called to be more and more the persons that Christ wants us to be, Ignatian spirituality calls us to a regular reflection (see the *Constitutions* 261, 342, 344) of where we are in our journey with Christ. The ongoing reflection is necessary so that by knowing our Lord and ourselves better we can better both determine the virtuous ends that we should be pursuing as well as assess the steps already taken. Since the virtues were first articulated the acquisition of virtue has been known as a dynamic, lifelong process of reflection and intended practice.

Exercises

The standard expression that Thomas uses to describe how one acquires a virtuous disposition is "exercise." The intended exercises of temperance, for instance, lead to the acquisition of temperance. Thomas even talks about "spiritual exercises" when he asks why all the effects of sin are not taken away by baptism. He writes, "This is suitable for our spiritual training (*spirituale exercitium*); namely, in order that by fighting against concupiscence and other defects to which he is subject, man may receive the crown of victory."[23]

This training is central, then, to both the spirituality of the *Exercises*, where the exercitant repeats meditations and contemplations to pursue the invitation to greater union with God, and to morality, where a person engages regularly in intended and repeated practices in pursuit of particular virtues. It is not coincidental that Ignatius appropriated a word known both among devotional movements in Spain as well as among proponents of the virtues in Paris.

A Prudent Director

Virtue theory, because it recognizes the difficulty in acquiring the virtues, acknowledges that the first sign of growth is the ability to find a prudent adviser.[24] In order to determine the mean in one's life one needs experience and reasoned insight but, to acquire that, one needs to depend on those who are able to appreciate one's own situation in life.

Both the life of Ignatian spirituality and the life of virtue require a mentoring companion. However, in both cases, the mentor is not teaching some propositional utterances about something, but rather is helping the apprentice understand how growth occurs in his or her particular life so as to find the right exercises that will lead them to greater discipleship and greater self-guidance.

An Appreciation for Human Feeling

Thomas always saw the passions as essential to the acquisition and development of virtuous passion.[25] Hugo Rahner points out in his important work[26] that the regular "application of senses" (a clear innovation in spirituality) taught the exercitant the importance of familiarity with one's feelings in order to discern properly.

A Vision of the End

Whereas the previous nine points highlight the compatibility of virtue ethics with Ignatian spirituality, this final one illustrates a dramatic point of intersection. The end of the *Exercises* is the First Principle and Foundation, that is, to serve God alone. That end is the same for a virtue ethics in the Christian tradition.[27]

There are other points of similarity, especially those that deal with specific virtues, like charity, gratitude, obedience, availability, and humility. But as we close we should recognize that though moral theology (see Slater) has had little interest in spirituality, it has had a need for it (see Mahoney). Spirituality, however, has always recognized its need for moral theology, but of a particular type. Spirituality, especially Ignatian spirituality, has always recognized the need for morality, perhaps not one of principles governing external acts, but rather one of the virtues (see *Constitutions* 308, 334, 338–40, 361, 401, 404, 423, 434, 481, 484, 486, 516, 518, 659) dealing with the development of character in service to God who is always calling us to follow Christ.

Notes

1. James Keenan, "Proposing Cardinal Virtues," *Theological Studies* 56, no. 4 (1995): 709–29; Keenan, *Virtues for Ordinary Christians* (Kansas City, MO: Sheed and Ward, 1996); Jean Porter, *The Recovery of Virtue: The Relevance of Aquinas for Christian Ethics* (Louisville, KY: Westminster John Knox, 1990).

2. Rigali's essays are numerous; a few salient ones are, "The Unity of the Moral Order," *Chicago Studies* 8 (1969): 125–43; "Christian Ethics and Perfection," *Chicago Studies* 14 (1975): 227–40; "The Future of Christian Morality," *Chicago Studies* 20 (1981): 281–9; "The Unity of Moral and Pastoral Truth," *Chicago Studies* 25 (1986): 224–32. Recent writers on the topic include Dennis Billy and Donna Orsuto, eds., *Spirituality And Morality: Integrating Prayer and Action* (Mahwah: Paulist Press, 1996); James Keating, "The Good Life," *Church* 11, no. 2 (1995): 15–20; James Keenan, "Morality and Spirituality," *Church* 12, no. 3 (1996): 40–42; Mark O'Keefe, *Becoming Good, Becoming Holy: On the Relationship of Christian Ethics and Spirituality* (Mahwah: Paulist Press, 1995).

3. John Mahoney, *The Making of Moral Theology* (Oxford: Clarendon Press, 1987).

4. John T. McNeill and Helen M. Gamer, eds., *Medieval Handbooks of Penance* (New York: Columbia University Press, 1990).

5. Henry Lea, *The History of Auricular Confession and Indulgences in the Latin Church* (Philadelphia: Lea Brothers, 1896), 1:230; see Kilian McDonnell, "The *Summae Confessorum* on the Integrity of Confession as Prolegomena for Luther and Trent," *Theological Studies* 54 (1993): 405–27; Thomas Tentler, *Sin and Confession on the Eve of the Reformation* (Princeton: Princeton University, 1977); Miriam Turrini, *La coscienza e le leggi: morale e diritto nei testi per la confessione della prima Età moderna* (Bologna: Società editrice il Mulino, 1991).

6. *Summa theologiae* IIa–IIae. Prologue, "*Sic igitur tota materia morali ad considerationem virtutum reducta.*" On Thomas see Leonard Boyle, *The Setting of the Summa Theologiae of Saint Thomas* (Toronto: Pontifical Institute

of Medieval Studies, 1982); James Keenan, *Goodness and Rightness in Thomas Aquinas' Summa Theologiae* (Washington, DC: Georgetown University Press, 1992); Keenan, "Ten Reasons Why Thomas Aquinas Is Important for Ethics Today," *New Blackfriars* 75 (1994): 354–63; James Weisheipl, *Friar Thomas D'Aquino* (Washington DC: Catholic University Press, 1983).

7. R. M. Henley, "Casuistry," in *Encyclopedia of Religion and Ethics*, ed. James Hastings, vol. 3 (New York: Charles Scribner's Sons, 1928), 239–47; Albert Jonsen and Stephen Toulmin, *The Abuse of Casuistry: A History of Moral Reasoning* (Berkeley: University of California Press, 1988); James Keenan and Thomas Shannon, eds., *The Context for Casuistry* (Washington DC, Georgetown University Press, 1995); Edmund Leites, ed., *Conscience and Casuistry in Early Modern Europe* (New York: Cambridge University Press, 1988).

8. Besides the important *Making of Moral Theology*, Mahoney's earlier *Seeking the Spirit* (London: Sheed and Ward, 1981) very powerfully makes this point.

9. Thomas Slater, *A Manual of Moral Theology*, 2nd ed., 2 vols. (New York: Benziger Brothers, 1908), 1:5–6.

10. Henry Davis, *Moral and Pastoral Theology*, vol. 1 (London: Sheed and Ward, 1941), 4.

11. This is a thesis that I am proving in a project entitled *Virtues, Cases and Consciences: The Unique Achievement of Early British Puritan Practical Divinity.*

12. Peter Milward, *Religious Controversies of the Elizabethan Age: A Survey Of Printed Sources* (London: Scolar Press, 1977), 73–74; Helen White calls it "incomparably the most popular book of spiritual guidance in sixteenth-century England," *The Tudor Books of Saints and Martyrs* (Madison, WI: University of Wisconsin Press, 1963), 205.

13. Brad Gregory, "The 'True and Zealous Service of God': Robert Parsons, Edmund Bunny, and *The First Booke of the Christian Exercise*," *Journal of Ecclesiastical History* 45 (1994): 238–68.

14. On the achievement of the Puritans see Kevin Kelly, *Conscience: Dictator or Guide? A Study in Seventeenth-Century English Protestant Theology* (London: Geoffrey Chapman, 1967); Henry McAdoo, *The Structure of Caroline Moral Theology* (New York: Longmans, Green, and Co., 1949).

15. Peter Holmes, ed., *Elizabethan Casuistry* (Thetford, Norfolk: Catholic Record Society, 1981).

16. Louis J. Puhl, *The Spiritual Exercises of St Ignatius: A New Translation Based on Studies in the Language of the Autograph* (Westminster, MD: The Newman Press, 1957), 44–45, exercises 97–98.

17. Ibid., 102, exercise 234.

18. Ibid., 6, exercise 15.

19. John O'Malley, *The First Jesuits* (Cambridge: Harvard University Press, 1993), 136–52; on Christian individualism and Jesuit spirituality see Thomas Clancy, *Papist Pamphleteers: The Allen-Persons Party and the Political Thought of the Counter-Reformation in England, 1572–1615* (Chicago: Loyola University Press, 1964), 142–58.

20. See *Summa theologiae* I–II, 64.1 and 2.

21. Puhl, *The Spiritual Exercises of St Ignatius*, 28, exercise 53.

22. Alasdair Macintyre, *After Virtue* (Notre Dame: University of Notre Dame Press, 1981).

23. *Summa theologiae* III, 69.3c.

24. See my "Parenting and the Virtue of Prudence," *Church* 10, no. 1 (1994): 40–42.

25. Simon Harak, *Virtuous Passions* (Mahwah: Paulist, 1993).

26. Hugo Rahner, *Ignatius the Theologian* (London: Geoffrey Chapman, 1990).

27. Joseph Kotva, *The Christian Case for Virtue Ethics* (Washington DC: Georgetown University Press, 1996).

7. Morality and Prayer

Enda McDonagh

This chapter appeared in Enda McDonagh, *Doing the Truth* (Dublin: Gill & Macmillan, 1979).

In the theological as distinct from the practical cooperation between the churches, which has become such a feature of our times, insufficient attention may have been paid to the characteristic of the churches which most impresses the ordinary believer and unbeliever, that they are worshipping or praying communities which uphold certain moral standards. Of course there has been extraordinary development in prayer shared between the churches and quite valuable growth in inter-church moral activity, particularly on social issues. But has there been adequate theological reflection on the relationship between prayer and morality as distinguishing characteristics, particularly in the light of the rather "radical" developments in both these which have taken place in recent years? The liturgical changes in the Roman Catholic Church in the wake of Vatican II[1] would have been almost inconceivable fifteen years ago. And they are now being followed—for some, overshadowed—by the renewal in personal and community prayer, described as "charismatic" or "pentecostal."[2] The changes in moral understanding are no less far-reaching and have long since crossed church boundaries. For two churches such as the Church of Scotland and the Roman Catholic Church in Ireland, where traditionally church attendance, personal prayer and a fairly rigid moral code have enjoyed great strength, the changes are, despite certain enriching and liberating effects, also the source of some confusion and pain[3] and place the traditional bonds between prayer and morality in urgent need of theological reconsideration.

Such reconsideration was inevitable. The age-old association between religion and morality,[4] which subsumed the relationship between prayer and morality, has had its own peculiar swings even within the Judeo-Christian tradition. While presumed to be mutually illuminating and supporting, in fact one frequently enjoyed periods of dominance at the expense of the other. Those who honored with their lips but not with their hearts (Isa 29:13) belonged to a long line of Hebrews and Christians for whom a certain distortion of religion suppressed or distorted morality. But moralism also had its turn in obscuring or reducing the central saving truth and power of the covenant of God and ultimately of Jesus Christ. The creative tension which ought to exist between the two and was proclaimed and lived by Jesus has frequently turned into a destructive exploitation of one or the other. It would be too much to expect that Christians and their churches today were not exposed to these perennial temptations and did not sometimes yield to them. The *semper reformanda* of the Reformed tradition, which the Roman Catholic Church has proclaimed once again as hers also, will provide the stimulus here as elsewhere for the theological task which is a necessary part of the reform and which has become all the more urgent in the face of radical change.

Such a theological attempt in its bearing on the day-to-day living of church members (in prayer and moral activity) could have the useful side effect of overcoming the divisions between Christian theologians and Christian preachers/practitioners which have appeared—and sometimes in ugly form. The ultimate goal of the theologian's task is to attempt, out of his study of the word and the Christian tradition, to assist ordinary Christians and Christian communities to understand and respond in prayer and life to the divine call offered to them in Jesus Christ. In grappling with the prayer-morality relationship in the new situations he will be attempting to provide assistance more directly than usual and finding himself more closely engaged in his reflections with daily Christian living.

It is hardly necessary to point out as a final introductory note that this is a theological and not a sociological exercise. No attempt will (can?) be made to correlate church attendance, personal and other prayer, statistically considered, with moral achievement, also statistically considered. Yet attention must be paid to experience, the obvious experience of changes in prayer and morality which require no statistical back-up and the personal experience, individual and shared, of new forms or needs in prayer and morality. It is with this kind of experience as stimulus that these theological reflections begin.

PRE–VATICAN II UNDERSTANDING OF PRAYER AND MORALITY

Scholarly qualifications can be fatal long before they reach their first century, let alone their first millennium. Yet it is necessary in reassessing the relationship between prayer and morality to define fairly exactly one's starting point. I am concerned here with pre–Vatican II understanding within the Roman Catholic tradition. It is with that tradition that I am most familiar and to it my professional competence is really confined. However, I hope that what I have to say will find traces of convergence as well as divergence across the denominational divide. I have deliberately selected the period prior to Vatican II, and the particular relationship between prayer and morality that characterised that period is well exemplified by the manuals of moral theology[5] which during that time enjoyed such influence in the training of Roman Catholic clergy and their subsequent preaching. It does not mean "traditional" which is much broader in scope and rightly should take us back to New Testament times. A prevalent (controversial) weakness is to identify one particular phase of tradition with all of tradition, the particular phase which happens to suit us.

However, before tackling the manual treatment of the association it is necessary to recall the popular understanding of prayer and morality which were dominant at least among Roman Catholics in that period and to a large extent still are.[6] Prayer was simply understood as speaking to God or communication with God (and this included listening to him). It did not, of course, confine itself to petition but included praise and adoration, thanksgiving and regret or sorrow, leading to repentance and reconciliation. For Roman Catholics, the public and central act of prayer was the Mass although it was an event (the word was not used and certainly not in any technical and theological sense) as were the other sacraments. There were other public prayers, paraliturgical as one might now call them, such as Benediction of the Blessed Sacrament, novenas, and devotions of numerous kinds. And there were private prayers for the individual, the family, or for a particular group on a special occasion. For completeness one would have to advert to a variety of practices of private personal prayer, oral and silent, meditative, contemplative, and mystical. But some elements of the more advanced forms were considered to reside in the more primitive types.[7] There was in addition the wider understanding of prayer as all that one does: *laborare est orare*. This was given concrete expression in the practice of the "morning offering" whereby one "consecrated" to God all one's activities for that day. It could also be expressed in terms of one's intentions to offer this or every work to God or by describing ones' work as always done for the love or glory of God in sound Pauline terms (1 Cor 10:13).

The morality[8] contemporary with the prayer-phase catalogued earlier was for the most part expressed in terms of a legal code of dos and don'ts, commands and prohibitions. God's will was the moral law and it was either directly revealed in the Judeo-Christian tradition (e.g., Ten Commandments) or accessible by reflection on human nature, the natural moral law (or both). The expression of these primarily in legal form and their intertwining (e.g., the content of the Ten Commandments was for the most part also natural law morality) were further compounded by the admixture of a voluminous code of canon or Church law, so that the prohibition of eating meat on Friday (a purely Church law) could be taken as morally equivalent to the prohibition of adultery—as both could be thought equally to involve serious sin and merit eternal damnation. The resilience of priests and people, more important perhaps of the Spirit of Christ, rose above many but by no means all of these confusions and limitations.

This rather obvious and simple outline of pre–Vatican II approaches to prayer and morality seemed a necessary introduction to considering how the relationship between them was understood.

Presuming an awareness of the tension and temptation between the prayer and morality poles discussed earlier and presuming that the tension was not always creative or the temptation always resisted, one still wants to know how the manual theologians and the people envisaged the relationship and so could hope to cope with it.

Prayer[9] as a duty of the virtue of religion was regarded as a moral obligation in various ways. This involved as usual a combination of divine (revealed and natural) and human ecclesiastical law. So Catholics were obliged by law to attend Mass on Sunday. They were also obliged to pray frequently throughout their lives (this was sometimes interpreted as daily or in terms of morning and evening prayers). And they were obliged to pray in particular situations for light to know their moral duty and strength to do it and to resist the temptation to evil.

One might not unfairly characterize the relationship as predominantly extrinsic in concept. There was a moral obligation to pray and this was couched in rather legal and so extrinsic terms—coming at the individual as it were from the outside, whether from God or the church. In relation to other moral obligations prayer was of assistance in seeking light from God to understand the obligation correctly and strength or grace from him to fulfill it as correctly understood. Undoubtedly the light and strength became internal to the person as granted by God, but the concept and image of the connection between them and the prayer for them was, I should say, also predominantly extrinsic. One asked God for help and the help came or it did not, but any inner connection between the asking and the help was not given much attention, at either a theological or popular level.

The prayer for forgiveness and the gifts of repentance and forgiveness for moral failure suggested a more intimate connection, but it was not expanded upon in other areas. The "morning offering" and "good intentions" consecrating of all one's activities to God were also intrinsic in concept as referring to God activities somehow foreign to him and so to communication with him through prayer.

There were appeals to experiences of inner illuminations and strengthening by God which did issue, for example, in special vocations, but these were not considered, for example, in the typical moral treatment, but as exceptions to be dealt with in theology of vocation, with criteria for distinguishing true from false or, in more advanced cases still, under the rubric of mystical theology. Moral theology and popular moral thinking were not concerned with such exceptional phenomena. The predominant links were extrinsic in moral obligations to pray or in the use of prayer to obtain light and strength to fulfill one's moral obligations, although in the prayer to obtain forgiveness the connection was understood in a more intrinsic way, but the potential for intrinsic connection in the "morning offering" was scarcely adverted to.

PRAYER AND MORALITY IN THE POST–VATICAN II ERA

The developments in understanding of prayer, particularly liturgical prayer, and of morality, which we attribute to this era had emerged in various ways to prepare for Vatican II itself. But they became predominant and official modes of teaching and practice after the Council.

The earlier simple and unscientific catalogue of types of prayer has been profoundly changed in content in the last decade. The community character of the Mass or Eucharist (a term in increasing use) has been newly emphasized for example by the use of the vernacular, the priest facing the people, the participation of laity in reading, bringing up gifts, bidding prayers, and the kiss of peace. These reforms have also been extended to the other sacraments. However, the other forms of public prayer in novenas and other devotions have undoubtedly declined, although they may be seen as increasingly replaced by prayer groups and developments such as the Charismatic Renewal movement, although without as yet the same clerical leadership or backing.

The most recent theological attempt to overcome the limitations of the manual approach to moral theology and its popular presentation began before World War II in Europe and reached its peak in the fifties and sixties.[10] A theology of Christian life, based on the human being called to share in Christ's sonship of the Father and brotherhood of all mankind, and derived more directly from the New Testament, began gradually to displace the legal system of the manuals although the undoubted achievement of these latter works provided a valuable challenge and corrective to some of the woollier forms of "love-ethic" which began to emerge.

This development of moral theology as a theology of the Christian life based on a Christian anthropology (ontology) is still far from complete.[11] Yet at the same time a quite different, if complementary rather than contradictory, approach is emerging, to which I shall have to return later.

The most striking consequence of these developments for our problem, the connection between prayer and morality, is the manifestation of inner and intrinsic connection between the liturgical activity of the Christian and his moral activity.[12] The liturgical activity explicitly proclaims his incorporation into Christ's response to the Father in self-surrender as Son, his resultant adoptive sonship of the Father and brotherhood of all men. And this is effected through the gift of the Spirit whereby we are buried with Christ to rise with him to a new life (Rom 6) in which we are empowered to cry, "Abba, Father" (Rom 8). The prayer which Jesus himself taught us to say begins "Our Father" (Luke 11). The moral living which he summarized as love of God and love of neighbour (Mark 12:28–31) finds its basis in this share in the gift and call to divine sonship of the Father and to the universal brotherhood of mankind which this entails. Each particular moral act and the moral life as a whole is to be a realization of that sonship and brotherhood which we explicitly recognize, manifest, and celebrate in liturgical and private prayer. The Christian life, like the Christian liturgy, has a basically trinitarian structure, directed toward the Father through sharing in the sonship of Jesus Christ by the sending of the Spirit. Our prayers for light and strength in moral situations are articulations of our need for the spirit of sonship within us to find expression in our moral understanding and in our moral response.

A good deal more might be said about the more precise content of such a Christian way of life and how one is to discover it, if one does not accept any simple theory of divine inspiration in every moral situation. However, that is a task for another time and place.

More relevant here is the theological basis with which such a trinitarian approach to moral theology could provide the prayer-renewal which is at present such a feature of the Roman Catholic and other churches. It must be admitted that the moral theologians themselves in their work did not anticipate such a powerful development or have the fully developed theological understanding adequate to the task. Despite a recognition of his essential place in the scheme of things, the Spirit remained the poor relation of the Trinity in the renewal of moral theology as well as in the renewal of the liturgy. The appeal to the Spirit in the new prayer movements has put the theologians on their mettle and one of the great practical advocates of shared prayer was one of the great pioneers in the renewal of moral theology, Bernard Häring. Other theologians writing in these islands too, such as Simon Tugwell[13] and Peter

Hocken,[14] have attempted to do fuller justice to the role of the Spirit, while keeping him within the Trinity. The temptation to treat him in isolation is not one all prayer enthusiasts can resist. Yet formidable work remains to be done in theological reflection on this prayer movement itself and its relation to daily living and morality. It would be impossible to deny the sense of liberation, which ought to be a feature of authentic prayer, which the movement has given to many people, as well as a sense of personal and communal integration at least as far as the group is concerned. (In this context the phenomenon of healing requires careful if positive evaluation.)[15] The dangers of excessive emotion undoubtedly exist, although the sheer lack of any emotional dimension in so much of even the reformed liturgy is not particularly praiseworthy either, given that the emotions are a God-given and integral part of man. More worrying from the ecclesiastical point of view are the dangers of elitism and sectarianism, although how far they exist is very difficult to judge. And for the moral theologian with his sensitiveness to the complexities of moral situations and to the mysteriousness of God's providential relationship with the world, there may appear to be for the less discerning a too easy temptation to appeal without question to what "the Spirit told me." Indeed there may be a deeper danger that the world in itself would be ignored in such an exclusively religious atmosphere.[16]

In my view these renewals in liturgy, shared prayer, and moral theology remain basically positive, and include solid achievements which will undoubtedly persist. It is perhaps too soon to offer any final theological analysis of the Charismatic Renewal movement, or balanced judgment on it, yet it might attend to some of the limitations which have emerged in the liturgical and moral theological renewal. And these limitations may lead in turn to posing the question of association in reverse form, that between morality and prayer, rather than prayer and morality.

FROM MORALITY TO PRAYER: A RECONSIDERATION OF THE BOND

The more obvious difficulty which renewal in prayer, liturgical, shared, and private, faces is what is rather loosely known as the phenomenon of secularisation. Without wishing to enter the tangled debate on this thorny issue, I think that it can be safely said that the cultural context in which our minds are shaped and so our prayer(s) learned and expressed has far fewer explicitly religious elements in it than it had even some decades ago, even in countries with such obvious public and private religious expressions as Scotland and Ireland. For many people this secular cultural context has made God, the transcendent and religious dimension of life, unnecessary or irrelevant or at any rate much more remote and obscure. It has made the traditional prayer concepts, formulae and structures, however renewed, strangers to one's daily thinking and living. A lack of inner connection which threatens a lack of inner conviction can sometimes be discerned even among those with a firm desire to maintain and develop their prayer life.

This would in part explain a certain sense of disappointment with the liturgical renewal in the Roman Catholic Church which some experience. Undoubtedly the expectations of many were raised too suddenly and too high, while the implementation by others has been partial and grudging.

More profoundly perhaps the expectations were simply mistaken at times. There was a suggestion that a community-based liturgy with fuller participation by the laity would quickly inspire and sustain the reform of society as a whole, breaking down the barriers of race or sex or nation in such places as twentieth-century America. When this did not happen except in particular groups and for individuals, the liturgy lost in significance for many earlier enthusiasts. The value of the liturgy in wider social renewal should not be ignored, but it is not a substitute for social moral action and the connection between prayer and moral action needs to be soundly based.

At a popular and more reflective level the problem of the relationship between morality and prayer, a facet, as I have said, of the relationship between morality and religion, has to face the reality that, while there has been a traditionally very close association between morality and religion/prayer, morality itself is older and wider than the Judeo-Christian tradition and that today it is taken for granted as essential to human living by people who reject or neglect religion and prayer. Confirmed and perhaps accelerated by the secularization process, however that is to be more precisely understood, morality both in its popular impact and as the subject of rigorous reflection is increasingly regarded as an autonomous human phenomenon.[17] Where the autonomy is absolute and no relationship to any transhuman or transcosmic reality is accepted, one is faced with one of the many brands of humanist morality. Accepting morality in its immediate and reflective state as autonomous does not however commit one to such absoluteness, which is basically derived from a philosophy of life which is not necessarily implicit in the analysis of morality itself but attempts to answer questions raised by, but going beyond what that analysis provides. Such questions are not answerable in terms of moral analysis alone although they open the way to a discussion of philosophies of life, including Christianity, as providing—or not providing—some satisfying answers for enquirers.

Among the many possible approaches to moral analysis, I prefer for the task in hand to concentrate on the moral experience as it occurs in the concrete situation. This experience is at its purest in the form of unconditional obligation to do or avoid something however unpleasant or disadvantageous it may be to me. And the final source of this obligation is another person or group of persons. In its most developed form the morality is an aspect of interpersonal relations (individual or group) which expresses an unconditional obligation or call, at least to recognize and respect the person(s) as person(s) and to make a particular response of food or shelter or education or comfort, according to the particular situation. The unconditionality that affects recognition, respect, and response as three not always distinguishable phases of the same reaction, is founded in the character of the personal source as constituting a world of its own, a creative center of knowing and loving, deciding and acting, which I as subject may not seek simply to use/abuse, to violate, to possess, to diminish or to eliminate. He is in that sense ultimately other than I am.

Because I am equally person and other, the call to recognition and respect is mutual, although the particular concrete response, for example, providing food, may affect me (the subject) more immediately than the other (source of the call). In the reciprocal interchange, recognizing or distinguishing the other in his otherness develops identification of the self; respect for the other involves accepting and respecting the self; responding to the other involves seeking potentialities in the self or self-development.

The other person is however not simply source of call and so of burden, but comes to one as a creative, new, and unique world, a gift or present in the literal sense of being given or presented to one and in the further sense of being (at least potentially) enriching for one. But this has to be qualified by our equally undoubted experience of the other as threat, potential or actual, at an individual or group level, provoking us to fear and self-protection. This ambiguity affects all our moral interchanges, although the direction of the overall moral call would seem to be to enabling the gift to triumph over the threat.

This moral or ethical analysis could be taken much further (and has been elsewhere)[18] as have meta-ethical questions which it raises, about the meaning of this human otherness with the unconditional obligations and inviolability which it involves; about the value or ability to go on attempting to enable the gift to triumph over the threat in a world which has experienced Auschwitz and Hiroshima and a thousand other lesser horrors; about the fulfillment available for subject or source even in the most favorable circumstances; and about the possible undermining of the whole moral enterprise by the absurdity of death. It is here, it seems to me, that Christianity corresponds and responds to the ethical analysis and meta-ethical questions: with its covenant structure relating God to man and man to man in a basically gift-call-compounded-by-threat-(sin) situation; with its understanding of human otherness as originating in the image of God the Father, the absolute other, and completed through its sharing in the divine sonship of Jesus Christ; and as finally assured of the triumph of gift over the most horrible threat, of meaning over absurdity, in the suffering, death, and resurrection of Jesus.

This mutual coherence, illumination, and intrinsic connection which the Christian can observe is not offered here as a proof from moral analysis for the existence of God or the truth of Christianity. The humanist of whatever type would try to answer the meta-ethical questions, supposing he accepted the ethical analysis, from his own worldview. The scope of my argument is to provide Christian believers with a way of accepting the autonomy of the moral experience, but then seeking to understand its deeper connection with their faith in Jesus Christ—their awareness and acceptance of the God of Jesus Christ which have been given to them in the gift of the Spirit at baptism.

Morality and faith is of course only a step away from morality and prayer. And it is by considering morality in terms of this analysis of human relationships and understanding our moral responses as between people, first at the genuinely moral and human level, that I believe our awareness of God, our prayer life, can be enriched and expanded.

The recognition and respect of the other as other, which are essential phases of genuine moral response, are often simply implicit and taken for granted. Yet precisely for the task in hand they deserve more attention. Sensitivity to the unique world of the other in its actuality and potential, that is to the mystery of the other, with the respect and even awe which this induces in one's best moments, are in themselves enriching for me and my relationship, implying enhanced self-awareness and self-acceptance; moral awareness and the awe it inspires enrich the humanity of the world generally and can provide in a changing and more secular culture a new context for religious awareness and awe.[19] Prayer may be formal and empty, lack inner connection and conviction because of the poverty of our human relationships and their moral implications. Unless more attention is paid to recognition and respect for the penultimate other, the recognition and respect for the ultimate may lack any real roots. The true basis for an intrinsic relationship between morality and prayer is to be found here.

In the Christian perspective the human otherness which demands this unconditional recognition and respect derives from, if it remains (inadequately) distinct from, the final other we call God.[20] Image and sonship are the Judeo-Christian ways of understanding of how the ultimate mystery is accessible to us in human form. So the moral response to the human other can and should by its own inherent dynamism expand into a response to the ultimate other; it can and should expand into prayer.

A fresh insight into this is provided by the Hebrew understanding of God as holy,[21] in a word which meant absolutely other, or as it was later (more obscurely) termed, transcendent. This holiness, with the awe it inspires, he shared with people. The renewal of holiness as awareness of and sensitivity to otherness will have to be alive for people with people if it is to be alive for people with God. Renewal in prayer is not just dependent on or related in some extrinsic fashion to a good moral life and relationship; it can be seen as an expansion of these relationships.

The reciprocity of such relationships and the dialectic of other-recognition/respect and self-identification/acceptance shed a certain light on a problem rendered acute at least at the popular level in our own time,[22] the contrast between the God-up-there or out-there or beyond and the God-within, between the transcendent and the immanent God. In recognition and respect for the human other one can and should be opened up to the God-beyond, while in the dialectic effect of further identification and acceptance of the self (also a human other) one can and should be opened up to the God-within, the immanent God. It is this God-within, the immanent God, which is also accessible to us in our community identification. By taking account of the historical character of human relations and moral responses as they build up and move into the future, one is summoned to an awareness of the Godhead, the eschatological God. And all this is dependent for its historical offer to each one and for its understanding on the original divine creation and incarnation. The absolute other, whose creating and saving deeds in the history of Israel and Jesus Christ gave human relations their divine significance, is also accessible in these relations as the God of the past as well as the present and the future, of man's origin and development as well as his present sustaining and transforming power and his future destiny.

In this necessarily compressed treatment of one aspect of moral analysis and its impact on understanding prayer, the perennial temptations to distortion and suppression are the more blatant. Clearly, sensitivity to human others may not in fact be expanded into awareness of the absolute and divine other. And for nonbelievers this seems undeniably true. (I do not wish to get engaged here with the quite different problem of how far this sensitivity may have an inevitable "implicit" or "anonymous" relationship with the God of Jesus Christ,[23] because even if one granted this, prayer in the strict and explicit sense does not arise for such people.) For Christians the temptation could be to reduce their Christianity and their prayer life to a similar "good neighborliness" on family, local, national, or world-scale. The penultimate would have obscured the ultimate, perhaps to the point of becoming the ultimate itself and so creating an idolatrous humanism.

Such temptation can only be avoided by insisting on the true meaning of the penultimate as derived from, dependent on, and directed toward the ultimate. And for this, of course, direct and explicit attention to the ultimate in liturgical and personal prayer, shared or individual, is essential. The close relationship between true and full other-recognition (including relationship to the absolute transcendent other) and true and full self-identification (including relationship to the absolute immanent other) means that the "idolizing" of the penultimate prevents true and full self-identification; and this in more traditional terms is called "damnation."

The other temptation, to which the earlier presentation in both pre– and post–Vatican II phases might seem more open, could easily arise here too; the distortion or suppression of the penultimate for the sake of the ultimate, the distortion or suppression of morality for the sake of religion or prayer. Where the human other is seen as finally derived from the ultimate other, the temptation to use him as a means to the ultimate other could become very real. Yet, unless the human other is taken fully seriously as a world in herself/himself and for her/his own sake, his true reality is lost and the God we seek at his expense is not the God of Jesus Christ, of creation and salvation. And as one, in the move toward God, suppresses the other, so one suppresses the self and there is no basis for a proper relationship between God and the self either. Like all other human and cosmic realities, the call to renewal of prayer and of awareness of God by a renewal of human relationships and of morality, has its threat as well as its gift elements and can never be entirely unambiguous.

It is worth recalling at this stage the gift and threat aspects of human relationships and their moral dimensions. Concentrating on the gift for the moment, I feel that one of the primary moral activities is simply that of thanksgiving for the presence of others, a celebration of their presence as gift. With the source and guarantee of this human otherness in mind, it is fairly easy to establish an inner connection between this primary moral call and activity and the thanksgiving for and celebration of the gift of the ultimate other. Where the Eucharist forms the explicit center of such thanksgiving and celebration, it is easily connected in mind if not in practice with thanksgiving and celebration parties for immediately human reasons. And proper understanding and genuine celebration of both can and should be mutually enriching. The mission which began with a (wedding) party concluded with a last (Eucharist) supper. The inner connection is based on the genuine humanity of the man who was God but was practically exemplified in the life of one who came eating and drinking, only to be accused of being a drunkard and a glutton (Luke 7:34).

The gift is always qualified and sometimes obscured and apparently overwhelmed by the threat. At both individual and group level, from battered babies and wives to football hooliganism to Northern Ireland or the Middle East, one can hardly escape noticing the prevalence and reality of the threat. The cry and the prayer are for peace and reconciliation, for the triumph of the gift over the threat. To many people these cries and prayers seem hollow and evidently fruitless. Perhaps once again the penultimate has been ignored for the sake of the ultimate, the moral situation misunderstood or ignored or inadequately responded to, while refuge is taken in prayer. At least a moral awareness of threat as obscuring gift and of the call to enable the gift to triumph over the threat would shift the prayer from the lips to the heart (Isa 29:13). Efforts at reconciliation begin by taking the others fully seriously with their own unique world, their limitations, fears and hatreds, as well as their actual and potential achievements. Such moral response may be rebuffed or inadequate or meet with what is for the present at least an intractable situation. Yet it has to go on, for the call is insistent and persistent that we should seek to enable the gift to triumph over the threat. And the battering husband or mother, the hooded gunman or hostile soldier, the football hooligan or threatening rapist, are also gifts whose enriching potential one cannot see (perhaps they cannot see) and yet must seek to discover and encourage to emerge.

"Love your enemies" (Matt 5:44) is how Jesus summarized the appropriate moral response to threat, the effort to transform it into gift. In pursuing this line, great risks may be involved and at the high point of moral response, one may have to lay down one's life even for one's enemies. The significance of this only becomes clear in the life and death of Jesus, but in the persistent attempts to reach the other as gift rather than threat, one is reaching for his mystery as image of God and Son of the Father. So, one is reaching for that divine mystery. The explicit prayer which one then voices for peace and reconciliation is the translation into words of what the search for God involves, as one seeks the true gift of humanity in one's enemy. Reconciliation is no cheap grace as Jesus showed, and it is frequently bought only at the price of human suffering as one or both individuals or groups persist in their efforts to overcome the threat element by the gift element, and so liberate true humanity and encounter its final mystery.

Such struggles today are conducted on the grand scale between exploiting or warring groups.[24] The efforts at reconciliation will be efforts to restore true recognition of and respect for the other group as gift rather than threat and then to find the appropriate solution which will embody that recognition and respect. The final argument against violence is that by eliminating one side to the dispute, it refuses ultimate recognition and respect and prevents mutual gift from replacing mutual threat. The immediate excuse for violence is that the powerful and entrenched (the basically threatening) refuse to recognize and respect the exploited and oppressed (the basically threatened) or to provide structures enabling such recognition and respect to grow into mutual enrichment and the removal of threat and exploitation. The commitment to overcome exploitation and oppression, with a sense of justice for all and readiness to undertake the same training program, the same risks as the men of violence (institutional or physical) will enrich our sense of human others and provide flesh and blood (incarnation) for the words of appeal for peace to God or to others, which flow so readily from the mouths of the comfortable. And in the faith which fuels the loving commitment, the committed discern and experience the mystery of God even as Jesus did; above all in the oppressed and the marginal people, while remaining aware of it in the oppressor, his needs, and even his particular impoverishment. Engagement in the pursuit of social justice at local, national, and international level is about recognizing, respecting, and responding to the inviolable otherness of all human beings; at the level of Christian understanding it is also an encounter with the absolute other in whose image and sonship all men share.[25]

It is, I believe, possible to consider other areas of moral activity, such as sexuality or verbal communication, and to discover the same kind of inner connection between the appropriate moral response to the other and the response to the ultimate other or God. From a different angle it is equally possible to take most of the traditional categories of prayer: adoration, thanksgiving, petition, contrition, in their vocal and silent forms or even more developed and mystical forms, and see how they have their parallels at the level of moral interchange between people and could be greatly enlivened and enriched by starting from the understanding of moral response and expanding into prayer. Along the same lines, the theological virtues which might well be called the "prayer" virtues in their traditional meaning of having God as their immediate object (unlike the moral virtues which relate directly to men) could be more richly understood by considering their human parallels, faith and hope in men as well as love of them, not simply as parallels, but as human realities relating human others but open to expansion to the ultimate other and to the transformation which that involves. However, if the point has not been sufficiently made by now that through moral experience and a deeper understanding of it, one is opened up to prayer experience and a fuller commitment to it, further elaboration will scarcely help.

CONCLUSION

Theologians are sometimes known to yield in arrogance to the temptations of exclusiveness or totalitarianism in their analysis and solution of difficulties. It is not a temptation which I experience particularly strongly here. I am too well aware of the strength of the prayer life and moral life of the people in that era which I have criticized as (inevitably) having a somewhat extrinsic understanding of the relation between prayer and morality, at least at the theological level. Again, I am very well aware of the achievements of liturgical reform in my own church and of the potential for good which the new prayer movement is already displaying, despite my reservations born of the inability of some very good people to connect inwardly with the predominantly religious thought and words used here. Threat elements are inseparable from gift elements in these movements, and could lead to liturgical and prayer communities estranged from, if not indifferent to the world in its "secularized" state. My object has been simply to complement these developments by endeavoring to show that a reconsideration of moral relationships and responses can provide the dynamism for a prayer development which avoids some of the limitations or threat-elements of the others discussed, while inevitably involving its own. And it is an approach which could increase communication between the "study-bound" theologian and the Christian on the street, while it would seem also to have the advantage of cutting across denominational boundaries.

Notes

1. The basis of these developments is contained in the first document issued by Vatican II, "Constitution on the Sacred Liturgy"; cf. *The Documents of Vatican II*, ed. Walter M. Abbot (New York: Guild Press, 1966), 137–77.

2. A useful account of the early developments of the movement in the Catholic Church is contained in Edward D. O'Connor, CSC, *The Pentecostal Movement in the Catholic Church* (Notre Dame: Ave Maria Press, 1971). Since then a flood of literature has appeared: the most prestigious, because of his office, is the book by Cardinal L. J. Suenens, *A New Pentecost* (London: Dartman, Longman and Todd, 1975). A thoughtful symposium on the Prayer and Renewal Movement in the Catholic Church appears in *La Vie Spirituelle*, 609 (July–August 1975). For the older movement outside the Roman Catholic Church, cf. W. J. Hollenweger, *The Pentecostals* (London: SCM Press, 1972).

3. In liturgical affairs a certain resistance to the developments has been associated with groups upholding the Latin and Tridentine form of the Mass. The charismatic prayer movement has also had its critics and opponents, but as it has not official status it does not cause the same difficulties.

4. Again there is a vast literature but quite a helpful recent collection of essays is to be found in Gene Outka and John P. Reeder Jr., *Religion and Morality* (Garden City, NY: 1973). Some of my own thoughts on this wider issue are developed in my recent book, *Gift and Call* (Dublin: Gill & Macmillan, 1975), particularly chaps. 1, 4, and 12.

5. Typical manuals in common usage at that time were H. Noldin and A. Schmitt, *Summa Theologiae Moralis*, 3 vols. (Barcelona: Herder, 1951), or M. Zalba, *Theologiae Moralis Compendium,* 2 vols. (Madrid: Editorial Catolica, 1958).

6. The various catechisms such as the Maynooth Catechism dealt with the matter in these terms and a fairly comprehensive account of the theology on which they were based is to be found in the article by A. Fonck, "Priere," *Dictionnaire de Theologie Catholique*, ed. A Vacant et al., vol. 13, part 1 (Paris: Letouzey et Ané, 1936), 169–244.

7. This point is made by Fonck, "Priere." I find it difficult to accept the very sharply distinguished and contrasting typologies in the classic study of Friedrich Heiler, *Prayer*, trans. Samuel McComb with the assistance of J. Edgar Park (London: Oxford University Press, 1932), particularly the total contrast between what he calls mystical and prophetic prayer. I would largely agree with criticisms of him by M. Nedoncelle, *The Nature and Use of Prayer* (London: Burns & Oates, 1964), 106–11.

8. For a description of the manual tradition and criticism of it see my

"Moral Theology: The Need for Renewal" in *Moral Theology Renewed*, ed. E. McDonagh (Dublin: Gill and Son, 1965), 13–30.

9. For this section cf. Noldin and Schmitt, *Summa Theologiae Moralis*, 2:132–47; M. Zalba, *Theologiae Moralis Compendium*, 1:531–62.

10. Two of the great pioneers of this work were: Fritz Tillman, in *Handbuch der katholischen Sittenlehre*, ed. Fritz Tillman, with Theodor Steinbüchel and Theodor Müncker, 4 vols. (Düsseldorf: Mosella-Verlag, 1934–8), particularly his own volume 3, *Die Idee der Nachfolge Christi*, first published in 1933 and in 4th ed. (Dusseldorf: Mosella-Verlag, 1953); and Bernard Häring, *The Law of Christ: Moral Theology for Priests and Laity*, trans. Edwin G. Kaiser, 3 vols. (Cork: Mercier Press, 1961–7). For some account of the background to these developments see my "Moral Theology: The Need for Renewal."

11. An attempt to provide such an "ontological" anthropology is found in the author's "The Law of Christ and the Natural Law," in *Duty and Discernment*, ed. G. R. Dunstan (London: SCM Press, 1975), 51–63.

12. I have developed this point elsewhere in the essay, "Liturgy and Christian Living," in *The Christian in His World*, ed. B. Devlin (Dublin: Gill and Son, 1968).

13. S. Tugwell, *Did You Receive the Spirit?* (London: Darton, Longman and Todd, 1972).

14. P. Hocken, *You, He Made Alive* (London: Darton, Longman and Todd, 1972). Cf. M. Thornton, *Prayer, a New Encounter* (London: Hodder and Stoughton, 1972).

15. The best "insider" account of this is probably Francis MacNutt, *Healing* (Notre Dame: Ave Maria Press, 1975).

16. These reservations are based on limited personal experience of the movement itself and so should not be exaggerated. Yet the history of not entirely dissimilar movements in the past would suggest that they may not be without some basis. P. Baelz, *Prayer and Providence* (London: SCM Press, 1968), would, together with some of the more classical treatments such as St Thomas Aquinas, *Summa Contra Gentes*, Bk 3, provide useful balance on this matter. R. A. Knox, *Enthusiasm* (Oxford: Oxford University Press, 1950), still provides a very valuable historical counterbalance to other temptations of such a movement.

17. This is the point of departure of my recent book *Gift and Call*. What follows is, in the analysis of morality, largely based on that work.

18. Ibid., particularly chaps. 4, 10.

19. Although I was helped by them at the time, I do not find very satisfactory as theological analyses the earlier attempts to deal with this challenge of prayer in a secular culture, by J. Danielou, *Prayer as a Political Problem*

(London: Sheed and Ward, 1967); and D. Rhymes, *Prayer in the Secular City* (London: Lutterworth Press, 1967).

20. The interesting work of M. Nedoncelle already cited does move from an analysis of prayer between men to prayer between men and God. But this is an entirely different approach from the one used here although it could have some useful connecting points.

21. This is obviously related to Rudolf Otto's *The Idea of the Holy*, trans. John W. Harvey (London: Oxford University Press, 1968). For more useful comments cf. John P. Reeder Jr., "The Relation of the Moral and the Numinous in Otto's Notion of the Holy," in Outka and Reeder, *Religion and Morality*, 255–92.

22. Whatever its ultimate theological limitations, John Robinson's *Honest to God* (London: SCM Press, 1963), and the ensuing debate did clearly find echoes of recognition among many Christians.

23. This problem was given considerable recent attention in Roman Catholic theology in the discussion of "anonymous Christianity" associated in particular with Karl Rahner.

24. As I have noted before (*Gift and Call*) there is still no fully satisfactory moral analysis of the relationships between groups.

25. Cf. my "Human Violence: A Question of Ethics or Salvation," chap, 10, *Gift and Call*, for a fuller discussion of this question.

8. Prayer and Ethics in the Thought of Karl Rahner

James Keating

This chapter first appeared as "Karl Rahner: Prayer and Ethics," in *Studies in Spirituality* 7 (1997).

There is a renewed effort in moral theology to articulate its relation with the emerging academic discipline of Christian spirituality. This effort of moral theologians to seek common ground with spiritual realities is clearly seen in the work of Bernard Häring, Enda McDonagh, and more recently Mark O'Keefe.[1]

In this essay I review the key ideas of Karl Rahner on prayer in order to associate his vision with Christian ethical discernment. In the end, Rahner appears as one who would encourage dialogue between ethics and spirituality in the context of the love of God and its clarifying effects upon moral reasoning.

THE CONTEXT OF AFFECTION AND CONNATURALITY

Harvey Egan is one of the most articulate promoters of Karl Rahner's theology as a body of thought which is at heart pastoral and sapiential rather than strictly academic in the pejorative sense of the term. "Those who dismiss Rahner as an abstract and convoluted thinker overlook the 'mysticism of everyday life,' which runs throughout his writings. Rahner the pastor, the homilist, the spiritual director, and the teacher of prayer is never far from the surface of even his most difficult works."[2]

Rahner places his "existential ethic" in the context of prayer and discernment. He draws heavily from the process of St. Ignatius' spiritual exercises, and respectfully places the unique individual person at the center of this ethic in the matrix of intimacy with God through the church. The moral tradition of the church, Rahner notes, is not addressed to some universal "instance" of human nature, but rather to uniquely loved persons with vocations all their own. God loves each individually, and thus one is beckoned to listen to God in the depths of prayer and conscience in order to discern how one ought to respond concretely to that love. However, this response to being loved is never to be in contradiction to general moral norms but may be construed as a summons to go beyond them, to that something "more" which one is called uniquely to do.[3] At bottom, universal norms are not sufficient to know what one's duty to the good is in the concrete.[4]

The ethical (love of others) and the mystical (love of God) are on a continuum which includes reason as a base and together they form the highest operation of the person, which Andrew Tallon calls "heart."[5] Utilizing St. Thomas in the context of Rahner's process of discernment, Tallon describes prayer's role in the heart's search for the good.

> Mystical life is the life of the spirit; the life of the spirit consists of prayer and action in reciprocal causation. Besides private and liturgical prayer time, there are times of decision and action in all realms of life that require discernment of spirits....The most perfect ethical action comes from discernment based on mystical attunement....And yet the mystical can fail to make an ethical difference if there is no change of heart; this could not be true were the ethical and mystical but operations of head and heart as separate faculties rather than degrees of actualization of one continuum. Affective connaturality applies to both the ethical and mystical because of their deeper unity.[6]

Affective connaturality (a knowing of the good, beautiful, and true by a felt reasoning out of a life of virtuous commitment) in distinction from rational analysis is seen by Aquinas, Ignatius, and Rahner as the normal way of knowing the good and loving God.

> Connatural knowing and loving are not the exceptions, the back-up system, as it were, for when discursive, conceptual knowledge and deliberative freedom fail..., but just the opposite: it is when discernment of spirits by affective connaturality in one's personal situation fails (when you just "don't have it in you") that you then must fall back by default on reasoning discursively from general principles.[7]

Loving Jesus is a fundamental virtue in any understanding of Christian prayer. What is most unique to this affection, as opposed to simply loving another person, is that loving Jesus can be unconditional and definitive, void of any fear of failure to measure up to the beloved's expectations. This is true because one's affections for Jesus are bolstered by "the God of faithfulness; his *own* unconditionality."[8] This love of Jesus is definitely affective and from the heart. The heart is to be understood as the fullness of the person in his or her freedom and knowing. Rahner once claimed that we must "throw our arms" around Jesus, and if we truly *want* to love him we can experience him "right up close to us as the concrete historical person he is."[9] This kind of affection which orients us toward fulfillment and salvation is the fruit of grace-filled prayer.[10]

Rahner has been recognized as the preeminent contemporary theologian of prayer and hailed by Harvey Egan as *Doctor orationis*.

> Rahner's theology attempts to evoke, to awaken, to deepen, and to strengthen the basic experience of the triune God that haunts every person's core....His theology begins and ends in a mystical moment: the experience of the lived, root unity of self-possessing knowledge and love penetrated by God's self-communication as mystery, revelation and love....Many theologians have learned from Rahner's Ignatian-flavored theology that theology must flow out of and then lead back into the prayer of silent surrender to the mystery of God's love for us in the crucified and risen Christ—and must do so without dissolving theology's necessarily critical function.

The theologian must have compassion for the human and worship God with his whole person, knowing when to "kneel his mind" before the incomprehensible God.[11]

In this context of connaturality, affection, and prayer I will now look at what Karl Rahner has specifically taught about the nature of prayer. I will then conclude with what his vision of prayer contributes to a vision of ethics and discernment.

KARL RAHNER ON PRAYER

Prayer Is Personal

Rahner stresses a creative tension in understanding prayer as somewhere between simple conversation, thereby "reducing the divine person to the level of other 'beings,'" and "undue stress" on God's transcendence which can "easily obscure the fact that we meet God in the man Jesus Christ."[12] Biblically we see the Hebrew Scriptures founding all prayer upon the faithfulness of God. God is seen as giving personal guidance which can be trusted because of God's majesty and goodness.[13] For Rahner, Jesus' prayer in the New Testament is seen as a revelation of the unity of his will with that of the Father. Both submission to the Father's will in prayer and petition in favor of some request are seen to be "indissolubly" united attitudes in the prayer of Christ. Christ is free in his prayers of petition for change and in his prayers which express submission and limits.[14]

Prayer is seen as the most "personal act" of any Christian spirituality and one of Christian history's "driving forces."[15] For prayer to be personal it must engage the whole person at his or her level of conscious freedom. This is why Rahner is suspicious of petitionary prayer which is only "reduced to abandonment to the divine will."[16] Prayer is a real human activity and yet exists in tension between an exercise and an attitude. These poles of prayer cannot be identified nor can they be severed, only distinguished. The Christian is seen as such, according to Rahner, only when he or she possesses an attitude of prayer, one which can be described as lifting one's heart to God "afresh on each occasion."[17]

The common element in any degree of prayer is the profound intimacy with God which it affords. Fundamentally, prayer is the recapitulation of the human identity. It is, says Rahner, "*The* great religious act."[18] Prayer is the most basic expression of humanity's belief that creation is sustained by a personal God to be addressed as "thou." Further, Rahner states that prayer is an expression of our longing for happiness, satisfaction, and fulfillment in personal intimacy with God. This personal object of prayer determines its dialogical character.

> The attempt to make abandonment to God's providence the quintessence of prayer ignores its character of dialogue. It stresses one truth, the immutability of God (which taken in isolation would mean that real prayer is impossible) and forgets the other, that God is 'personally' concerned with our affairs. This immutability of God…must be kept open for the truth of the incarnation and crucifixion, for the truth that God 'changes' for the sake of man. This is the only possible source of a dialogical character of prayer.[19]

Prayer, Fidelity, and the Human Identity

This dialogical sense of prayer is truly a manifestation of the greater and more basic structure of creation itself. Prayer is a grace, a response to God's prevenient love. However, prayer is also an act of human freedom. In fact, it is in this intersection between grace and freedom that prayer operates and comes to its richest meaning—the call of the Divine and the response of the human in love.[20]

This call and response is received and acted upon in a community of persons and by a person in community.[21] Prayer has both an individual thrust and a communal, public reality. "[One] must not forget that the prayer of the individual relies on the community which it serves, and that the only ultimate meaning of community prayer is to lead the individual to God."[22] Individualism is an aberration of the duty to pray; prayer's very nature is expressive of a person opening up to the Holy Spirit who, in turn, opens one to other humans in their need. Prayer is receptivity and the explicit realization of one's relatedness to the Divine.[23]

In a real sense, says Rahner, "Prayer is already given to us in the depths of our existence."[24] The fullness of prayer's meaning can only be assessed by those who actually pray. This experience of praying is as old as human history and hence part of the fundamentals of human existence such as love and loyalty. These fundamentals, like prayer itself, are also questioned today for their contemporary relevance and yet persist, if simply as questions.[25] Along with these fundamentals prayer stands as witness against the exclusive view of truth held by the sciences which promote only the measurable and calculable as constituting reality. Suppressing these fundamentals as "dreams and optional opinions" only fosters their return in unconscious, aberrant, irrational, and "savage" activity.[26]

In her study of the prayer of the early founders of monasticism, Roberta Bondi concludes:

> It is a fundamental theological conviction that reality itself
> is grounded in God, whose basic being is love. To be made
> in the image of God means that we cannot see anyone or
> anything else as it truly is without seeing as God sees, that
> is, through the lens of love. [The early monastics] were con-
> vinced that rather than a commitment to the truth excluding
> love, only the presence of real love could be the basis of see-
> ing the truth at all. Love and rationality…must be all of a
> piece. Reasoning…is only reliable when it is grounded in
> love.[27]

The refusal to see anything true outside materiality has influenced the spread of modern-day atheism, thus promoting the denigration of prayer's relevancy.[28] However, Rahner sees prayer as a corrective to materialism and any narrow conception of humankind as object. Prayer, as a fundamental indicator of humankind's nature, confirms our basic openness to the "ground of our existence" and therein affirms our iden-tity as beings who, in worship, say "thou" to God.[29] The essential feature of all prayer, even prayer of petition, is "man's absolute surrender to the sovereign decrees of God's will." Without this full embrace of openness to God's will, any request in prayer is "at most the projection of a vital need into a void."[30] In light of God's incomprehensible mystery even a denied petition must be acknowledged as possibly salvific in the context of God's universal will for salvation. The goal is for persons not to be dominated by desires for material or spiritual goods but rather to surrender themselves to God.

In petitionary prayer, "man is mindful not only of who *God* is, but also who *he himself* is" [needy].[31] Most convincingly, Rahner holds that prayer is the explicit expression of our consciousness of being grasped by God, evidenced in such experiences as doing good despite any lack of recognition or gratitude on the part of others. One finds the ground for prayer in the experience of being faithful to the truth despite the lack of any sensate feedback. This, Rahner says, is "the experience of eternity" in time.[32]

The ground of any prayer is found in the reality that God actually addresses us in prayer, that the eternal approaches us from eternity in time. How is it that prayer is to be understood not merely as a monologue with oneself? Most profoundly, Rahner thinks that the authentic content of all our praying is not some inserted idea or inspiration by God into our hearts but rather that "we experience ourselves as the ones spoken by God." What God "primarily says to us is ourselves in our decreed freedom."[33]

> God's most original word to us in our free uniqueness is not a word arising momentarily and categorically *in addition* to or separate from other objects of experience within a wider area of our consciousness, but is we ourselves as integral total entities....The person then hears himself as God's address....He does not hear "something" in addition to himself.[34]

In this sense prayer is understood as dialogue. God addresses us in our radical openness and in so doing constitutes us as the content of his message. Jules Toner expresses this understanding of persons as prayer's content in the context of understanding Ignatius' vision of God's will.

> It is clear, then, that for Ignatius the glory of God which we should will in every act of willing is God's glory *in us* and...*for us*. The Glory of God...is human persons insofar

as they are alive with God's life in Christ and are manifesting that life in the world. Not only is God's glory coming to be in human persons; it is achieved by God through the free decisions and actions of human persons.[35]

God addresses us in the very depths of our freedom and intellect as we discern how best to give God glory in our categorical choices. Prayer is not a simplistic telegraphic mode from God but a profound weighing of the truth in the communion of divinity and humanity. Toner reports that for Ignatius prayer is to be entered when one is making difficult decisions and that one should trust that God will answer.[36] Rahner sees God answering prayers of petition, in the context of a specific choice, only in unrestricted openness to God. This choice for a certain object can be seen as "a movement" in the larger dialogical relationship constituted by the subject's "unlimited and unconditional openness" to God who addresses his most radical word to us in our own availability, our own intelligent freedom.[37]

Donal Dorr sees Jesus' prayer of petition in the garden before his arrest as paradigmatic of all who would confront God in their open neediness.

> "Not my will but yours be done." This act of commitment was the climax of hours of struggle in prayer. The Gospels make it perfectly clear that what Jesus was struggling to do in that prayer was not to *abandon* his own deepest will but to be *faithful* to it—despite the horror of…his…death.[38]

Public Prayer

Fidelity to one's deepest intelligent freedom before God indicates well the direction of Rahner's understanding of prayer. His sense of prayer is inclusive of private and liturgical prayer, and also a "midway" variety of prayer which he calls community prayer.[39] Community prayer is likened to a couple sharing their needs with a third party in order to "receive relief and consolation."[40]

At public events (Rahner mentions meetings, Scripture reading and teaching theology), community prayer is seen as a "heartfelt prayer for the enlightenment of the Holy Spirit." Community prayer is seen as an expression of humanity's deepest creative tension, to love God and neighbor. This community prayer must be rooted in a common experience so that it might truly be "the *common* dialogue of human beings with God."[41]

Rahner concludes that due to the power of this kind of prayer it is "a grave and sacred task." He argues that community prayer is not more frequently engaged in due to embarrassment on the part of believers. He calls upon these believers to reflect on why sharing prayer is humiliating if, in fact, we truly love the God and Lord we commonly claim as our own. "Lovers are not ashamed in each other's presence. They allow each other into the inmost mystery of their life and being. Then why should they be embarrassed to pray together?"[42]

This call to community prayer confirms the social nature of each person. In the realm of religion one brings that faith and identity to the community and finds it confirmed in the community of believers. Community prayer is summoned at those times and places of everyday life when insight and strength of faith is needed in the context of shared existence and duties. Private prayer alone does not touch our social nature and public liturgy alone does not tangibly fill our everyday moments of needs within community. A person can discover his or her personhood "only within his social nature and in function of this social nature....We are aware today in a quite new and inescapable way that man is a social being, a being who can exist only within such intercommunication with others throughout all of the dimensions of human existence."[43]

Since the time of Christ's life, death and resurrection, history carries more than an implicit hope of salvation. The church represents humanity's explicit grasp of salvation in the person of Jesus. Because Christians explicitly live in Christ, their devotion to him can prudently manifest itself in public prayer at the appropriate times and places.[44]

The experience of God, however, is normally implicit in the daily events of knowing and choosing. Prayer and worship is simply the "explicit celebration of the divine depth of [one's] ordinary life."[45] One is called to become a mystic as he or she apprehends the hidden presence of God in the ordinary experiences of knowledge, freedom, limit, and love. Michael Skelley summarizes Rahner's thinking on the inner structure of prayer by noting that "every moment of every day has the potential to become an explicit, mutual experience of God, in which God chooses to become present to us and we choose to become present to God."[46] We do not, however, experience God in exclusively religious ways. Our salvation is offered, accepted, or rejected in the fully human engagement of our free and intelligent choices. The life of any human, then, reveals the presence of God in his or her exercise of transcendence. This transcendence becomes an explicitly religious act when interpreted in light of God's word. However, "worship is not primarily what happens when we gather together to celebrate Eucharist: it is primarily what happens when we cooperate together with God in history."[47]

Worship assists us in avoiding spiritual amnesia. By this I mean that in worship, whether communal or private, one is affirmed in or reoriented to, if need be, one's fundamental identity as beloved of God. The self-offering of God in the routine of daily living is hidden for the most part. In history God calls forth a response from persons in their transcendental nature contextualized in ordinary experience. It appears from Skelley's study that Rahner sees public manifestations of worship as simply the explicit revelation of what is going on at the core of life itself—a passionate exchange of divine and created desire.[48]

Rahner describes this exchange in an analysis of the human identity. For Rahner, each human is not "merely the sameness of the repeated universal and not merely a case of the law." Rather, the human being is held in a creative tension existing in common with others and yet is always more than the others or their expressed values in universal norms. "Man is really also (not only) *individuum ineffabile*, whom God has called by name, a name which is and can only be unique, so that it really is worthwhile for this unique being as such to exist for all eternity."[49]

Prayer and Moral Norms

Eternal life is going to have real meaning only because real, unique choices were made in the moral realm as responses to the self-offering of God in history. Eternal life is, in fact, tasted in the uniquely chosen free acts of the moral person.[50] If Rahner is correct in saying that there is an "individual ethical reality of a positive kind which is untranslatable into material universal ethics (but not contradictory to them)," then prayer, which is the explicit acknowledgment by a person of being called by name, is to be a feature in discerning ethical responsibilities.[51]

In fact, Rahner sees his existential ethic as a method of moral discernment. His method respects the uniqueness of the individual-community tension, rather than deductively applying norms exclusively, so that it can be more open to the "personal-individual love of God." In connection with this, Rahner understands the conscience as that deliberate power which does not "merely" apply norms but grasps "as such what has to be done by me individually," and integrates the personal love of God with the search for truth (conscience). This reflects the Second Vatican Council's vision of conscience as the divine voice which echoes in the deepest part of our hearts (*Gaudium et Spes* 16).[52]

Rahner's approach to ethical decision making is imbued with respect for the process of discernment as articulated by Ignatius of Loyola. In Rahner's explication of this method of discernment, he outlines two possible modes of choice: application of norms, or secondly, God making his will known to an individual "within the framework of Christian principles applied to the particular situation."[53]

Why would one need God to show the way from within the framework of Christian principles? Why not simply follow the principles? Dave Roncolato has articulated this question very clearly and as an answer concludes that Ignatius operated under a deontological moral methodology. In this, Ignatius determined that discernment was not applicable to options in violation of any external norm of morality.[54] Ignatian spiritual discernment and moral discernment are not the same processes. "The Ignatian process seeks to discriminate volitional impulses according to their origin." Are they inclinations from the Holy Spirit or from that which is opposed to God? Alternately, the process of moral discernment seeks "relevant data or insights into anyone particular moral dilemma."[55]

If, according to Ignatius, normative ethics is primary and prevents discernment from collapsing into unbridled mysticism, prayer's role would be to simply confirm, through consoling impulses, what reason has already defined. The role of confirming what reason has discovered, however, is not to be belittled. In fact, confirmation through the affect is necessary for reason to gain its full confidence.

A central task of theological inquiry is to insure that persons—not just "heads" nor just "hearts"—keep the internal relations between theology and prayer clear and resilient. Prayer…is not the kind of activity which concentrates attention upon analytic refinement. It concentrates upon God….It can be a deeply intuitive activity precisely because it sustains an insightful context for the stories…concepts and doctrines which are the stuff of theology. Prayer provides a placement and a ground for disciplined thinking about scripture and theology. This implies more than the spiritual admonition that prayer is an aid to understanding; it has something to do with the very logic of religious believing.[56]

Don Saliers further notes that prayer "informs" the believers with the specific concepts theology is concerned with: God's will, creation, faith, grace, and so on. "The so-called 'objective' study of theology and learning to describe the concepts does not inform in the same way. The struggle to pray and to worship God informs our very person and gives determinative shape to Christian character."[57]

Prayer, Reason, and Affect

To really think theologically, Saliers believes one must do it in the context of religious experience, of faith. Out of this faith one embraces prayer and prayer "is more than thinking, more than subjective communion. It is a ground or telos for theological reflection."[58] And so there is a mutually interpenetrating existence for thinking and prayer. Karl Rahner has grounded his understanding of worship in the person of Jesus Christ.[59] For him Christ is the explicit manifestation of the "Liturgy of the World" which is the implicit structure of reality. The essence of this structure is the offer of divine self-giving and its corresponding acceptance in the same person of Jesus Christ.

In Christ the self-giving of God and the human response to this giving is "present in the world in a historical and communicable way."[60] Thinking and prayer can be understood analogically within this Christic identity of receiving divinity and responding, within the tension of divinity and humanity. In Christ, at the core of his identity, is a unity between human and divine which founds the very condition of the possibility for prayer and the discovery of what is true. Thus the preeminent stance of being human, at one's core, is a unity of thinking and praying, not, however, a uniformity. This unity can be seen as an expression of love, if humanity is understood as a yearning or desiring for God. Worship is the "religious" expression of this love as experienced in the fullness of one's human identity. Richard Viladesau speaks of this unity between knowing and loving (prayer):

> Love is knowledge in its full state. This implies that the truest form of knowledge is not the "objective," in the sense of uninvolved, impersonal, uncommitted apprehension of realities, but is rather "subjective," in the sense of involving the disposition of the free person....Indeed we have insisted that we are dealing not with concepts, but the performance of the living subject; and anyone who has appropriated his/her own intellectual life in its full reality knows it, not as an "abstract" and lifeless immersion in ideas or concepts, but as a vital dynamism which is finally identical with love, and which demands the commitment and decision of the whole person...to seek for the good in the culminating moment of rationality...and to love [the good is an implicit choice for God].[61]

John Macquarrie has called this intermingling of prayer and thinking "passionate thinking." "Such a thinking is not content to learn what is, but considers what ought to be...such a thinking is sometimes intermingled with painful longing."[62] For Macquarrie, to search out what is real and true is prayer since what faith calls reality is God. One of prayer's effects is to clarify a believer's grasp of reality as interdependent. Prayer breaks down barriers between individuals and reminds us that we are more than our societal functions.[63] Finally, prayer is seen as responsible thinking as it directs us out to others and the ultimate other. Our prayer is our response to God; it "is our responsible thinking in the presence of God."[64]

For Rahner, this responsible thinking in the presence of God becomes a deeply ingrained virtue of being, which acutely affects the believer as he or she responds to the intimacy known in the free self-offering of God. Andrew Tallon explicates:

> A major reason we are given to pray is to become someone whom God can affect. "Being affected" is a necessary condition for any affective response, and love is above all essentially an affective response. Being affected by God is grace, and grace is a gift affecting the human person by actualizing the person's nature. The gifts *gratis data* are habits: habits as virtues perfect the nature by improving performance of the acts of knowing and loving.[65]

Tallon continues,

> Rahner has a wider sense of feeling than particular emotions: he means feeling more as mood consonant with fundamental options and as the highest achievement of the human spirit become habits, i.e. virtues; they have sunk their roots deep into the structure of the spirit.[66]

This felt sense carries consolations which help the individual recognize God's will. As mentioned above, decisions of great import are made more on the basis of this felt sense of consolation and peace than on any rational analysis. Prayer is part of the fabric which holds the reasonableness of this affective sense from tearing or unraveling into idiocy.

For Ignatius and Rahner, recognizing consolation as having divine origin is essential in Christian discernment. It is not enough to simply apprehend a moral quality in any decision involving one's unique vocation choice, but rather it is vital to recognize if one's decision has its source in God or in the devil;[67] hence the necessity of consolation as a means of recognizing this origin.[68] This consolation resides at the "heart" of the person, and as Tallon describes it, is a continuity of affect, reason, and intellect. The whole person is coming to a decision about God's will, not isolated segments of the person. When God addresses the individual person, God addresses him or her in that person's complete context.[69]

From this call God bids persons to enact their greatest potential as God's beloved by their loving and knowing and choosing the good in a unified actualization of their heart.[70]

For Rahner, the context for decision making is paramount in considering one's ethical choices and ultimate object, God.[71] This context is the unity of loving neighbor and loving God in Christ. From out of this context, whether implicitly or explicitly, all decisions of loving, knowing freedom reach the divine mystery and call the person to participation in it through Christ's pascha.[72] The communal context is the arena within which one receives the unique and unrepeatable call from Christ. This context includes personal prayer and one's fidelity to conscience in ethical decisions. Loving God and neighbor are on the same continuum and experienced in the concrete commitments of daily experience. Similar to the mediation of divinity in Christ's humanity, we find the mediation of Christ in our encounters with neighbors in need (Matt 25:40).

> If, according to the gospel, love for our neighbor can be understood as the absolute sum of all moral obligations, and if at the same time it is something which basically always transcends an ethic of laws...and if love for God and neighbor can only be exercised in one and the same love for our fellow man, then this also implies the intrinsic unity between morality and religion.[73]

The unity of faith and ethics is experienced in the depths of one's own freedom and when one regards neighbor in dignity and serves real needs. Prayer becomes the expression of ultimate truth which recognizes that in the human condition any good one discerns is at once the fruit of dependence upon grace (gift) and the work or discipline of intellect (task).[74] This fruit, which is sown in prayer (devotion) and reason (truth), carries the confirmation of consolation ("a peace which surpasses all understanding"). Ultimately, the whole, the truth, which is initially grasped by the human in community can only be tested and interpreted properly from within this same network of relationships, commitment, and love.

For Maurice Nedoncelle, prayer is "contemplation of God and the resulting dialogue with him." "The end of prayer is prayer, the situation in which God's self-manifestation stirs up the living answer of the human will."[75] As with Rahner, Nedoncelle holds that prayer can be understood as a "remedy for selfishness" as it relocates the human in his/her authentic condition as beloved, dependent and open toward mystery. Prayer is an engagement of presences. We are called to look at the face of God, to contemplate, to reverence God's freedom in the offering of our own to him.[76]

CONCLUSION

Rahner's work in existential ethics intimates a characteristically Christian value in decision making which ought to be respected in theological ethics. Egan comments that for Rahner, "Christian decisions must often be made in a way that transcends the application of general and universal principles."[77] This respect for the uniqueness of persons and circumstances can be seen in Rahner's own personal prayers as he wrestles with the tension between law and obedience on the one hand, and love or spirit on the other. "Are you truly the spirit of freedom in my life, or are you not rather the God of law? Or are you both? Your laws…are commands of freedom…they awaken in us the freedom of loving You."[78]

Moral decisions cannot be made by some universal formula. Even in the midst of reasoned principles a person is always confronted with a decision of love. Logic and rational deliberation are necessary but not sufficient in discovering reality: "Not by knowledge alone, but by the full flower of knowledge, love." Discursive knowledge is said to only give us "some little help" in dealing with life's challenges and decisions.[79] The knowledge that truly remains is intimacy with God. God speaks to us [prayer] in our individual choices that strengthen or weaken our openness to God.[80]

Rahner's analysis of the Ignatian *Spiritual Exercises* explicitly links consciousness of God to decision making. "For [Ignatius] the whole sense of his precepts for making the election depends on the moral value of the relevant object of choice *being recognized* from its being inspired by God or the devil. The discernment of its *origin* is therefore the radical condition of the possibility of distinguishing its moral value."[81]

Rahner's conclusions about Ignatian discernment have implications for the role of prayer in decision making, especially regarding the necessity of, and/or occasion for, the use of explicit prayer, explicit openness to the divine origin of one's moral decisions. Rahner distinguishes between any explicit religious act and "those fundamentally human in character."[82] The link between the two is love. "One is only freely in possession of one's own being which in turn is to be entrusted to God, when and if one surrenders oneself to love for another being."[83]

Thus by loving God and others and expressing it in prayer, for example, we more clearly know or possess ourselves and thus are liberated to be ourselves. In such a state of liberation one might better grasp the truth of the decisions before him or her and be better able to direct them in fidelity to that truth.

Notes

1. Bernard Häring, *Free and Faithful in Christ* (New York: Seabury, 1978); Enda McDonagh, *Doing the Truth* (Notre Dame, IN: University of Notre Dame Press, 1979); Mark O'Keefe, *Becoming Good, Becoming Holy: On The Relationship of Christian Ethics and Spirituality* (New York: Paulist, 1995).

2. Harvey Egan, "Translation Editor's Preface," in Karl Rahner, *The Content of Faith: The Best of Karl Rahner's Theological Writings*, ed. Karl Lehmann and Albert Raffelt (New York: Crossroad, 1992), xi.

3. Jeremy Miller, "Rahner's Approach to Moral Decision Making," in *Louvain Studies* 5 (1975): 350–9.

4. Karl Rahner, *The Dynamic Element In the Church* (New York: Herder & Herder, 1964), 16.

5. Andrew Tallon, "The Heart in Rahner's Philosophy of Mysticism," in *Theological Studies* 53 (1992): 713. See also "Affection, Cognition, Volition: The Triadic Meaning of Heart in Ethics," in *American Catholic Philosophical Quarterly* (Spring 1994): 211–32.

6. Ibid., 707–9.

7. Ibid., 704, 711. Rahner, *Dynamic Element*, 166.

8. Karl Rahner, *The Love of Jesus and the Love of Neighbor* (New York: Crossroad, 1983), 40–44.

9. Ibid., 23.

10. Ibid., 24.

11. Harvey Egan, "Karl Rahner: Theologian of the Spiritual Exercises," in *Thought* 67 (September 1992): 261.

12. Rahner, "Prayer," in *Encyclopedia of Theology: A Concise Sacramentum Mundi*, ed. Karl Rahner (London: Burns & Oates, 1975), 1268.

13. Ibid., 1268–9.

14. Ibid., 1269.

15. Ibid., 1270.

16. Ibid., 1271.

17. Ibid., 1272.

18. Ibid.

19. Ibid., 1273. This idea that God "changes" and thus conditions the possibility for any *real* dialogical prayer is also mentioned in Rahner's "Apostolate of Prayer," in *Theological Investigations*, vol. 3, trans. Karl H. and Boniface Kruger (Baltimore: Helicon, 1967), 209–11.

20. Rahner, "Prayer," 1274.

21. Ibid. See also Karl Rahner, *Christian at the Crossroads* (New York: Seabury, 1975), 59; and Enda McDonagh, *Invitation and Response: Essays in Christian Moral Theology* (New York: Sheed and Ward, 1972), 43, 49, 52.

22. Rahner, "Prayer," 1274. Roberta C. Bondi, *To Pray and to Love: Conversations on Prayer with the Early Church* (Minneapolis: Fortress, 1991), 39; and James Keating, "Privacy, Public Commitment and the Spiritual Life," in *Spiritual Life* 38 (Winter 1992): 214–8.

23. Rahner, "Prayer," 1275.

24. Rahner, *Christian at the Crossroads*, 49.

25. Ibid., 49–50.

26. Ibid., 51–52.

27. Bondi, *Pray and Love*, 36. Don Saliers, *The Soul in Paraphrase: Prayer and the Religious Affections* (New York: Seabury, 1980), 12–13, has made a similar point in analyzing one's affections toward God and in general, stating that Western culture and science have seen affections as peripheral to the task of seeking the truth.

28. Rahner, *Christian at the Crossroads*, 52.

29. Ibid., 55.

30. Ibid., 57.

31. Ibid., 59.

32. Ibid., 61.

33. Ibid., 66.

34. Ibid., 66–67.

35. Jules Toner, *Discerning God's Will: Ignatius of Loyola's Teaching on Christian Decision Making* (St. Louis: Institute of Jesuit Sources, 1991), 16–17.

36. Ibid., 73. Toner seems to think Rahner's vision of how God addresses the human being is too focused on human deliberation. "Rahner does not seem to see consolation as a matrix from within which the discerner experiences a volitional movement, a conative impulse, from God toward a proposed alternative" (321).

37. Rahner, *Christian at the Crossroads*, 67–68.

38. Donal Dorr, *Integral Spirituality: Resources for Community, Justice, Peace, and Earth* (Maryknoll: Orbis, 1990), 275.

39. Rahner, *The Practice of Faith: A Handbook of Contemporary Spirituality*, ed. Karl Lehmann and Albert Raffelt (New York: Crossroad, 1983), 97.

40. Ibid.

41. Ibid., 98.

42. Ibid., 99.

43. Karl Rahner, *Foundations of Christian Faith: An Introduction to the Idea of Christianity*, trans. William Dych (New York: Seabury, 1978), 323.

44. Ibid., 322, 430.

45. Karl Rahner, "On the Theology of Worship," in *Theological Investigations*, vol. 19, trans. Karl H. Kruger (New York: Crossroad, 1983), 149.

46. Skelley, *Liturgy of the World: Karl Rahner's Theology of Worship*, (Collegeville, MN: The Liturgical Press, 1991), 85.

47. Ibid., 94.

48. Ibid., 104–5. See also Rosemary Haughton, *The Passionate God* (New York: Paulist, 1981), 214; and Rahner, *Theological Investigations*, vol. 19, 147.

49. Karl Rahner, "On the Question of a Formal Existential Ethic," in *Theological Investigations*, vol. 2, New York: Crossroad, 1990, 226–7.

50. Rahner, *Foundations of Faith*, 437.

51. Rahner, *Theological Investigations*, vol. 2, trans. Karl H. Kruger (New York: Crossroad, 1982), 222–3, 229; and Richard M. Gula, SS, *Reason Informed By Faith: Foundations of Catholic Morality*, (Mahwah, NJ: Paulist Press, 1989), 318–23.

52. See also Michael Allsopp, "Conscience, the Church, and Moral Truth: John Henry Newman, Vatican II, Today," in *Irish Theological Quarterly* 58 (1992): 192–208; Timothy O'Connell, *Principles for a Catholic Morality* (San Francisco: Harper, 1990), 112; and Rahner, "Formal Existential Ethic," in *Theological Investigations*, vol. 2, 229–33.

53. Rahner, *Dynamic Element*, 91.

54. Dave Roncolato, "Ignatian Discernment and Catholic Normative Ethics," unpublished paper, Duquesne University, 1992, 17. See also Mark

O'Keefe, "Discernment and Moral Decisionmaking," in *Journal of Spiritual Formation* 15 (February 1994): 68, where the author writes: "There are, of course, many situations in which there are no clear rules or in which it is not clear how relevant rules might apply. Similarly, the deductive, rule-based method does not seem to give sufficient attention to the unique qualities present in every concrete historical situation with wide possible variables in the persons involved and in the surrounding circumstances of time and place. Further this method seems to suggest that 'blind' obedience to rules can be held up as a virtue, a notion that runs contrary to a richer sense of Christian moral living as a response to other persons and to God with adult freedom and responsibility."

55. Roncolato, "Ignatian Discernment," 27. He contends moral decision making and discernment are distinct yet converge in the obvious shared goal of knowing God's will, 28.

56. Saliers, *Soul in Paraphrase*, 81–82.

57. Ibid., 83–84.

58. Ibid., 86.

59. Egan, "Karl Rahner," 267–8.

60. Rahner, *Foundations of Faith*, 195.

61. Richard Viladesau, *The Reason for Our Hope: A Theological Anthropology* (New York: Paulist, 1984), 149–51. See also Harvey Egan, *Christian Mysticism: The Future of a Tradition* (New York: Pueblo, 1984), 377.

62. John Macquarrie, "Prayer is Thinking," in *Southwestern Journal of Theology* 14 (1972): 43.

63. Ibid., 51–52.

64. Ibid., 45.

65. Tallon, "Rahner's Philosophy of Mysticism," 709.

66. Ibid., 717.

67. Rahner, *Dynamic Element*, 162–4.

68. Ibid., 158–63.

69. Ibid., 150, 169.

70. Tallon, "Rahner's Philosophy of Mysticism," 727–8.

71. See Karl Rahner and Johann B. Metz, *The Courage to Pray* (London: Burns & Oates, 1980), 55–56.

72. Rahner, *Foundations of Faith*, 310–1.

73. Ibid., 410.

74. Ibid., 79.

75. See Maurice Nedoncelle, *God's Encounter with Man: A Contemporary Approach to Prayer* (New York: Sheed & Ward, 1964), 103.

76. Ibid., 8, 10, 12–13.

77. Egan, "Karl Rahner," 15.

78. Karl Rahner, *Prayers for a Lifetime*, ed. Albert Raffelt (New York: Crossroad, 1987), 26.

79. Ibid., 17.

80. Rahner, *Dynamic Element*, 163–4.

81. Ibid., 163.

82. Rahner and Metz, *Courage To Pray*, 55.

83. Ibid., 56.

9. The Saint as Moral Paradigm

Donna L. Orsuto

This chapter first appeared in *Spirituality and Morality: Integrating Prayer and Action*, ed. Dennis Billy and Donna L. Orsuto (New York: Paulist Press, 1996).

The postmodern world presents particular challenges to authentic Christian discipleship. The apparent breakdown of a coherent moral or religious consensus which typifies postmodern culture necessitates a critical reflection on how Christians present and live the Gospel. In a time when abstract theories and ideas seem to have lost their compelling force,[1] it is not enough simply to explicate the demands of Christian discipleship. In and of themselves, they do not hold and attract followers to Christ. New modes of communication are necessary. The moral confusion and spiritual disorientation which characterize contemporary society cry out for the proclamation of the good news. The problem is to find a mode of communication which is comprehensible to contemporary men and women, a language which responds to their often unarticulated religious yearning.

This chapter suggests that the most effective way to transmit the good news is through the personal witness of disciples. Not only through their words, but most especially through their actions, they provoke a response in people. Mother Teresa of Calcutta, a woman whom many would consider a living "saint," exemplifies this point. Without a doubt, she has made and is making a powerful impact on contemporary society. What attracts people to her, though, is not so much what she says, but who she is and what she does. As an authentic disciple of Christ, she communicates the good news with her life. She radiates Christ's pres-

145

ence and draws people to God. In diverse situations over the centuries, people like Mother Teresa, including both the more restricted category of canonized saints and other exemplars, have embodied Christian values and ideals to such an extent that they have become moral paradigms. Their lives challenge others with the demands of Christian discipleship, but they do so in a pretheoretical language that transcends mere theories and ideas.

CHRISTIAN DISCIPLESHIP IN THE WORLD OF JURASSIC PARK

This pre-theoretical communication is particularly important in postmodern society because of the pointed disillusionment with theories and ideas. In many ways, the epitome of the postmodern crisis is the story of *Jurassic Park*. In the world of Jurassic Park, scientific experiments with DNA allow dinosaurs to come back to life in the rationally "controlled" environment of an island theme park. However, in a terrifying turn of events, the dinosaurs escape human mastery and wreak havoc. As in Jurassic Park, so in current society, theory no longer appears to have the capacity to bring order to the postmodern world.[2]

One does not have to embrace the current abandonment of theory that marks so much of contemporary philosophy to recognize that theory by itself does not bring about moral change in society. Past attempts to establish dialogue with secular culture on moral issues seem to have reached an impasse. The shift to postmodernity marks a recognition that the church and the world no longer share a common set of moral values.[3] The Christian in postmodern society is similar to Kierkegaard's story of the clown in the burning village. As one author explains, when the clown tries in vain to convince the villagers of an impending fire, his words are not taken seriously because he is "ticketed and classified," so to speak, by his role:

> Whatever he does in his attempt to demonstrate the seriousness of the position, people always know in advance that he is in fact just a clown. They are already familiar with what he is talking about and know that he is just giving a performance which has little or nothing to do with reality.[4]

In this context, contemporary culture poses a serious challenge to Christians: how to present the Christian ideal of discipleship in a setting where moral theories seem to have lost their force.

One point is clear: theories in and of themselves rarely compel one to moral or religious conversion.[5] As John Paul II says, "People today put more trust in witnesses than in teachers, in experience than in teaching, and in life and action than in theories" (*Redemptoris missio* 42).[6] Perhaps this is one of the reasons why he has beatified and canonized an unprecedented number of people during his pontificate.[7] In his most recent encyclical letter, *Veritatis splendor*, John Paul II specifically refers to the saints as moral paradigms: "By their eloquent and attractive example of a life completely transfigured by the splendor of moral truth, the martyrs and, in general, all the Church's Saints, light up every period of history by reawakening its moral sense" (*Veritatis splendor* 93).[8]

WHO ARE THE SAINTS?

The Postmodern Philosophical Debate

Is the saint though an effective witness in postmodernity? In the field of moral philosophy, there are diverse opinions about who the saints are and their role as moral paradigms. This is exemplified in the exchange between Susan Wolf and Robert Adams. Wolf argues that saints, with their morally good actions, are unattractive as models because they seem bland and dull. Her three criteria for moral sainthood include the following: (1) every act of that person is "as morally good as possible"; (2) the person himself or herself is as "morally worthy as can be"; and (3) "one's life be dominated by a commitment to improving the welfare of others or of society as a whole."[9] Fulfilling these three criteria is such an all-consuming task that other "nonmoral virtues as well as many of the interests and personal characteristics" of a "healthy, well rounded richly developed character" would be excluded.

Consequently, the saint emerges as a "strangely barren" and boring person.[10] In critiquing Wolf's somewhat narrow perception of sainthood, Adams suggests that "actual saints" (and there actually are saints) are "immensely attractive" and "intensely interesting" to others. He

insists that sainthood must ultimately be seen as a religious phenomenon; the central focus is the saint's relationship with God.[11] He stresses
that "the substance of sainthood is not sheer willpower striving like
Sisyphus (or like Wolf's Rational Saint) to accomplish a boundless task,
but goodness overflowing from a boundless source."[12]

Another important contribution in the field of moral philosophy is
Edith Wyschogrod's *Saints and Postmodernism*. She argues for a
"hagiographical ethics" as a compelling alternative to reliance upon
moral theory. Her ideas are quite complex and far beyond the scope of
this study. Nevertheless, her definition of a saint, though much broader
than the Christian understanding, does give some insight into the direction of her "hagiographical ethics." She defines

> the saint—the subject of hagiographic narrative—as one
> whose adult life in its entirety is devoted to the alleviating of
> sorrow (the psychological suffering) and pain (the physical
> suffering) that afflicts other persons without distinction of
> rank or group or, alternatively, that afflicts sentient beings,
> whatever the cost to the saint in pain or sorrow. On this view
> theistic belief may but need not be a component of the
> saint's belief system.[13]

Among her numerous contributions, she considers two major questions:
how the saints exemplify "what moral lives are" and how they demonstrate concretely how "one might go about living a moral life."[14]

The Saints in the Christian Tradition

This chapter proposes to explore these two points specifically
from a Christian perspective. In the Christian tradition, the saints are not
the dull, unfulfilled individuals described by Wolf; rather they are paradigms of human authenticity. The saints reflect human fulfillment par
excellence. As Karl Rahner suggests, the saints are "initiators and the
creative models of the holiness which happens to be right for, and is the
task of, their particular age."[15] They also serve as teachers and models of
Christian morality. Bernard Häring suggests that we should turn to the

"magisterium of the saints" for guidance—they can teach us how to respond to the call of discipleship today.[16]

In the New Testament, the followers of Christ were called saints (Acts 9:13, 32, 41; Rom 1:7; 16:2; Phil 1:1).[17] They were set apart as a people or community for God alone. Over the centuries, the term gradually developed to refer specifically to certain deceased believers who were honored in a special way because of their faithful witness to Christ, even unto death (the martyrs) or because of their exceptional holiness. In a broad sense, saints refer to those persons whose experience of intimate union with Christ so transforms them that they are conformed to his image and likeness. Their lives are transparent: in their being and acting, the divine love and presence shines through them to such an extent that others recognize this and look to them as paradigms of Christian discipleship. Because of their intimate communion with Christ and with all members of the Body, others are drawn to turn to them in intercession and veneration. Some, who through martyrdom or through the exercise of heroic virtue, whose writing has undergone careful scrutiny and who have been proven to be intercessors (through miracles), are officially recognized by the Roman Catholic Church as "blessed" or "saints."[18]

Since the martyr is the "highest mark of love" (*Lumen gentium* 42),[19] we shall use it as a specific example to show precisely how the saint is a moral paradigm. What does the martyr tell us about living a moral life? The word "martyr," which literally in Greek means "witness," represents the ideal of discipleship. From earliest times to today, the martyrs were honored as those who sacrificed their lives in an ultimate act of love and fidelity to Christ and his teaching:

> Condemned, tortured, bloodied, and executed, martyrs were perceived by other Christians as entering in a graphic way into the dying of Jesus, and so into his rising. They were icons of Jesus Christ, awesome signs of the victory of his power in the face of the evil of this world.[20]

In the period from apostolic times to 312, an epoch interspersed with great persecution in the church, the martyrs were perceived as authentic disciples. They were models for other Christians of how they should act when faced with hostility for their Christian faith. This is particularly evident in *The Acts of the Christian Martyrs*.[21] For example, in the moving account of "The Martyrdom of Saints Perpetua and Felicitas," Perpetua stands out as model of unwavering commitment to Christ. Despite pressure from her family and the pain of eventually being separated from her baby, she had only one reply to her pleading father:

> "Father," said I, "do you see this vase here…"
> "Yes, I do," said he.
> And I told him: "Could it be called by any other name than what it is?"
> And he said: "No."
> "Well, so too I cannot be called anything other than what I am, a Christian."[22]

Sometimes in the romanticization of the early martyrs, the concrete reality of fear and isolation is overlooked. The readiness of Perpetua to sacrifice her life for her convictions in spite of the suffering that she endured surely poses a challenge to men and women of postmodern society. Though martyrdom is a gift to which few are called, part of the Christian vocation is to be ready to offer a "consistent witness" even in the midst of suffering and sacrifice (*Veritatis splendor* 93).[23] As Lawrence Cunningham has noted:

> The willingness to die for one's faith is the ultimate test of faith commitment. The threat of death is so powerful that it becomes the touchstone by which we measure what we hold as ultimate and nonnegotiable in life. What is it we would die for? Honor? Country? Family? Possessions? Love? When we read of the religious martyrs, they remind us—they test us—about the degree to which we have or have not accepted the discipleship of Jesus. They force us to ask: Would we go that far?[24]

The saint, and more specifically the martyr, exemplifies what the moral life is. The moral life is not simply following rules, it finds its meaning in a loving relationship with Christ, a relationship which shapes one's actions.

The Identification and Recognition of the Saints in Cult

The historical development of the cult of the saints is quite complex, and beyond the scope of this study. However, a brief review of salient points will demonstrate how the saints emerged as moral paradigms. Up until the beginning of the fourth century, the only persons who were venerated as saints were the martyrs.[25] Eventually, non-martyrs or "confessors" were recognized for their heroic witness to Christ in the midst of persecution. With the cessation of persecution, other outstanding holy persons, especially monks and virgins, were venerated.

Peter Brown has shown that in late antiquity the saints were seen as exemplars who re-presented Christ. In that period, the aim and effect of the *imitatio Christi* was to make "Christ present by one's own life in one's own age and region."[26] As John S. Hawley so succinctly suggests when introducing Brown's essay:

> Their personhood was the crux of the morality they taught—
> often implicitly rather than discursively—and what they
> sought to imitate and perfect was no specific aspect of the
> life of Jesus…but the unfallen Adam that waits to be redis-
> covered within us all. They were not examples typifying
> aspects of the whole, they were convincingly the whole; as
> exemplars they contrasted markedly to a world of shards
> and fallen fragments by which they were surrounded. They
> showed the way through to a level of being so coherent that
> in contrast to the dimness or at best reflected glory of ordi-
> nary existence it seemed able to generate its own light.
> Hence the language of luminosity pervades descriptions of
> them. Their impact was registered in "flashes of signal
> light" and "shining visions," not in what is usually meant by
> moral instruction.[27]

During this period, the cult of the saints was very much a grass-roots movement under the authority of the local bishops, and it was only in the tenth century that the pope became more officially involved.[28] Eventually, it became more centralized and the process of recognition of saints developed into a formal and somewhat complex ecclesiastical exercise.

The formal process leading to canonization has been developing since the Middle Ages. Key moments in the development include the formation in 1588 by Sixtus V (1585–90) of the Congregation of Rites which took responsibility for the identification of saints, the complex procedure developed by Urban VIII (1623–44), Prospero Lambertini's (Benedict XIV, 1740–58) study of beatification and canonization, the critical study of the saints by the Jesuit Bollandists which was started in the seventeenth century by Jean Bolland (and particularly inspired by Leribert Rosweyde, 1569–1629), the 1917 Code of Canon Law, and the formation of the Congregation for Causes of the Saints in 1969, which was formerly a part of the Congregation of Rites.[29] The most recent reform, which simplified the process, took place in 1983 with John Paul II's Apostolic Constitution, *Divinus perfectionis magister*.[30]

Throughout the development of the canonization process, the main purpose was and is to provide models of holiness. Holiness, which is nothing other than union with Christ in love, necessarily has an effect on one's moral actions. This is evident when considering the two traditional categories of saintliness: namely, martyrdom and heroic virtue. Martyrdom, considered "the highest gift and supreme test of love," is of course the apex of Christian heroism (*Lumen gentium* 42).[31] Other candidates for beatification or canonization, though not gifted with martyrdom, must exercise heroicity of virtue.[32] Heroic or exceptional virtue implies that one is so radically transformed by God's own love as to live profoundly and in an exemplary way the theological virtues of faith, hope, and charity and the four cardinal moral virtues of prudence, justice, fortitude, and temperance. Whether for the martyr or others who have exemplified heroic virtue, the operative word is love: the key is to live a life of exceptional love toward God and neighbor.

Lex Orandi, Lex Credendi, Lex Vivendi

The liturgical prayer of the church regularly presents us with the challenge of the saints as models for Christian living. For example, Vatican II's "Constitution on the Sacred Liturgy" says that the church proposes the martyrs and other saints to the faithful "as examples" who draw all to God (*Sacrosanctum concilium* 104).[33] Further, in the first eucharistic preface for Holy Men and Holy Women I (The Glory of the Saints), the church prays:

> Father, all powerful and ever living God…you are glorified in your saints, for their glory is the crowning of your gifts. *In their lives on earth, you give us an example.* In our communion with them, you give us their friendship. In their prayer for the Church you give us strength and protection. *This great company of witnesses spurs us on to victory* to share their prize of everlasting glory, through Jesus Christ our Lord.[34]

Likewise, in the second eucharistic preface, Holy Men and Holy Women II (On the Activity of the Saints), the faithful are encouraged to look to the saints as models:

> You (Father) renew the Church *in every age by raising up men and women outstanding in holiness, living witnesses of your unchanging love. They inspire us by their heroic lives, and help us by their constant prayers to be the living sign of your saving power.*[35]

The proper of saints in the *Roman Sacramentary* emphasizes the particular ways that each martyr or other saint acts as an exemplar. This specific focus is accompanied by a prayer that the faithful would be inspired to act in the same way. For example, on January 28, when the Roman Catholic Church celebrates the memorial of St. Thomas Aquinas, the opening prayer is as follows: "God our Father, you *made Thomas Aquinas known for his holiness and learning. Help us to grow in wisdom by his teaching, and in holiness by imitating his faith.*" Again on June 3, the feast of Charles Lwanga and Companions, we pray, "Father, you have made the blood of the martyrs the seed of Christians. *May the witness of St. Charles and his companions and their loyalty to Christ in the face of torture inspire countless men and women to live the Christian faith.*" Both of these, and other similar opening prayers for saints, begin by recognizing the source of the exemplary life, namely God. Then a particular characteristic of the saint's witness is emphasized (for St. Thomas Aquinas, his holiness and learning; for St. Charles and his companions, their loyalty to Christ in the face of persecution and death). Finally, it is accompanied by the petition that the faithful might be inspired by the example of the saint. There is a movement from *lex orandi* to *lex credendi* to *lex vivendi*: prayerful contact with the saint's witness which is proclaimed in the liturgy is meant to transform one's life.

WHAT THE MORAL LIFE IS: DISCIPLESHIP

So far we have determined who the saints are and that they are presented as models both in the historical development of cult and in liturgy. In light of this, the obvious question is, precisely how do the saints show us what the moral life is? The answer is simple, yet profound: *they do so by manifesting to us what it means to be a disciple of Christ.*

In recent years, the theme of discipleship has been proposed as a "powerful paradigm for Christian living."[36] In his book, *A Church to Believe In: Discipleship and the Dynamics of Freedom*, Avery Dulles, SJ, argues persuasively that an appropriate model of the church for this age is that of the "Church as a Community of Discipleship." He introduces this proposal by quoting from John Paul II's first encyclical *Redemptor hominis*:

> Therefore, if we wish to keep in mind this community of the people of God, which is so vast and so extremely differentiated, we must see first and foremost Christ saying in a way to each member of the community: "Follow me." It is the *community of the disciples*, each of whom in a different way—at times very consciously and consistently, at other times not very consciously and very consistently—is following Christ. This shows also the deeply "personal" aspect and dimension of this society (21).[37]

In light of this focus on the church as a community of disciples, two particular questions arise: What do we mean by discipleship and how is it a manifestation of the moral life? How can those who have "very consciously and consistently" followed Christ serve as models for the rest of us? Of the ninety times that the word "disciple" occurs in the New Testament, seventy-nine are in the Gospels.[38] Though each of the four Gospels has its own particular point of view,[39] they converge on the description of discipleship as a personal and intimate relationship with and total adherence to Jesus Christ (Mark 8:34–38; Matt 16:24–26; Luke 9:23–26; John 15:1–12). The moral life is best characterized by discipleship which has the following three characteristics. Firstly, this relationship begins with a divine initiative: Jesus calls individuals to a personal and intimate relationship with him ("to be his regular companions," [Mark 3:14, TLB]), an invitation that is often heard in the midst of ordinary activities. Secondly, discipleship implies a radical break with the past and a new commitment to Jesus' way of being and acting. Thirdly, the experience of discipleship empowers one to carry on Jesus' mission, even in the midst of persecution.

After the death, resurrection, and ascension of Jesus, the notion of discipleship changed dramatically. As Dulles notes:

> For the first time a community of disciples existed without the visible presence of the Master. One might imagine that in that case the apostles would replace their absent Lord, and would themselves become Christ to their followers. To some extent this did occur. They spoke in his name, so that Jesus could say of them, "Whoever hears you hears me" (Lk 10:16). "As the Father has sent me, I send you" (Jn 20:21). Paul could write to his Corinthian converts: "Be imitators of me as I am of Christ" (1 Cor 11:1). But the disciples never really took the place of Jesus, who alone remained, in the full sense, Master and Lord.[40]

Paul's attitude is fundamental for understanding the challenge of discipleship in the early church. While each follower was called into an intimate and personal relationship with the risen Lord, certain members of the community, like Paul himself, were exemplars of how concretely this could be done in diverse circumstances. It is for this reason Paul could say, "Imitate me as I imitate Christ" (1 Cor 11:1).

LEARNING TO LIVE THE MORAL LIFE: SAINTS AS PARADIGMS

This Scripturally rooted focus on discipleship is particularly relevant while facing the challenge to be a Christian in a post-Christian and postmodern society. The call to discipleship is just as definite today as it was when Jesus was walking along the Sea of Galilee. Today as in the past, discipleship implies that there is no cheap grace.[41] Total adherence to Jesus means following him and incarnating his way of being and acting in one's own life. The challenge is to respond to this call in diverse historical and cultural situations. The saints stand out as exemplars of Christian discipleship by incarnating gospel values existentially in time and space.[42] In considering the saints as paradigms of discipleship, it is important to understand in what sense they are an example. As John S. Hawley notes:

> The key term is example, a word whose meanings diverge in two directions that are only distantly related. In one sense an example is an instance, an illustration, a case in point. In the other, an example is not a subset of something larger but a paradigm that sets the shape for a series of imitative phenomena that follow in its wake. It is a model, a prototype, not merely an example but an exemplar. Both these usages help us to state the moral impetus so often present in hagiographical traditions. On the one hand, saints can be examples of something, or even of someone; on the other, they can be examples to someone.[43]

Indeed, as Lawrence Cunningham notes, "the life of the saint should act as a parable. It should shock us into a heightened and new sense of God's presence (and judgment) in our own lives."[44] We might add, the lives of the saints should shock us into embracing the demands of Christian discipleship. If not only individuals, but the church as a whole is a community of disciples, it must be stressed that this community includes also Mary, the "perfect disciple,"[45] and the communion of saints, those who have constantly and consistently responded to the call of discipleship. As noted above, discipleship is intimately intertwined with one's personal relationship with and adherence to Jesus Christ.

More than anyone else, Mary and the saints have responded to this challenge. They are icons of Christ. They mirror Christ by taking on his way of being and acting in diverse historical and cultural situations.[46]

CONCLUSION

The saints have not only gone before us as models to be imitated, they are also our companions on the journey. This is a profound truth: as part of the body of Christ, we do not have to go on the journey alone. There are a host of companions, living and dead, who share with us, who celebrate with us, who help us on our way. Indeed, we invoke the saints in liturgy as companions of prayer. "It is for that reason we pray at the liturgy to have 'some share in the fellowship of your apostles and martyrs'; that we beg to praise God 'in union with them,' and why, finally, we are bold to ask 'to share in the inheritance of all your saints.'"[47]

Notes

1. See *Anti-Theory in Ethics and Moral Conservatism*, ed. Stanley G. Clark and Evan Simpson (Albany: State University of New York Press, 1989).

2. I got this image of *Jurassic Park* from Timothy Radcliffe, "Challenges to Our Mission in the First World," *Sedos Bulletin* 26 (1994): 148–50. He uses it to contrast the world of Jurassic Park, a world of violence, competitive consumerism, isolation, and fatalism with the way of Christ. As he notes (148) and as I agree, there are also positive elements of contemporary society that should be taken into account, including "a cherishing of the individual, human rights, a tolerance of those who are different, etc."

3. On this theme, see Walter Kasper, *The God of Jesus Christ* (New York: Crossroad, 1987), 3–75.

4. Joseph Ratzinger, *Introduction to Christianity*, trans. J. R. Foster (San Francisco: Ignatius Press, 1990), 15–16. As Ratzinger notes, the story was popularized by Harvey Cox's book, *The Secular City* (New York: Macmillan, 1966).

5. Walter Conn, *Christian Conversion: A Developmental Interpretation of Autonomy and Surrender* (New York: Paulist Press, 1986), esp. 158–268. In speaking of Thomas Merton's conversion experience, he comments (179): "A life of self-transcendence does not grow and flourish into conversion without the

nourishment of a strong model." He is speaking of Merton's personal friends, but it seems that the idea can be broadened to consider saints as exemplars.

6. John Paul II, *Encyclical Letter on the Permanent Value of the Church's Missionary Mandate* (Vatican City: Libreria Editrice Vaticana, 1991).

7. See Patrick de Laubier, "Sociologie des saints," *Revue thomiste* 91(1991): 34–67; Jean Evanou, "Les saints et bienheureux proclamés par Jean Paul II (1978–1988)," *Esprit et vie* 99 (1989): 200–7; Kenneth Woodward, *Making Saints* (New York: Simon and Schuster, 1990), 120–2.

8. John Paul II, *Encyclical Letter, The Splendor of Truth Shines* (Vatican City: Libreria Editrice Vaticana, 1993).

9. Susan Wolf, "Moral Saints," *Journal of Philosophy* 79 (1982): 419–39, esp. 420.

10. Ibid., 421.

11. Robert Adams, "Saints," *Journal of Philosophy* 81 (1984): 392–401.

12. Ibid., 398. See also Owen Flanagan, *Varieties of Moral Personality* (Cambridge, MA: Harvard University Press, 1991).

13. Edith Wyschogrod, *Saints and Postmodernism* (Chicago: University of Chicago Press, 1990), 34.

14. Ibid., 4. For a description of postmodernism and a summary and critique of Wyschogrod's position, see David Matthew Matzke, "Postmodernism, Saints and Scoundrels," *Modern Theology* 9 (1993): 19–36.

15. Karl Rahner, "The Church of the Saints," in *Theological Investigations*, vol. 3, *The Theology of the Spiritual Life*, trans. Karl H. and Boniface Kruger (New York: The Seabury Press, 1974), 100.

16. Bernard Häring, *Free and Faithful in Christ: Moral Theology for Priests and Laity*, vol. 2, *The Truth Will Set You Free* (Middlegreen, Slough, UK: Saint Paul's Publications, 1979), 218. For introducing me to this theme in Häring's writings, I am grateful to William Thompson, *Fire and Light: The Saints and Theology* (New York: Paulist Press, 1987), 28n4. From a Methodist tradition, Stanley Hauerwas also recognizes the importance of saints. In "Ethics and Ascetical Theology," *Anglican Theological Review* 61 (1979): 98, he says: "Attending to the lives of the saints is for Christians the means of moral growth on which all other aspects of moral life depend." For this and further references to Hauerwas' position that the saints are models of the Christian life who represent "what we are about," see Kevin O'Neil, *What Should We Be? A Study of Stanley Hauerwas's Christian Tradition-Dependent Character Ethics* (STD. diss., Accademia Alfonsiana, 1989), 256–8. For a survey of recent research on saints, see Lawrence Cunningham, "A Decade of Research on the Saints: 1980–1990," *Theological Studies* 53 (1992): 517–33.

17. Otto Procksch and Karl G. Kuhn, "Hagios," in *Theological*

Dictionary of the New Testament, ed. G. Kittle and G. Friedrich, 10 vols. (Grand Rapids: Eerdmans, 1964–76), 1:88–115.

18. For a history of the process of canonization, see William J. McDonald, gen. ed., *New Catholic Encyclopedia* (New York: McGraw-Hill, 1967), s.v. "Canonization of Saints, History and Procedure," by Paul Molinari. The process was simplified in 1983, as we shall indicate further in the text.

19. See *Vatican II: The Conciliar and Post Conciliar Documents*, ed. Austin Flannery (Collegeville, MN: Liturgical Press, 1975), 401; Paul Molinari, "Martyrdom: Love's Highest Mark and Perfect Conformity to Christ," *The Way Supplement* 39 (1980): 14–24; *Nuovo Dizionario di Spiritualità*, ed. Stefano De Fiores and Tullo Goffi (Rome: Edizioni Paoline, 1979), s.v. "Martire."

20. Elizabeth A. Johnson, "Saints and Mary," in *Systematic Theology: Roman Catholic Perspectives*, ed. Francis Schüssler Fiorenza and John P. Galvin (Minneapolis: Fortress, 1991), 2:149.

21. *The Acts of the Christian Martyrs*, intro. and trans. Herbert Musurillo (Oxford: Clarendon Press, 1972). See also W. H. C. Frend, *Martyrdom and Persecution in the Early Church: A Study from the Maccabees to Donatus* (Garden City, NY: Doubleday, 1967).

22. *The Acts of Christian Martyrs*, 109.

23. John Paul II, *The Splendor of Truth Shines*.

24. Lawrence S. Cunningham, *The Catholic Heritage* (New York: Crossroad, 1983), 23.

25. Agostino Amato, "Culto e canonizzazione dei santi nell'antichità cristiana," *Antonianum* 52 (1977): 38–80, esp. 38–43. Also important for the early period is the excellent study by Peter Brown, *The Cult of the Saints: Its Rise in Latin Antiquity* (Chicago: University of Chicago Press, 1981).

26. Peter Brown, "The Saints as Exemplar in Late Antiquity," in *Saints and Virtues*, ed. John S. Hawley (Berkeley: University of California Press, 1987), 7.

27. Hawley, *Saints and Virtues*, xv.

28. Johnson, "Saints and Mary," 147. In 1993, Pope John XV was the first pope to canonize a saint. See also Michael Downey, ed., *The New Dictionary of Catholic Spirituality* (Collegeville, MN: The Liturgical Press, 1993), s.v. "Saints, Communion of," by Shawn Madigan.

29. See Christopher O'Donnell, ed., *Ecclesia: A Theological Encyclopedia of the Church* (Collegeville, MN: Liturgical Press, 1995), s.v, "Saints" by Christopher O'Donnell; McDonald, *New Catholic Encyclopedia*, s.v. "Bollandist," by P. Roche; Pierre DeLooz, "Towards a Sociological Study of Canonized Sainthood in the Catholic Church," trans. Jane Hodgkin, in *Saints and Their Cults: Studies in Religious Sociology, Folklore and History*, ed. Stephen Wilson (New York: Cambridge University Press, 1983), 186–216.

30. John Paul II, *Divinus perfectionis magister, Acta Apostolicae Sedis* 75 (1983); 349–55. The English translation of this document by Robert J. Sarno as well as "Norms to Be Observed by Bishops in the Causes of Saints" and the "General Decree," both documents of the Congregation for the Causes of the Saints, is published in *New Laws for the Causes of the Saints* (Rome, 1983). For a commentary and guide to the new legislation, see Fabijan Veraja, *Le cause di canonizzazione dei santi* (Vatican: Libreria Editrice Vaticana, 1992). On how the new legislation affects diocesan inquiries, see Robert J. Sarno, "Diocesan Inquiries Required by the Legislator in the New Legislation for the Causes of Saints," (JCD diss., Gregorian University, 1988).

31. In Flannery, *Vatican Council II*, 401; Molinari, "Martyrdom," 14–24.

32. Paul Molinari and Peter Gumpel, "Heroic Virtue: The Splendour of Holiness," *The Way Supplement* 39 (1980): 25–34.

33. In Flannery, *Vatican Council II*, 29.

34. *The Roman Missal: The Sacramentary* (New York: Catholic Book Publishing Co., 1985), 511. In this and subsequent quotations, the emphasis is mine. The focus on saints as models is also a helpful approach in ecumenical dialogue; see Michael Whalen, "The Saints and Their Feasts: An Ecumenical Exploration," *Worship* 63 (1989): 194–209; George Tavard, "The Veneration of Saints as an Ecumenical Question," *One in Christ* 26 (1990): 40–50.

35. *The Roman Missal: The Sacramentary*, 513.

36. See Keith J. Egan, "The Call of the Laity to a Spirituality of Discipleship," *The Jurist* 47 (1987): 71–85. In light of the post–Vatican II era and the new Code of Canon Law, Egan suggests that the most appropriate spirituality of the laity is precisely a spirituality of discipleship.

37. John Paul II, *Redemptor hominis*, March 4, 1991, as quoted in Avery Dulles, *A Church to Believe In: Discipleship and the Dynamics of Freedom* (New York: Crossroad, 1992), 7 [emphasis mine].

38. David Noel Freedman, ed. in chief, *The Anchor Bible Dictionary*, 1st ed. (New York: Doubleday, 1992), s.v. "Disciple, Discipleship," by Hans Weder.

39. See Fernando F. Segovia, ed., *Discipleship in the New Testament* (Philadelphia: Fortress Press, 1985).

40. Dulles, *A Church to Believe In*, 9.

41. Ibid., 10.

42. Lawrence Cunningham, *The Meaning of Saints* (San Francisco: Harper and Row, 1980), 2.

43. Hawley, "Introduction" in *Saints and Virtues*, xiii.

44. Cunningham, *Saints*, 79.

45. Mary is also referred to as the prototype of the "believer-disciple." See Dulles, *A Church to Believe In*, 9. For a further development of Mary's discipleship, especially as developed in Luke's Gospel, see Raymond E. Brown et

al., *Mary in the New Testament* (New York/Mahwah, NJ: Paulist Press, 1978), 105–77.

46. Cunningham, *Saints*, 75.

47. Lawrence Cunningham, *Catholic Prayer* (New York: Crossroad, 1989), 141.

10. The Formation of Conscience

Kenneth R. Himes

This chapter first appeared as "The Formation of Conscience: The Sin of Sloth and the Significance of Spirituality," in *Spirituality and Moral Theology: Essays from a Pastoral Perspective*, ed. James Keating (New York: Paulist Press, 2000).

Conscience is at the heart of the moral life. The term *conscience* is, however, famously vague and is often used by people in ways that are not easily reconciled, if not outright contradictory. Yet the word *conscience* remains central to most descriptions of the moral life. In what follows I will highlight one of the connections between the spiritual life and the moral life by showing spirituality's importance for the formation of conscience. First, I will clarify the various meanings of *conscience* and indicate the understanding of conscience that I consider especially important for linking spirituality and morality. Then I will note the threat to the formation of a good conscience by what the tradition has called the capital sin of sloth. In the third part of the paper, I shall suggest how a vibrant spiritual life serves as an antidote to the danger of sloth in the moral life. Finally, I will close with some pastoral implications for the moral formation of people.

The Meanings of Conscience

A difficulty that theologians and philosophers have with the term *conscience* is that in the English language the same word is used to describe diverse yet related aspects of our moral experience. As the Irish

162

moral theologian Sean Fagan has written, "The word 'conscience' has had such a complex, ambiguous history and has been used with so many meanings that it is difficult to confine it to a simple definition."[1] In the classical world, the Greek word *syneidesis*, literally, a "knowing with," was the term used by philosophers to describe "the experience of self-awareness in the forming of moral judgements [*sic*]."[2] Centuries later, in the New Testament, the term had come to mean the ability of human beings to "evaluate the moral worth of their behavior in the light of their beliefs."[3] It was, for Paul, "the moral personality, the centre of the soul where choices are worked out and responsibilities undertaken."[4]

Patristic authors "relied heavily upon Paul, stressing the idea he adopted from Old Testament prophetic literature of a moral law written by God on men's hearts."[5] Jerome, however, introduced a rare Greek term—*synteresis* or *synderesis*—to describe the power of conscience that survived even the fall. This *synteresis* was understood as the person's inner call to authenticity and pursuit of the human good.

Later medieval theologians who sought "to do justice to both authorities…applied the Pauline term to the actual exercise, or judgment of conscience, while reserving Jerome's term for the idea of conscience as an innate permanent capacity" within each individual.[6] In effect, Jerome's *synteresis* became the human being's intuitive grasp of the first principles of the moral life, while Paul's *syneidesis* was used to designate the practical reasoning ability of a person applying the principles to specific actions.

Over time, as moral theology became focused on the resolution of pastoral problems, various theological authors placed conscience at the center of their ethical theories. Concurrent with this positioning of conscience in moral experience, theologians struggled "to distinguish carefully different states of conscience in view of law and freedom: the firm conscience, the doubtful conscience, the broad conscience, the scrupulous conscience, and so forth."[7]

By the time of the manualists, the experience of conscience was largely described in terms of states pertinent to the process of decision making: (1) true and false conscience; (2) certain and doubtful conscience; (3) perplexed conscience; (4) scrupulous conscience; (5) lax conscience; (6) probable conscience.[8] In order to assist people in sorting through the details of moral decision making, and to enable the person

to avoid the pitfalls of conscience formation suggested by some of the
categories noted above, an array of moral systems was created. The
details of these moral systems need not concern us here, but their role in
the formation of conscience was to help an individual determine freedom or obligation relative to a particular precept. We need only note
that, by the mid-point of the twentieth century, conscience had come to
be largely identified in popular idiom and by many moral theologians
with concrete judgments in decision making.[9]

With the renewal of moral theology, we have seen growing interest in retrieval of a richer notion of conscience than simply that of *syneidesis*, a faculty of decision making. A quick survey of commonly used
texts within American Catholic moral theology today suggests a fairly
popular set of distinctions. Timothy O'Connell has suggested that we
understand conscience in three ways, generally corresponding to the traditional categories of *synteresis*, moral science, and *syneidesis*.[10]
According to O'Connell, the first understanding of conscience is "as an
abiding human *characteristic*,...an awareness of human responsibility....It is to be a being in charge of one's life," a "human capacity for
self-direction."[11] Conscience in the second sense "is the process which
that characteristic demands,...the ongoing process of reflection, discernment, discussion, and analysis."[12] The third sense of conscience
described by O'Connell is as "an *event*,...the concrete judgment of a
specific person pertaining to her or his own immediate action."[13]

Richard Gula closely follows O'Connell in the description of conscience. Instead of O'Connell's terms—*characteristic*, *process*, and
event—to designate the different aspects of conscience, Gula suggests
capacity, *process*, and *judgment* but means by the terms the same moral
phenomena.[14] Gula emphasizes that he is not talking about "three different realities...but simply the three senses in which we can understand
the one reality of conscience."[15]

In her recent volume, which is described as a feminist exploration
in Catholic moral theology, Anne Patrick writes, "Conscience is simply
a *dimension of the self*, one central to our experience of moral agency."
She goes on to say:

> I define it as personal moral awareness, experienced in the
> course of anticipating future situations and making moral

decisions, as well as in the process of reflecting on one's
past decisions and the quality of one's character, that is, the
sort of person one is becoming.[16]

Here Patrick combines elements of what the tradition called "antecedent"
and "consequent" conscience and alludes to the different dimensions of
conscience as "moral awareness," the "course of anticipating future situations," and "making moral decisions." These latter expressions would
seem roughly to coincide with the threefold framework of O'Connell
and Gula.

Lest one conclude that the agenda behind this differentiation of
conscience is a liberal or revisionist reading of the tradition, let me cite
an influential conservative voice in Catholic moral theology. In the first
volume of his multivolume work on Christian morality, philosopher
Germain Grisez notes that for Vatican II "conscience refers at once to
awareness of principles of morality, to the process of reasoning from
principles to conclusions, and to the conclusions, which are moral judgments on choices made or under consideration." He further recalls that
Thomas Aquinas used the terms *synteresis* for the sense of conscience as
"awareness of principles," *practical reasoning* for "the process of reasoning," and *conscience* for the concluding "moral judgments on
choices."[17]

Thus, within the tradition, the one English word *conscience* may
allude to different dimensions of moral experience. Whether they use
classical or contemporary terminology, recent authors have sought to
distinguish the various types of moral experience that are lumped
together under the popular designation *conscience*. The purpose of
recalling these various aspects of our moral experience and the reason
for citing the Catholic tradition's semantics on the topic are to emphasize that we can ignore a central role for spirituality in the moral life if
we do not expand the discussion of conscience to include more than
decision making. In addition, directing our attention to conscience in the
sense of the person's serious search for value, truth, and the good will
alert us to a significant pastoral obstacle that stands in the path of moral
growth: the vice traditionally called sloth.

SLOTH AS THE ENEMY OF CONSCIENCE

In the medieval period, there was no settled list of capital sins, although there was considerable redundancy among many lists. Two sins, *tristitia* (melancholy) and *acedia* (apathy), were seen to be closely related, with the former understood as a component of the latter. *Acedia* was a word covering a "jumble of notions" that referred to mental (boredom), spiritual (indifference), moral (apathy), and physical (laziness) states.[18] *Acedia* eventually was translated as "sloth" in English-language lists of the capital sins. Unfortunately, sloth has come to be understood in modern usage as laziness or shiftlessness, missing the other medieval senses of the term beyond the physical. As a result, the real evils that earlier generations of Christians sought to name by the Latin words have slipped into the background.

When used in the moral sense, the person seized by *acedia* is the affect-less individual, one incapable of investment or commitment, a person who cannot get deeply involved in any cause or relationship. Such an individual is unable to take an interest in or to care about things that normally one would. It is this understanding of sloth that I consider to be the real enemy of sound conscience formation. Sloth as moral apathy is what hinders a person from pursuing that which is good. It is a refusal to seek the good because it is difficult and demanding. As one modern writer put it, sloth "is a refusal to be moved, and to be moved especially to any real endeavor, by the contemplation of the good and the beautiful."[19] This way of looking at sloth presumes that the moral agent "has a duty to do more than resist evil; he must also undertake to do good."[20]

The radical evil of sloth can be seen in the heart of Catholic teaching on conscience. The Catholic understanding of the person is that we are endowed by God with an ability to be self-transcendent; there is within the person a moral summons to be transformed into a more authentic human. Another recent textbook in moral theology describes the full meaning of conscience to be "not just the ability to make decisions about ethical questions confronting us in the present moment," but rather conscience is

> a deep and abiding hunger within us to move beyond ourselves, a moral appetite constantly urging us on beyond all

our limits and boundaries, calling us to stretch ourselves beyond our selfish and petty concerns, reaching out for others, for the moral good and ultimately for God.[21]

Conscience as *synteresis* is the moral dimension of the call to self-transcendence. To hear the call of conscience is to be aware of the divine invitation to become more fully and authentically human. At one level, conscience is the call to be an imitator of Christ, since it is Jesus alone who has plumbed the depths of what it means to be human. For the disciple, being truly one's self means being in Christ. Therefore, in seeking to understand the meaning of conscience, we can say that it has to do with our awareness of what it means to become authentically human.

Sloth is a capital sin precisely because we are creatures graced with the capability of growth into a deeper and richer participation in life, and sloth undercuts the drive to self-transcendence. Sloth permits the voice of conscience to be muted so that the moral quest for goodness ceases. An individual's passion for the good dissolves, and the conscience of the slothful person permits self-satisfaction instead of inviting self-transcendence. Those who are morally mature experience a deep attraction for the good, are drawn to it, and fall in love with it; but those who are slothful experience what the biblical writers called "a hardening of the heart," a developing indifference to the good.

SPIRITUALITY AND THE STRUGGLE AGAINST SLOTH

Sloth as moral apathy requires a diagnosis and remedy that is different from sloth viewed as laziness. When sloth is reduced simply to laziness, the remedy becomes obvious: we ought to work harder. Moral indolence is cured by the discipline of diligent and persistent performance of good deeds. Viewed this way, sloth is something we can control and combat by our own efforts. If, however, sloth is best understood as apathy, as a loss of feeling for the good, then the challenge is of a different kind: we need to care again. If care is absent, however, if we are without passion, lacking a desire for the good, it becomes evident that we cannot correct the problem solely by ourselves. What is needed for the person is to be moved once again, to have passion reawakened. It is in this regard that spirituality becomes important for combating sloth. According to the early monastic tradition, which gave rise to the listing of capital sins, sloth can only be overcome through the indwelling of God. It is by having God move within us that we experience a rebirth of desire and care.

Of course it is not possible to force God's action, to summon God to come into our lives in a new and revivifying way. The early monks knew that truth well. They also thought it possible, however, to engage in various practices that opened up interior space for the Spirit of God to move, for instance, *lectio divina*, contemplation of nature's beauty, and fasting. It is spiritual renewal that rekindles our longing for God, a God whom we may experience as all-caring, concerned, and loving toward oneself, others, and creation.

There are a variety of ways in which a living spirituality counteracts the dangers of sloth. By a living spirituality I mean more than an affect-less acknowledgment of God's existence or a passive recitation of prayers. First and foremost, spirituality entails an encounter with the one who is holy and who is known in the world about us. For Christians, this encounter with God is most clearly experienced in the person of Jesus who reveals a God who is love. Discipleship is an expression of spirituality, our response to this personal God who is revealed in the life of Jesus of Nazareth. We follow Jesus so that we may come to know the living and true God. Seen in this way, the moral life of a believer is but a dimension of discipleship, the grace-empowered response to God's action in the world through Jesus and others.

Thus, Christian morality can never be mere external obedience to a legal norm or abstract ideal. Rather, it must be a response to God that engages the total self, both internal and external. As disciples, we are to love God, not just obey God. As Edward Vacek reminds us, "Love is not only an affirmation. Love also means receiving the beloved into one's self, that is, being affected. God's love of us implies that we make a difference to God. When one embraces, one is also touched."[22] The spirituality of the disciple involves the experience that we matter to God, "that our simplest and most complex strivings" are of significance not only to ourselves but to God. A living spirituality takes us beyond an intellectual acknowledgment that our God is a God of self-offering to an acceptance both intellectual and affective that "we belong to God" (1 John 4:6).

Such a love transforms us, for we now live with an awareness that our lives are not simply ours alone.[23]

There is a second way that spirituality helps us counteract sloth. Central to a vibrant spiritual life is the practice of prayer that maintains the distinctive tone of moral activity that ought to be characteristic of disciples. As the new Israel, the church has been called into the intimacy with God in Jesus that is recorded in the Gospel of John (e.g., 10:30). For the good to have an appeal that is stronger than the attraction of vice, it is necessary for followers of Jesus to develop a covenantal relationship with God. The offer of covenant is a grace that we do not deserve, but Scripture tells us that God freely chose to enter into such a relationship with creation. As a result of the divine initiative, the life of discipleship requires more than conformity to a code of ethics. Personal encounter with the God of Jesus Christ prevents a covenantal morality from becoming a contractual ethic, that is, a legalistic approach to the moral life concerned with not violating rules or commandments. Prayer helps us appreciate that the goal of our moral action is not loyalty to an abstract ideal but a grateful praise of God for what we have received in love.

Through prayer, the believer maintains the proper interior disposition for the moral life. Prayer prevents us from losing sight of God amidst all the preoccupations that fill our lives. Eucharistic rituals, for example, reinforce the dialogic character of life. We are caught up in a blessing of God, a sacrifice of praise for all that God does. The gift-response nature of the moral life is kept before our eyes by participation in such a ritual.

Cultivation of a personal relationship with God avoids the trap of becoming deists in our moral lives, acknowledging some sort of distant responsibility and accountability to an impersonal creator. Rather, Christian morality places all the values and norms of the moral life within the context of a loving and intimate kinship with Jesus and the God he reveals. Spirituality is necessary both *as an aid* to the moral life, permitting the moral response to be an interior one, and *as the fruition* of the moral life, once we realize that nothing we can do adequately responds to divine love, and so we must stand before God in praise and worship.

A third dimension of how spirituality counteracts sloth is seen in the area of motivation. Spirituality empowers us to act in a morally appropriate manner, and this is evident in two ways. On the one hand, we all act out of mixed motives (love, vainglory, desire for reward, fear of punishment, shame, peer and societal pressures, compassion, etc.). Part of moral growth is to examine what it is that encourages us to do the good. A vibrant spirituality helps us to purify our motive, for it encourages us to act out of a desire to respond in love to the love that we experience. Moral action flowing from love must be rooted in ongoing encounter with the God who is love, the God who touches our hearts and fires our spirit. If such moments of prayerful contemplation of God are absent, it becomes far easier for other motives to move to the foreground. When higher motives for morality are diminished and inferior motives predominate, it becomes possible for the believer to gradually lose the desire and longing for the good. It is not likely that lesser motives can sustain the disciple in the struggle against apathy when one faces disappointment and difficulty and the moral life demands sacrifice and suffering.

This leads to the other aspect of motivation in the moral life. Besides purifying our motives, the spiritual life provides a depth of passion and zeal that moves us more powerfully than intellectual appeals to an ideal known only in the abstract. The moral life is not just something cerebral but visceral. Moral action requires a struggle of the will as well as of the mind. To move the will, what is required is not only an appeal to alleged facts but an encounter with Christ. Disciples are not in love with "truth" or the "good"—they are in love with a personal God who is truth and goodness.

Meditation on the Gospels, participation in sacramental rites, and individual and group devotions are ways in which we come to know Jesus. By knowing Jesus experientially, we can be inspired by him, fired with love to follow him, and serve him. Oftentimes it does little good for us to tell ourselves to stop our participation in a destructive lifestyle, to "just say no." We need to reorient ourselves to a new source of energy, something that moves us, draws us in the direction of the good despite the appeal of vice. We must find something to which we can devote ourselves. Prayer, understood broadly as attending to God, helps us to do that, to fall in love with God. Liturgical symbols, hymnody, good preaching—all have the power to evoke a response that is affective and compelling.

Prayer and other elements of the spiritual life can school our emotions so that we are drawn to the good, while also providing us with emotional energy to seek and choose the good, despite obstacles and suffering. Unless we love the good, unless we care about the morally right thing to do, it is hard to imagine that we will be able to sustain the life of discipleship. Sloth deadens the passions and leads us to indifference to the good. A life marked by regular practices of personal prayer and frequent participation in the liturgical life of a community offers an antidote to sloth, since it will be a life in which we are taught to care deeply about the good, for we know the good experientially as it is found in the living God.

In sum, the formation of a Christian conscience must entail not merely tools for clear thinking but also the training of our passions, so that we truly desire the good and want to do what is right. Spirituality is instrumental in this process, for conscience must integrate both cognitive and affective dimensions of human personality.[24]

THE FORMATION OF CONSCIENCE

In the present state of Roman Catholic teaching, the dignity of conscience is held as the highest personal norm. At Vatican II the bishops proclaimed that "conscience is the most secret core and sanctuary" of a person. To listen to one's conscience and follow it "is the very dignity" of the person. The bishops' emphasis on the primary importance of conscience is such that they acknowledge that a conscience may be in error "from invincible ignorance without losing its dignity" (*Gaudium et Spes* 16).[25] To make sense of this latter statement, we must remember that "appeal to conscience as a moral authority for one's actions presupposes a 'good conscience.'"[26] That is, the conciliar teaching presumes that *synteresis*, conscience as inner call to moral responsibility, is what each person must follow. We must pursue the good as we see it. Provided that we have made an honest effort to learn what we can about the matter under review, we are bound to follow our conscience. This is so even if others see my action to be wrong. As long as I do not know it to be wrong, but believe myself to be right, I must follow the truth as it speaks to me in the sanctuary of conscience. Being faithful to the truth, as best I can know it, is the measure of being in good conscience.

The distinction between the pairs of words "good/bad" and "right/wrong" is a familiar one to Catholic moral theologians. Good/bad refers to *synteresis*, and as long as one is acting in good conscience, one is not morally blameworthy even if one is wrong at the level of conscience as *syneidesis*. People may sincerely search for the good while not always making right decisions. Honest mistakes do occur. Hence, we see the wisdom of Anne Patrick's observation that conscience is not some sort of moral radar, always honing in on the correct judgment. Rather, it is more like intelligence—we all have some of it; we all could use more of it; and even a lot of it does not mean we are always right.[27] Disciples can make wrong decisions (*syneidesis*) without being dishonest or insincere in their quest for the good (*synteresis*).

Even as the conciliar teaching makes clear, however, the supremacy of conscience can be challenged when a person "who cares but little for truth and goodness" is in error. It is this aspect of the Council's teaching I am concerned with in this paper. Generally, it has received less attention than the conciliar teaching that correctly exalts the dignity of conscience. That high view of conscience was a needed clarification about the Catholic teaching, since the church has not always been seen in the modern era as a protector of the freedom of conscience. Yet, the situation today suggests that we must remember: "Emphasis on the freedom of conscience and the right and obligation to *follow* it should not blur the fact that there is an equal obligation to *form one's conscience*."[28]

The reason moral theology distinguishes among the various meanings of conscience is not only for the purpose of linguistic precision. Depending on what one means by conscience, there are diverse approaches to what is involved in the formation of conscience. In some cases, for example, conscience as practical judgment, the emphasis will be on *informing* the conscience, acquiring the necessary knowledge in order to make wise judgments. Often when teachers and pastors speak about the need for people to have an informed conscience before making moral choices, it is the attainment of information that they have in mind. One should know what the church teaches about a particular issue, what reliable information from scholarly disciplines about it is available, how this issue impacts human well-being, and so on. In this context, the contribution of spirituality to conscience is akin to learning methods of discernment. That is, spirituality's contribution in this example is largely limited to helping us decide wisely. The dimension of conscience that is pastorally most problematic is not the need people have for information. In our information-rich culture, all sorts of information are abundantly available.

Unfortunately, much of the information to which we have access in American society is misleading and even false; it is presented without context, overhyped, irrelevant to human well-being, and peripheral to our experience. Thus, the task of separating wheat from chaff is as important as ever. Indeed, the wise person in the future will not be the person with the ability to access information but the individual with the skill to screen out and filter information. I wish to argue, however, that what is presumed by those who advocate an *informed* conscience is instead an adequately formed conscience, that is, a conscience that has been motivated and trained to desire the good so that the person will work at being informed.

Pastoral Implications

A pastoral problem for our age is that we readily assume the fact of good conscience. Those who have worried about informing conscience have stressed knowing right and wrong, developing prudence and skills in decision making, without taking sufficient note of the duty to form one's conscience. A corollary of viewing conscience mainly as *syneidesis* is to see the human person as a problem solver. The valued traits then become analytic reasoning, rational discourse, disinterested judgment. Other qualities—imagination, openness, creativity, passion, self-criticism, compassion—may be undervalued in such a framework. We have seen this skewed approach in the mistaken operational assumptions of social scientists, for instance, who act as if the best way to observe moral growth is to assess people's judgments in hypothetical cases. Precisely because they are hypothetical, such exercises are of limited value. They remove us from actual involvement in a situation; our answers do not reveal anything about what we would really do or even actually think in real life.

Pastorally, the much-needed task is to help each other love the God who is good. Therefore, at the pastoral level, we may misplace our energies if we focus too much on the conscientious person as decision maker. What is needed today is a renewed interest in the conscientious person as the sincere seeker of truth and the consequent pastoral strategy of evoking passion for the good by schooling people in practices of prayer, both personal and communal. We need to deepen and transform our desires, to train our affections to love properly. Only if that is done well will we avoid the apathy that stunts the moral quest and makes talk of good conscience doubtful. I would like, then, to suggest a couple of the pastoral implications of the argument that sloth is the enemy of good conscience and that spirituality is the needed counter force to foster growth in the moral life of the disciple.

Before doing so, let me be clear that I am aware our job as a church is not completed by creating a love for moral goodness, as important as that is. We must also sharpen our ability to make moral judgments that are correct, to become not just people who love, but people who love well. As I have made clear, however, we have spent much time and effort in recent years dealing with conscience and right decision making. Indeed we have so focused on *informing* the conscience, stressing knowledge of right from wrong, that we have paid inadequate attention to *forming* the conscience, of desiring the good and shunning the bad. As a church we have presumed that people were sufficiently zealous and in love with the good so that the processes of prudent discernment would be practiced. Yet, too often the moral difficulty is not lack of knowledge, for we know what it is we should do; the real difficulty is doing the right thing and, even more profoundly, wanting to do it.[29] Having the capacity to reason to correct moral judgments is insufficient if we lack any real commitment to seek and do the good. So I underscore two pastoral implications of my viewpoint.

First, people can come to learn that the morally good life is both possible and attractive. Thus, stories of exemplary figures are worth reading; news accounts of heroic activity should be highlighted and exposure to admirable persons sought. What people need, in part, are standards of heroism, examples of compassion, experiences that challenge their taken-for-granted world of self-interest.

The community of believers must hold up the lives of ordinary persons who display a quiet heroism in the way they live out their commitments, care for their neighbors, and struggle to maintain personal integrity. At the same time, biographies of figures such as Dorothy Day,

Thomas More, Bartolomé de Las Casas, Pierre Toussaint, Joan of Arc, Oscar Romero, Francis of Assisi, Mother Teresa, and Thea Bowman are examples of well-known persons whose witness can inspire and guide Christians in their moral growth. The community of faith needs to instill in believers a desire to do the good and to assist disciples in becoming more attuned to the nature of the good life. The goal is to facilitate persons' commitments to be faithful in seeking out the good.

Our moral experience can find us in tension between our sense of ourselves and a life that does not live up to that self-image. A possible reaction is to be spurred into action so as to close the gap between the reality and the moral ideal, for example, being a good parent, teacher, friend, and the like. A properly formed conscience drives us to bring our self-understanding into accord with professed ideals. The incorrect solution for the apathetic, however, is to revise our ideals downward. A conscience captivated by sloth will allow us to avoid the moral tension of conversion by ignoring the call to embrace the good or by convincing us that the moral ideal to which we aspire is too demanding. Seeking the good, loving the good, encourages transformation of the self, such that persons are encouraged to live up to ideals rather than surrender them.

As a community of faith, we need to instill in people a love for goodness, encourage in them a sense of moral idealism whereby they do not succumb to skepticism or cynicism about moral values. Young people especially need to know adults who are committed to excellence in the moral life in the same way that skilled workers are dedicated to excellence in their craft, athletes are committed to excellence in performance of their sport, or musicians devoted to their music.

Second, in considering conscience as an inner call to authenticity and diligence in pursuing the good, an important formative task is to awaken and sharpen moral sensitivity. We respond only to what we experience, to what enters into our consciousness. Too often people who are insufficiently sensitive to moral values do not even grasp the moral dimensions of an experience. How often have we seen a person not even realize how his or her words or actions cause another person's pain? How often do people fail to see what is really at stake in a decision, unable to focus on anything but what is of immediate and direct satisfaction? This is a deficiency in moral sensitivity. It is not that some individuals consciously choose poorly; instead, they are not even capable of grasping all that is embedded in the experience to which they are being asked to respond.

In order to sharpen and deepen sensitivity, a variety of elements can be utilized. Largely these will focus on the affective dimensions of moral growth, for what is at stake is the inability to feel people's pain, the discipline to delay immediate gratification for a higher purpose, the courage to withstand the pressure of peers or societal expectations. Iris Murdoch writes of the grave need to discipline what she calls the "fat relentless ego" and the moral struggle involved in that effort.[30] Sloth always tempts us to complacency in the moral life. It is much easier to remain within a world that does not challenge us to change, that shields us from those who are different from us, a world that allows us to create self-deceiving myths about moral goods and evils. Challenging disciples to sacrifice, to sharing their talents and possessions, to working cooperatively, to denying themselves for the sake of another, to working with persistence and care on a project that has only future rewards, to living up to promises—all these are disciplines that restrain the ego and make room for moral growth.

Developing sensitivity is also facilitated by expanding our range of experiences, since in this culture it is relatively easy for many to insulate themselves from what is unpleasant or unrewarding. In more affluent suburban areas, for instance, many people are shielded from the sufferings of the economically deprived. Service projects that introduce us to people in need can awaken feelings of compassion. In many of our homes and neighborhoods, children may not frequently encounter examples of gentleness, patience, or caring. Barraged by larger-than-life images of sports figures, gun-toting superheroes, and slick entrepreneurs, the search for true moral examples can be difficult in this culture.[31]

CONCLUSION

My aim in this essay has been to stress an obligation that might be called *forming* rather than *informing* conscience. In meeting this obligation, there is a significant role for spirituality, since the first task of conscience formation is to teach people a love, even a passion, for the good. Only then can we move to the aspect of conscience that is concerned

with making wise and prudent decisions. Looking at conscience formation, as I have used the expression, the major obstacle is sloth, a moral
apathy, which permits one to be complacent about rather than passionate for the good. Spirituality's contribution to the formation of conscience as *synteresis* is to deepen our love, our desire, for the God who
is goodness.

Notes

1. Sean Fagan, "Conscience," in *The New Dictionary of Catholic
Theology*, ed. J. Komonchak, M. Collins, and D. Lane (Wilmington, DE:
Michael Glazier, 1987), 226.

2. John Mahoney, *The Making of Moral Theology: A Study of the
Roman Catholic Tradition* (New York: Clarendon Press, 1987), 185.

3. Ibid., 187.

4. Ibid., 187–8, quoting Philippe Delhaye, *The Christian Conscience*
(New York: Desclee, 1968), 42.

5. Mahoney, *The Making of Moral Theology*, 186.

6. Ibid., 187.

7. Servais Pinckaers, *The Sources of Christian Ethics* (Washington,
DC: Catholic University of America Press, 1995), 272.

8. See, for example, Henry Davis, *Moral and Pastoral Theology*, vol. 1
(London: Sheed and Ward, 1935), 65–80.

9. In such a framework, it was not easy to see the role or significance
of spirituality for the moral life. Indeed, prayer often was treated as one more
legal obligation that might bind a person, and the same sort of moral calculus
used for resolving the force of a law in other areas of life was employed when
discussing the legal obligations relevant to the spiritual life.

10. Timothy O'Connell, *Principles for a Catholic Morality*, rev. ed. (San
Francisco: Harper & Row, 1990), 109.

11. Ibid., 110 (emphasis in original unless noted otherwise).

12. Ibid., 111.

13. Ibid., 112.

14. Richard Gula, *Reason Informed by Faith* (Mahwah, NJ.: Paulist
Press, 1989), 132.

15. Ibid., 131.

16. Anne Patrick, *Liberating Conscience: Feminist Explorations in
Catholic Moral Theology* (New York: Continuum, 1996), 35.

17. Germain Grisez, *The Way of the Lord Jesus*, vol. 1 (Chicago: Franciscan Herald Press, 1983), 76.

18. Stanford Lyman, *The Seven Deadly Sins: Society and Evil* (New York: St. Martin's Press, 1978), 5.

19. Henry Fairlie, *The Seven Deadly Sins Today* (Washington, DC: New Republic Books, 1978), 126.

20. Lyman, *The Seven Deadly Sins*, 9.

21. Russell Connors Jr. and Patrick McCormick, *Character, Choices and Community: The Three Faces of Christian Ethics* (Mahwah, NJ: Paulist Press, 1998), 137.

22. Edward Vacek, *Love, Human and Divine: The Heart of Christian Ethics* (Washington, DC: Georgetown University Press, 1994), 123.

23. Ibid., 127.

24. There are other aspects of the relationship between morality and spirituality that could be explored, for example, the role of discernment in decision making, or the way images of God shape our moral attitudes. I only wish to suggest here that there is a clear contribution that spirituality makes to the formation of conscience once we consider conscience as more than a faculty for practical moral judgment. Concerning discernment see John Haughey, "The Role of Prayer in Action/Reflection Groups" in *Tracing the Spirit*, ed. James Hug (Mahwah, NJ: Paulist Press, 1983), 103–21. For the moral import of our images of God, see James Gustafson, "Spiritual Life and Moral Life," in *Theology and Christian Ethics* (Philadelphia: Pilgrim Press, 1974), 161–76.

25. Vatican Council II, Pastoral Constitution on the Church in the Modern World. See, for example, Austin Flannery, ed., *Vatican Council II: The Conciliar and Post Conciliar Documents* (Wilmington, DE: Scholarly Resources, 1975).

26. Fagan, "Conscience," 229.

27. Patrick, *Liberating Conscience*, 35.

28. Fagan, "Conscience," 228.

29. As has been pointed out in a recent text, the danger is that without a desire to seek conscientiously for the good we become "moral 'couch potatoes.'" See Connors and McCormick, *Character, Choices and Community*, 135.

30. Iris Murdoch, *The Sovereignty of Good* (London: Routledge and Kegan Paul, 1970), 52.

31. There are, of course, many other implications that could be drawn out, but I have not done so in the interest of space. One obvious point to be developed is the importance of communal prayer and the celebration of the sacrament for conscience formation. Patricia Lamoureux has explored in a thoughtful way the import of communal celebration of the Liturgy of the Hours for morality. In particular, she discusses the moral vision and virtue of solidarity as developed through such prayer. See "Liturgy of the Hours and the Moral

Life," *New Theology Review* 10 (February 1997): 40–57. Timothy O'Connell's new book has several important insights for the topic of sacramental celebration and morality, especially his comments on gesture, music, and the simple fact of being gathered with others. See *Making Disciples: A Handbook of Christian Formation* (New York: Crossroad, 1998), esp. chaps. 11 and 13.

Part Three

REFOCUSING
ETHICAL TOPICS

11. Spirituality and Justice

Walter J. Burghardt

This chapter first appeared as "A Spirituality for Justice," in *Handbook of Spirituality for Ministers*, vol. 2, ed. Robert Wicks (New York: Paulist, 2000).

Almost a decade ago, I had a dream. Nothing quite as revolutionary as the vision of Martin Luther King Jr., but still, not insignificant for the future of our church, our country, our way of life, our spirituality.

It was springtime 1989. I was in my twelfth year as Georgetown University's theologian in residence, my twenty-third year as editor of the scholarly journal *Theological Studies*, my forty-fourth year on its editorial staff. I sensed it was time to resign both positions. I was touching seventy-five, increasingly aware of the psalmist's warning, "The days of our life are seventy years, or perhaps eighty, if we are strong" (Ps 90:10). And yet, my mind was still active and insatiably curious, my imagination free and flowing, my emotions spirited. On what should I focus for however many years God might have in store for me? An apostolic area that would engage my background, talents, and interests? Background? Theology, specifically the so-called fathers of the church. Talents? Communication: preaching, lecturing, writing, editing. Interests? People, especially and increasingly Jesus' "little ones," the poor and the powerless, the distressed and the downtrodden.

I was then a senior fellow of the Woodstock Theological Center, had in fact been a fellow since its inauguration in 1974. A research organization located at Georgetown University in the District of Columbia, the center was founded by the New York and Maryland Provinces of the Society of Jesus, to put theology to work on social, economic, and political issues. It proved to be the seedplot for my dream. The center had been, and still is, doing impressive work in touching theology to the neuralgic problems of our time, through research and writing, conferences and workshops. An admirable approach indeed. And yet, I worried. This approach reaches only a relatively small number of our people. How might we expand the center's influence, stimulate American Catholics *as a whole* to live and spread our social gospel?

It was then that the dream took on flesh and blood. The heart of the matter? Preaching. Where do American Catholics gather regularly in largest array, even more than for pro football? At weekend liturgies. True, actual head counts show regular weekend Mass attendance ranging from only 27 to 36 percent; still, an audience of millions a TV network might profitably barter its soul to win. Not preaching in general, but proclaiming "the faith that does justice." What the president of Catholic Charities, Inc., Jesuit Fred Kammer, integrated as the title of his book *Doing Faithjustice*.[1] It is the inseparable unity our 32nd General Congregation (1974–5) called "the mission of the Society of Jesus today."[2] It is the mission the then-Superior General of the Jesuits, Pedro Arrupe, confessed was the concept most difficult of all to put across to his society.[3]

The dream, however, had a nightmarish aura. Granted that effective Catholic preachers are not absent from our pulpits, preaching is by common consent not our pride and glory, is all too often dull as dishwater. I cannot forget a pertinent phrase from Dennis O'Brien, a former president of the University of Rochester in New York. In a book engagingly entitled *God and the New Haven Railway and Why Neither One Is Doing Very Well*, he observed that on Monday morning most people on the train station are not likely to see church service as "one of the livelier, more salvational times of week"; their appraisal is more likely to be "Saturday Night Live, Sunday Morning Deadly."[4]

If our proclamation of God's word is to instill new life into the relationship between faith and justice, (1) the minds and imaginations of our preachers must be captivated by a fresh vision, and (2) their hearts must be set afire with a fresh flame. As we shall see, the first demand has to do with a well-preserved Catholic secret: biblical justice. The second demand was strongly urged by Fr. Philip Murnion, director of the National Pastoral Center in New York City. He insisted that our project "Preaching the Just Word" would fail of its purpose if its exclusive or overriding priority were information, data, skills, or strategies, important as these are. Undergirding all these must be a spirituality, a conversion process that turns the preacher inside out, shapes a new person, puts "fire in the belly." Not two separate, disparate segments; rather a unique wedding of head and heart, of thinking and loving, that would shape a unique retreat or workshop.

But is it only the preacher the project has in mind? Hardly. A homily simply begins the justice project. Once captured by the homily, by biblical justice, each community of Christians must gather to ask three questions: (1) What are the justice issues in our area? (2) What resources do we command to confront these issues? (3) Since we cannot do everything, what concretely shall we do?

Hence the two main structural features of this essay: (1) the justice that should dominate not only our proclamation of the gospel but our individual and communal living; (2) the spirituality that must penetrate the justice if justice is to come alive.

JUSTICE

When I say *justice*, the philosopher in me, the ethicist, has in mind a virtue that impels me to give every man, woman, and child what each deserves, what each can claim as a right. Not because they are Jews or Christians, brilliant or beautiful, prosperous or productive. Only because they are human beings, all shaped of the same dust and spirit. Simply as humans, they can, for example, lay claim to food, a job, a living wage, decent housing, can demand to be treated with respect.

When I say *justice*, the lawyer, the jurist, the judge thinks of Lady Justice, the woman with scales and a sword, her eyes blindfolded or closed in token of impartiality, swayed neither by love nor by prejudice, moved only by what is laid down in law. Legal justice sees to it that just laws foster the common good, that human rights written into law are protected, that the scales of Lady Justice are not weighted in favor of the rich and powerful, that the indicted remain innocent until proven guilty, that the punishment fits the proven crime.

The Hebrews of old knew all that, tried with varying success to live by it. Such justice, they knew, is indispensable for civilized living.

They sensed, as we do, that unless we give people what they deserve and what has been written into law, life becomes a jungle, the survival of the fittest, the rule of the swift, the shrewd, the savage. Even so, they lived by something more important still. It is a justice that Yahweh wanted to "roll down like waters" (Amos 5:24). It is actually a justice too rich, too opulent, to be easily imprisoned in a definition. Still, back in 1977 biblical scholar John R. Donahue shaped a working definition with admirable succinctness:

> In general terms the biblical idea of justice can be described as *fidelity to the demands of a relationship*. In contrast to modern individualism the Israelite is in a world where "to live" is to be united with others in a social context either by bonds of family or by covenant relationships. This web of relationships—king with people, judge with complainants, family with tribe and kinfolk, the community with the resident alien and suffering in their midst and all with the covenant God—constitutes the world in which life is played out.[5]

It is in this context that we must read what the prophet Micah trumpeted to judges who accepted bribes, to princes and merchants who cheated and robbed the poor, to priests and prophets who adapted their words to please their hearers.[6]

> With what shall I come before the LORD,
>   and bow myself before God on high?
> Shall I come before him with burnt-offerings,
>   with calves a year old?
> Will the LORD be pleased with thousands of rams,
>   with ten of thousands of rivers of oil?
> Shall I give my firstborn for my transgression,
>   the fruit of my body for the sin of my soul?
> He has told you, O mortal, what is good;
>   and what does the LORD require of you
> but to do justice, and to love kindness,
>   and to walk humbly with your God? (Mic 6:6–8)

"Do justice." Like Isaiah and Jeremiah, like Amos and Hosea, Micah proclaims to Israel that the Lord rejects precisely those things the Israelites think will make God happy. Not because such offerings are unacceptable in themselves; rather because two essential ingredients are missing: steadfast love and justice. And the justice is not simply or primarily what people deserve. The prophets trumpeted fidelity. To what? To the demands of relationships that stemmed from their covenant with God. What relationships? Primarily three: to God, to people, to the earth.

Love God Above All Else

This command did not originate with Jesus. It was God's primary demand on Israel: "Hear, O Israel: The LORD is our God, the LORD alone. You shall love the LORD your God with all your heart, all with your soul, and with all your might. Keep these words that I am commanding you today in your heart. Recite them to your children and talk about them when you are at home and when you are away, when you lie down and when you rise" (Deut 6:4–7). This, Jesus declared, is "the greatest and first commandment" (Matt 22:38).

Negatively, the first commandment forbade other gods: "You shall have no other gods before [or: besides] me. You shall not make for yourself an idol, whether in the form of anything that is in heaven above, or that is on the earth beneath, or that is in the water under the earth. You shall not bow down to them or worship them; for I the LORD your God am a jealous God" (Exod 20:3–5). The command did not lie long in abstraction; for when Moses delayed coming down from Mt. Sinai with the two tablets of the covenant, the people cast an image of a calf from gold and said, "These are your gods, O Israel, who brought you up out of the land of Egypt!" (Exod 32:4).

Love Your Neighbor as Yourself

Again, not a command that originated with Jesus. It occurs first not in Matthew but in Leviticus (19:18). And the neighbor was not just the Jew next door. The Lord had commanded, "You shall not oppress a resident alien; you know the heart of an alien [you know how an alien feels], for you were aliens in the land of Egypt" (Exod 23:9; see 22:21). More than not oppressing, "you shall also love the stranger, for you were strangers in the land of Egypt" (Deut 10:19; see 24:17–18). More basically, behind the law lies the covenant, "the great God, mighty and awesome, who is not partial and takes no bribe, who executes justice for the orphan and the widow, and who loves the strangers, providing them food and clothing" (Deut 10:17–18).

Not an easy command. Not only difficult to obey, but difficult to interpret. I cannot believe God meant some sort of psychological balancing act: as much or as little as you love yourself, so much love or so little love shall you lavish or trickle on your neighbor. I cannot disregard the conviction of a solid Scripture scholar: with the words "as yourself," Jesus is speaking of "a right form of self-love."[7] Still, I resonate to other biblical experts who suggest that each of us must love every other image of God, however flawed, like another "I," another self, as if I were standing in his or her shoes, especially the paper-thin shoes of the downtrodden and disadvantaged. Here Isaiah is blunt and to the point:

> Is not this the fast that I choose:
> > to loose the bonds of injustice,
> > to undo the thongs of the yoke,
> to let the oppressed go free,
> > and to break every yoke?
> Is it not to share your bread with the hungry,
> > and bring the homeless poor into your house;
> when you see the naked, to cover them,
> > and not to hide yourself from your own kin?
> > > (Isa 58:6–7)

Not to hide yourself from *your own kin*.

It brings us back to the kings of the Old Testament. As God's vicegerents, they had a special obligation to the poor, to those in need, to the helpless. Psalm 72 is instructive:

> Give the king your justice, O God,
> > and your righteousness to a king's son.

> May he judge your people with righteousness,
>> and your poor with justice....
> May he defend the cause of the poor of the people,
>> give deliverance to the needy....
> For he delivers the needy when they call,
>> the poor and those who have no helper.
> He has pity on the weak and the needy,
>> and saves the lives of the needy.
> From oppression and violence he redeems their life,
>> and precious is their blood in his sight. (Ps 72:1–2, 4,
>> 12–14)

What did Jesus add to Leviticus? "This is my commandment, that you love one another as I have loved you" (John 15:12). This is New Testament justice: love as Jesus loved. I mean the God-man who not only urged us to love our enemies and pray for those who persecute us (Matt 5:44), but lived what he urged unto crucifixion.

The point I emphasize here is the social focus of Scripture. Those who read in the sacred text a sheerly personal, individualistic morality have not understood the Torah, have not sung the psalms, have not been burned by the prophets, have not perceived the implications and the very burden of Jesus' message, and must inevitably play fast and loose with St. Paul.

That social focus of God's book is evident on its opening pages. On the sixth day of creation our incredibly imaginative God did not have in mind isolated units, autonomous entities, scattered disparately around a globe, independent each of every other—entities that might one day decide through a social contract to join together for self-aggrandizement, huddle together for self-protection. God had in mind a people, a human family, a community of persons, a body genuinely one. The exodus itself was not simply a liberation from slavery. "While liberation from oppression is a fundamental aspect of the Exodus narrative, it is not simply *freedom from* which is important, but *freedom for* the formation of a community which lives under the covenant."[8] John Donahue has summed it up with powerful simplicity: "Men and women are God's representatives and conversation partners in the world, with a fundamental dignity that must be respected and fostered. They are to exist in interdependence and mutual support."[9]

It is this divine dream for human living that the Second Vatican Council stated unambiguously: "God...has willed that all men and women should constitute one family." Again, "God did not create man and woman for life in isolation, but for the formation of social unity." And "this solidarity must be constantly increased until that day on which it will be brought to perfection. Then, saved by grace, men and women will offer flawless glory to God as a family beloved of God and of Christ their brother" (*Gaudium et Spes* 24, 32).[10]

Our Earth: All that Is Not God or the Human Person

Here we encounter a serious challenge to justice. I mean God's directive to the humankind just shaped in the image and likeness of the divine: "Fill the earth and subdue it; and have dominion over the fish of the sea and over the birds of the air and over every living thing that moves upon the earth" (Gen 1:28). Here the Hebrew Testament calls for careful discernment. What is it that Genesis says, and what does it mean?

The creation stories in Genesis 1—2 literally ground humans in the dust and dirt of creation itself. "The LORD God formed man from the dust of the ground" (Gen 2:7). "You are dust, and to dust you shall return" (Gen 3:19). At the same time, God gives these dirt creatures called humans authority to shape and direct nature. The human tills and keeps the garden of Eden (Gen 2:15). The human names and defines the animals (Gen 2:20). The human is commanded to have "dominion" over the creatures God has made (Gen 1:28; cf. Ps 8:6).[11]

"Have dominion"? Little wonder that some critics have taken this biblical command as the origin of the Western world's exploitation of nature. In a classic 1967 article, Lynn White Jr. argued that from Genesis 1 "Christianity...not only established a dualism of humans and nature, but also insisted that it is God's will that humans exploit nature for their proper ends."[12] Granted that Genesis 1:28 has been thus interpreted over the centuries, the text and its context do not in fact justify exploiting nature for human convenience. In Psalm 72, for example, quoted in part previously, the Hebrew term for "have dominion" is used (v. 8; see also Ps 110:2) in a context that describes not only the care that should characterize a king as God's viceregent, with especial concern for the most vulnerable and fragile, for the widow, the orphan, and the alien. The broader context includes "abundance of grain in the land," grain waving "on the tops of the mountains" (v. 16), fertility in the land associated with prayer for the king (v. 15).

The mandate given humanity in Eden is not exploitation but reverential care for God's creation.[13] The very context "suggests that this human dominion is to be carried out 'in the image of God,' an image that suggests nurture, blessing, and care rather than exploitation, abuse, and subjugation."[14]

Almost a decade ago, Douglas John Hall expressed our relation to material creation with an insight that still attracts me mightily.[15] He rejected a model that struck him as excessively idealistic: humans are in nature. Rejected it because it denies humans any role in shaping the natural environment. He rejected a model that seemed to him excessively imperialistic: humans are above nature. Rejected it because here nature is exploited for human purposes with little or no concern for its injurious impact and no sense of responsibility to a higher authority. Hall opted for the biblical model: humans are with nature. Opted for it because here humans stand to nature in a relationship of steward or caretaker. A steward is one who manages what is someone else's. A steward cares, is concerned, agonizes. Stewards may not plunder or waste; they are responsible, can be called to account for their stewardship. As the psalmist phrased it, "The earth is the Lord's and all that is in it" (Ps 24:1).

SPIRITUALITY

Now to the heart of the matter as it touches this volume: What has biblical justice to do with spirituality? No response will be intelligible unless we understand what we mean by spirituality. Not a simple matter, for spirituality has a history; more accurately, has histories.[16] For my purposes, some basics will be sufficient.[17]

What do I mean by a spirituality? St. Paul sparks a useful beginning: The spiritual person is one whose whole being, whose whole life, is influenced, guided, directed by "the Spirit that is from God" (1 Cor 2:12). Not some ghostly apparition in outer space, but the third person of the Trinity, the divine person given us by the Father and the Son, alive within us, shaping us into images of Christ, shaping us increasingly as sisters and brothers in Christ, as children of the Father.

How does the Holy Spirit effect this? By infusing into us incredible gifts we could not possibly produce by our naked human nature. I mean a faith that at its best is a total self-giving to God, a hope that is a confident trust in God's promises, a love that enables us to love our sisters and brothers as Jesus has loved us (1 Cor 13:13). I mean what Paul called "spiritual wisdom and understanding, so that you may lead lives worthy of the Lord, fully pleasing to him, as you bear fruit in every good work and as you grow in the knowledge of God" (Col 1:9–10). I mean what Paul termed "the fruit of the Spirit:" "love, joy, peace, patience, kindness, generosity, faithfulness, gentleness, and self-control" (Gal 5:22–23). I mean charisms that build up the Christian community, different gifts to different persons, but "all…activated by one and the same Spirit, who allots to each one individually just as the Spirit chooses" (1 Cor 12:11).[18]

Now, within Catholicism there are spiritualities and spiritualities. Basically, each spirituality lives up to the description I have attempted. Each is a living-out of the Christian life under the inspiration of the Holy Spirit, through the gifts the indwelling Spirit produces in us for our personal sanctification and our contribution to the life of the community.

But different social situations, different cultures, different religious communities, different personalities lay special stress on different facets of the richness, the breadth and depth, that Catholic spirituality encompasses. And so we have a *cursillo* spirituality, a charismatic spirituality, a lay spirituality, a liberation spirituality, a feminist spirituality. We find Franciscans stressing Lady Poverty, Benedictines emphasizing the common life (community), Jesuits laying particular stress on service. We have individuals imitating the lady mystic Julian of Norwich, Teresa of Avila or Thérèse of Lisieux, Dorothy Day or Thomas Merton, Swiss theologian Hans Urs von Balthasar or Jesuit paleontologist Teilhard de Chardin. Special emphases within the one basic spirituality, to suit different needs, desires, tasks, persons.[19]

Of high significance for my approach here is another recent emphasis. For all too long and for all too many, spirituality has been identified with our interior life: what goes on inside of us. A holistic spirituality includes both the inner experience of God and its outward expression in relationships.[20] That is why I was delighted to discover, not long ago, a definition that attracts me mightily: spirituality is a "process of being conformed to the image of God for the sake of others."[21] For the sake of others.

Biblical Justice

In the light of this, I can only conclude that biblical justice is itself a spirituality. How could it fail to be? Take a man or woman who loves God above all else, to the exclusion of all earth's idols, pleasure and power, wealth and wisdom; who sees in every other, in friend and foe, in Saddam Hussein as well as John Paul II, a reflection of God, a link with God that even sin cannot totally undo; whose life is a ceaseless effort to help the less fortunate, to "send the downtrodden away relieved" (Luke 4:18); who touches each "thing," each product of God's imaginative creation, earth and sea and sky, with respect and reverence. That man or woman is a "spiritual" person in St. Paul's sense. For such an approach to life is impossible unless the Holy Spirit is directing it. Know it or not, this man or woman is "being conformed to the image of God for the sake of others."

What, then, is there to add? A specifically *Catholic* dimension and a systematic method for achieving spiritual growth that centers on the process of *conversion*.

Ecclesial Spirituality

A Catholic spirituality of justice must be ecclesial. I mean, it takes place within a distinctive community, within the church Jesus founded to continue his work of salvation. That mission was intimately concerned with justice, with the program Luke has Jesus express in the synagogue of his home town: "The Spirit of the Lord is upon me, because [the Lord] has anointed me to bring good news to the poor. He has sent me to proclaim release to captives and recovery of sight to the blind, to let the opressed go free, to proclaim the year of the Lord's favor" (Luke 4:18–19; cf. Isa 61:1–2).

That mission, the mission Jesus laid on his disciples after his resurrection (John 20:21), is the commission conveyed to every person baptized into Christ. We are sent not as rugged individualists, but as part and parcel of a people, members of a body where, as St. Paul insisted, no one can say to any other, "I have no need of you" (1 Cor 12:21). A body wherein the gifts vary (wisdom, knowledge, healing, miracles, administration) but the giver is the same (the same Holy Spirit living within us and ceaselessly shaping the one body).

Negatively, this means that a Catholic spirituality of justice is not a process developed in a sheer me-and-Jesus relationship. That relationship is indeed vital, indispensable; for unless we branches abide in the vine that is Christ, we "can do nothing" (John 15:5). Still, ever since the Holy Spirit descended upon the infant church at the first Pentecost, St. Paul's declaration to the Christians of Corinth is basic for Christian living: "In the one Spirit we were all baptized into one body—Jews or Greeks, slaves or free—and we were all made to drink of one Spirit" (1 Cor 12:13). Of that body Jesus is indeed the head, but he is head of a body; and it is within this body that God's grace circulates like a bloodstream. Not only are the sacraments—from the waters of baptism to a final oiling—communal experiences, experiences that bring the church together, encounters with Christ in the context of the community. By God's gracious giving, we are commissioned to be channels of grace to one another.

Over the years I have been thrilled by an insight of a gifted Presbyterian novelist and preacher, Frederick Buechner. Three decades ago he compared humanity to a gigantic spider web:

> If you touch it anywhere, you set the whole thing trembling....As we move around this world and as we act with kindness, perhaps, or with indifference or with hostility toward the people we meet, we too are setting the great spider web atremble. The life that I touch for good or ill will touch another life, and that in turn another, until who knows where the trembling stops or in what far place and time my touch will be felt. Our lives are linked. No man [no woman] is an island.[22]

It would be unfortunate, however, if we were to see justice as a one-way street, where the haves affect the have-nots—the rich are generous to the poor, the learned teach the ignorant, the powerful bend down to the powerless, the more gifted evangelize the less endowed. No. Crucial for a justice spirituality is an expression heard repeatedly in Latin America: "The poor evangelize us."[23] Not only the economically poor but so many of the AIDS-afflicted and recovering alcoholics, refugees and the displaced, women and blacks, Hispanics and Native Americans, political prisoners like Africa's Mandela and enslaved electricians like Poland's Walesa have helped the churches discover what a 1979 conference of Latin American bishops called "the evangelizing potential of the poor."[24]

How do "the poor" actualize that potential? They challenge the churches. By their sheer numbers, by their Christlike endurance under domination and persecution, by their underlying gospel goodness. By their openness to God and what God permits, they have compelled us to look with ourselves, have at times stimulated profound conversion. Theologian Jon Sobrino expressed it clearly and succinctly:

> When the Church has taken the poor seriously, it is then that it has become truly apostolic. The poor initiate the process of evangelization. When the Church goes out to them in mission, the paradoxical result is that they, the poor, evangelize the Church.[25]

The poor are not simply recipients of apostolic ministry; they are our teachers and educators. Not only recipients of our spirituality; they help shape it.

Still, a Catholic spirituality of justice is not ecclesial if it is not eucharistic. Simply because, in the words of Vatican II,

> The liturgy is the summit to which the Church's activity is directed; at the same time it is the source from which all her power proceeds....From the liturgy, therefore, and especially from the Eucharist,...that sanctification of men and women in Christ and the glorification of God, to which all other activities of the Church stretch and strain as toward

their goal, are most effectively achieved. (*Sacrosanctum Concilium* 10)[26]

Paradoxically, it is not primarily by inserting an ideology that the liturgy becomes a force for justice. I am not downplaying the power of the homily, which, as Vatican II asserts, is "part of the liturgical action" (ibid., 35) is "part of the liturgy itself" (ibid., 52).[27] In season and out, I have insisted that an effective justice homily, even though it cannot solve complex social issues, can and must raise a congregation's consciousness, its awareness. Still, the liturgical action effects change above all by its own inner dynamic. For the temporal order can be changed only by conversion, only if men and women turn from sin and selfishness. And for Catholics the primary source of conversion is the Mass, which extends through time and space the cross through which the world is transfigured. I have stated this forcefully elsewhere:

> The Mass should be the liberating adventure of the whole Church, the sacrament which frees men and women from their inherited damnable concentration on themselves, loosens us from our ice-cold isolation, fashions us into brothers and sisters agonizing not only for a church of charity but for a world of justice as well.[28]

Many years ago Jesuit John C. Haughey recaptured for me a remarkable insight expressed by government people engaged in a Woodstock Theological Center project on government decision making. As they saw it, good liturgy facilitates public responsibility not because it provides principles of resolution, not because it tells the worshipers precisely what to think about specific conflicts, but rather because an effective celebration of the transcendent puts them in touch with that which transcends all their burning concerns, their particular perplexities. Good liturgy frees us to sort out the issues we have to decide, because it makes us aware of our addictions and our illusions, casts a pitiless light on myopic self-interest, detaches us from a narrow selfishness, facilitates Christian discernment. It can be, in short, a powerful force for conversion. Good liturgy is not so much didactic as evocative; it lets *God* come to light, allows *God* to be heard.

Very simply, the primary way in which the liturgy becomes a social force is through its own inner dynamism, by its incomparable power to turn the human heart inside out, free it from its focus on self, fling it out unfettered to the service of sisters and brothers enslaved.

In a related way, I have often emphasized that the Eucharist's purpose is not only to link us more intimately with Christ—the traditional "You are what you have received"—but to transform us into Eucharists. For what is the Eucharist? A presence; a presence of Christ; a real presence; a presence of the whole Christ, body and blood, soul and divinity; a presence that stems from love, from the love of a God-man, and leads to love, a crucified love for every man and woman born into our world. This Eucharist can make of us, demands that we become, genuine Eucharists. I mean that we are present to our sisters and brothers; really present; a presence of the whole person, not only mind and money but flesh and spirit, emotions and passions; a presence that springs from love and leads to love: "Love one another as I have loved you" (John 15:12).

An unexpected contribution to an ecclesial spirituality for justice has reached me from Fordham University's Elizabeth Johnson. Ever on the alert for fresh interpretations of expressions most of us take for granted, she has discovered an intriguing ambiguity in the age-old *communio sanctorum*. The latter word could mean either "holy persons" or "holy things," participation in sacred realities, especially the eucharistic bread and the cup of salvation, the meaning when the phrase was first used in the Eastern Church. Medieval theologians, she notes, "played with both meanings." Actually, "there is no need to choose between the two for they reinforce one another." And then Johnson's insight into a profound application today:

> In the light of the contemporary moral imperative to treat the ever-more damaged earth as a sacred creation with its own intrinsic rather than instrumental value, the elusive quality of the phrase's original meaning is a happy circumstance. At its best, sacramental theology has always drawn on the connection between the natural world and the signs of bread, wine, water, oil, and sexual intercourse which, when taken into the narrative of Jesus' life, death, and resurrection, become avenues of God's healing grace. Now, in the

time of earth's agony, the *sancta* can be pushed to its widest meaning to include the gifts of air, water, land, and the myriad creatures that share the planet with human beings in interwoven ecosystems—the brothers and sisters of Francis of Assisi's vision. For the universe itself is the primordial sacrament through which we participate and communicate with divine mystery. Since the same divine Spirit who lights the fire of the saint also fuels the vitality of all creation, then "communion in the holy" includes holy people and a holy world in interrelationship. By this line of thinking, a door opens from within the symbol of the communion of saints itself to include all beings, sacred bread and wine certainly, but also the primordial sacrament, the earth itself. Once again, this symbol reveals its prophetic edge as its cosmic dimension calls forth an ecological ethic of restraint of human greed and promotion of care for the earth.[29]

Conversion

Integral to a comprehensive spirituality for justice, for anyone who proclaims justice or simply lives justly, is a conversion. Conversion, like spirituality, is not easy to define.[30] I am not directly concerned here with the sudden, swift, almost instantaneous turnabout, for example, from Saul to Paul, from strict Pharisee to Christian believer. For my purposes, I recommend a more complex approach. I suggest the approach of Jesuit Bernard Lonergan (1904–84). Lonergan has left us a systematic method for understanding spiritual growth that centers on the process of conversion. But we shall not grasp that process unless we recall several background realities.

The work of justice has for its purpose to fashion community. For community is "the ideal basis of society. Without a large measure of community, human society and sovereign states cannot function. Without a constant renewal of community, the measure of community already enjoyed easily is squandered."[31] For Christians, the profound call to shape community stems from Jesus' prayer to his Father on the eve of his crucifixion that those who believe in him may be "completely one,"

one as he and his Father are one (John 17:20–23). From a Christian perspective, the ideal community is God's kingdom, a social reality: as the liturgy of Christ the King has it, "a kingdom of truth and life, a kingdom of holiness and grace, a kingdom of justice, love, and peace." Injustice—in the biblical sense, lack of love—is what tears community apart, sunders relationships, and divides society into rival sectors.

It is precisely this call to community that gives sin its most significant characteristic. In Scripture, sin involves not only our traditional "offense against God," but also the sundering of community. The whole of Scripture from Genesis to Revelation is the story of struggle for community, of lapses into division, disintegration, enmity. If biblical justice is fidelity to the demands of a relationship, then sin is a refusal of responsibility; sin creates division, alienation, dissension, marginalization, rejection; sin dis-members the body.

In a sinful world our mission is reconciliation. I suggest that all Christians may apply to themselves what Paul says of himself:

> If anyone is in Christ, there is a new creation: everything old has passed away; see, everything has become new! All this is from God, who reconciled us to himself through Christ, and has given us the ministry of reconciliation; that is, in Christ God was reconciling the world to himself...and entrusting the message of reconciliation to us. So we are ambassadors for Christ. (2 Cor 5:17–20)

As believers, as faith-filled Christians, our task is to help people to recognize, understand, value, and live accurately the various relationships they have to one another so that they might heal the ruptures that alienate, that destroy relationships. In short, to promote justice.

Healing these ruptures is the function of conversion. What succinctly is the conversion? For Lonergan, a conversion to exact fidelity to four transcendental precepts. What precepts? (1) Be attentive: focus on the full range of experience. (2) Be intelligent: inquire, probe, question. (3) Be reasonable: marshal evidence, examine opinions, judge wisely. (4) Be responsible: act on the basis of prudent judgments and genuine values. This last, for Lonergan, includes being in love: wholehearted commitment to God as revealed in Jesus Christ. Why are these

precepts called transcendental? Because they are not limited to any particular genus or category of inquiry, for example, science or theology;
they are simply a normative expression of the innate, God-given, spontaneous, and invariably unfolding operations of human intentional consciousness.

The transcendental method does not permit easy explanation; one
has to absorb Lonergan's *Method in Theology*, a challenging invitation
to self-awareness, self-understanding, self-appropriation. For our purposes, two aspects are especially significant. First, "in a sense everyone
knows and observes transcendental method. Everyone does so, precisely
in the measure that he is attentive, intelligent, reasonable, responsible."[32]
Second, "in another sense it is quite difficult to be at home in transcendental method, for that is not to be achieved by reading books or listening to lectures or analyzing language. It is a matter of heightening one's
consciousness by objectifying it," that is, "applying the operations as
intentional to the operations as conscious."[33] Concretely, how does one
do that with the four precepts? It is a matter of

> (1) *experiencing* one's experiencing, understanding, judg-
> ing, and deciding, (2) *understanding* the unity and relations
> of one's experienced experiencing, understanding, judging,
> deciding, (3) *affirming* the reality of one's experienced and
> understood experiencing, understanding, judging, deciding,
> and (4) *deciding* to operate in accord with the norms imma-
> nent in the spontaneous relatedness of one's experienced,
> understood, affirmed experiencing, understanding, judging,
> and deciding.[34]

In connection with those four precepts Lonergan identifies three
conversions: intellectual, moral, and religious.

Intellectual conversion is "a radical clarification" of experience. It
eliminates a misleading myth about human knowing: that to know is to
see, hear, touch, taste, smell, feel. On the contrary, "the world mediated
by meaning is a world known not by the sense experience of an individual but by the external and internal experience of a cultural community,
and by the continuously checked and rechecked judgments of the community. Knowing, accordingly, is not just seeing; it is experiencing,

understanding, judging, and believing." Liberation from the myth, discovering the self-transcendence proper to the human process of coming to know, is to break through ingrained habits of thinking and speaking. "It is a conversion, a new beginning, a fresh start. It opens the way to ever further clarifications and developments."[35]

Moral conversion involves shifting our criteria for decisions and choices from satisfactions to values. It "consists in opting for the truly good, even for value against satisfaction" when they conflict. But "deciding is one thing, doing is another." What remains? To root out biases in the self, in culture, in history; to keep scrutinizing our responses to values; to listen to criticism; to learn from others.[36]

> So moral conversion goes beyond the value, truth, to values generally. It promotes the subject from cognitional to moral self-transcendence....He still needs truth...the truth attained in accord with the exigencies of rational consciousness. But now his pursuit of it is all the more secure because he has been armed against bias, and it is all the more meaningful and significant because it occurs within, and plays an essential role in, the far richer context of the pursuit of all values.[37]

Similarly, religious conversion goes beyond the moral. It occurs when we are "grasped by ultimate concern." It is a falling in love, unqualified self-surrender; it means loving "with all one's heart and all one's soul and all one's mind and all one's strength." It means accepting a vocation to holiness. "For Christians it is God's love flooding our hearts through the Holy Spirit given to us. It is the gift of grace." It involves replacing the heart of stone with a heart of flesh, and then moving gradually to a complete transformation of all my living and feeling, my thoughts and words, my deeds and omissions.[38]

Not a rigid order of conversions—first intellectual, then moral, then religious. Normally, religious conversion is prior to moral, which in turn is prior to intellectual. The experience and acceptance of God's love, the Holy Spirit poured into our hearts, is the beginning of genuine apprehension of what is good, accurate understanding of what is true.

Now Lonergan's approach to conversion is not ivory-tower philosophical theology. As far as justice is concerned, it keeps the underlying spirituality I commend so strongly from being reduced to more and more prayer, fidelity to daily meditation, resistance to temptations, and avoidance of the near occasions of sin—the psalmist's "clean heart" (Ps 51:10). It has to do with truth, with values, with love, with "the eros of the human spirit," with suffering, with a transformation not only of my innermost self but of my relationship to people and the earth, to culture and history.[39]

Awesome? Yes indeed. But only through such transformation can God's creative dream for community, for the kingdom, be realized. Lonergan saw so clearly that what makes for community, its "formal constituent," is common meaning. Conversely,

> as common meaning constitutes community, so divergent meaning divides it. Such division may amount to no more than a diversity of culture and the stratification of individuals into classes of higher and lower competence. The serious division is the one that arises from *the presence and absence of intellectual, moral, or religious conversion.* For man is his true self inasmuch as he is self-transcending. Conversion is the way to self-transcendence. Inversely, man is alienated from his true self as he refuses self-transcendence, and the basic form of ideology is the self-justification of alienated man.[40]

Here, for me, is a type of conversion (not the only one) that is crucial for a profound spirituality of biblical justice. For its high point, religious conversion is conversion "to a total being-in-love as the efficacious ground of all self-transcendence, whether in the pursuit of truth, or in the realization of human values, or in the orientation man adopts to the universe, its ground, and its goal."[41] It is a conversion not defined by a definite date but enduring and developing through a lifetime. It involves my relationship not only to God and people but to the earth that sustains me; not only a spiritual soul but my mind and heart, my emotions and passions. It is critical not only for individual holiness but for the building of community, for the church's mission to promote the human family, the church's "redemptive role in human society inasmuch as [self-sacrificing] love can undo the mischief of decline and restore the cumulative process of progress."[42]

To sum up: Take biblical justice, that is, fidelity to relationships that stem from our covenant with God—loving God above all idols, seeing in each flawed human an image of Christ, touching every facet of earth and sea and sky with reverence. Link that to life within the *ecclesia*, life within the body of Christ, a life of faith and hope and love, life in ever-widening communities (parish, diocese, universal church) for the building of the human family, life nourished by the body and blood of the risen Christ. Introduce into that complex a ceaseless, never-ending conversion to a communal search for an intellectual value called truth, a communal opting for what is truly good against self-satisfaction, a communal self-surrender to Love incarnate.

With such a spirituality we might begin edging back to storied Eden, to that brief shining moment when humanity was at peace with God, humans at peace with one another, humans at peace with the rest of God's creation. It is still a dream divine. And if the kingdom is not yet—not yet what God had in mind when the Lord looked on everything created and "indeed, it was very good" (Gen 1:31)—it just might stimulate our search together for a spirituality that makes us more attentive, more intelligent, more reasonable, and more responsible. In a word, more Christlike.

Notes

1. Fred Kammer, *Doing Faithjustice* (New York / Mahwah, NJ: Paulist, 1991).

2. See "Decrees of the 32nd General Congregation," no. 48, in *Documents of the 31st and 32nd General Congregations of the Society of Jesus* (St. Louis: Institute of Jesuit Sources, 1977), 411. The exact sentence reads, "The mission of the Society of Jesus today is the service of faith, of which the promotion of justice is an absolute requirement."

3. See Arrupe's homily at the Ateneo de Manila, Quezon City, Philippines, on the feast of St. Ignatius Loyola, July 31, 1983, commemorating the fourth centenary of the arrival of the Jesuits in the Philippines, in *Recollections and Reflections of Pedro Arrupe, S.J.*, trans. Yolanda T. De Mala, SC (Wilmington, DE: Michael Glazier, 1986), 128.

4. (Boston: Beacon, 1986), 121.

5. John R. Donahue, SJ, "Biblical Perspectives on Justice," in *The Faith That Does Justice: Examining the Christian Sources for Social Change*, ed. John C. Haughey, SJ, Woodstock Studies 2 (New York: Paulist, 1977), 69. More recently, Donahue has stated that his "earlier reflections should be supplemented by the reflections of J. M. P. Walsh" in the latter's *The Mighty from Their Thrones* (Philadelphia: Fortress, 1987). Specifically, see Donahue's "What Does the Lord Require? A Bibliographical Essay on the Bible and Social Justice," *Studies in the Spirituality of Jesuits* 25, no. 2 (March 1993): 20–21.

6. See Léo Laberge, OMI, "Micah," in *The New Jerome Biblical Commentary*, ed. Raymond E. Brown, SS, Joseph A. Fitzmyer, SJ, and Roland E. Murphy, OCarm (Englewood Cliffs, NJ: Prentice-Hall, 1990), 16:2 and 5, p. 249.

7. So Benedict T. Viviano, OP, "The Gospel according to Matthew," *New Jerome Biblical Commentary*, 42:133, p. 666.

8. Donahue, "What Does the Lord Require?" 14.

9. Ibid., 12.

10. "Constitution on the Church in the Modern World."

11. Dennis Olson, "God the Creator: Bible, Creation, Vocation," *Dialog: A Journal of Theology* 36, no. 3 (1997): 173.

12. Lynn White Jr., "The Historical Root of Our Ecological Crisis," *Science* 155 (1967): 1205.

13. See Olson, "God the Creator," 173; Donahue, "What Does the Lord Require," 8; also James Limburg, "The Responsibility of Royalty: Genesis 1–11 and the Care of the Earth," *Word & World* 11 (1991): 124–30; James Tubbs, "Humble Dominion," *Theology Today* 51 (1994): 543–56, linking dominion with the NT image of Christ and the humble character of his dominion.

14. Olson, "God the Creator," 173–4.

15. See Douglas John Hall, *The Steward: A Biblical Symbol Come of Age* (Grand Rapids, MI: Eerdmans, 1990). My summary reflects that given by Olson, "God the Creator," 174.

16. Useful here are two summaries: Walter H. Principe, CSB, "Spirituality, Christian," *The New Dictionary of Catholic Spirituality*, ed. Michael Downey (Collegeville, MN: Liturgical Press, 1993), 931–8; and Richard Woods, OP, "Spirituality, Christian (Catholic), History of," ibid., 938–46.

17. Here I am borrowing from my "Characteristics of Social Justice Spirituality," *Origins* 24, no. 9 (July 21, 1994): 159.

18. See also 1 Cor 12:4–11, 28–30; Rom 12:6–8; Eph 4:11–13.

19. Worth reading in this connection is James J. Bacik, "Contemporary Spirituality," in Downey, *Dictionary of Catholic Spirituality*, 214–30.

20. See Michael H. Crosby, OFMCap, "Spirituality," in *The New*

Dictionary of Catholic Social Thought, ed. Judith A. Dwyer (Collegeville, MN: Liturgical Press, 1994), 918.

21. See M. Robert Mulholland, Jr., *Invitation to a Journey: A Road Map to Spiritual Formation* (Downers Grove, IL: InterVarsity, 1994), quoted by Lawrence S. Cunningham in a brief review *Commonweal* 121, no. 1 (1994): 41.

22. Frederick Buechner, *The Hungering Dark* (New York: Seabury, 1969), 45–46.

23. See the article, primarily concerned with Latin America, by John F. Talbot, SJ, "Who Evangelizes Whom? The Poor Evangelizers," *Review for Religious* (November–December 1993): 893–7.

24. From the Puebla conference's "Preferential Option for the Poor" (no. 1147), quoted by Talbot, "Who Evangelizes Whom?," 894.

25. Quoted by Talbot, "Who Evangelizes Whom?," 896, from Sobrino's *Resurrección de La Verdadera Iglesia* (Santander, Spain: Sal Terrae, 1984), 137–8.

26. "Constitution on the Sacred Liturgy."

27. Ibid.

28. Walter J. Burghardt, SJ, *Preaching: The Art and the Craft* (New York / Mahwah, NJ: Paulist, 1987), 129.

29. Elizabeth A. Johnson, "Community on Earth as in Heaven: A Holy People and a Sacred Earth Together," (Santa Clara Lectures 5, no. 1, Santa Clara, CA: Santa Clara University, 1998), 13.

30. See Richard N. Fragomeni, "Conversion," *Dictionary of Catholic Spirituality*, 230–5, stressing four categories helpful for understanding the process: autobiographical, biblical, liturgical, and theological (Lonergan's approach is summarized under the last category).

31. Bernard J. F. Lonergan, SJ, *Method in Theology* (New York: Herder and Herder, 1972), 363.

32. Ibid., 14.

33. Ibid.

34. Ibid., 14–15.

35. Ibid., 238–40.

36. Ibid., 240.

37. Ibid., 241–2.

38. Ibid., 240–1.

39. Ibid., 242.

40. Ibid., 357; emphasis mine.

41. Ibid., 241.

42. Ibid., 55.

12. Spirituality and Ecology

Mary Frohlich

This chapter first appeared as "Under the Sign of Jonah: Studying Spirituality in a Time of Ecosystemic Crisis," in *Spiritus* 9 (Spring 2009).

INTRODUCTION

The people of Jesus' day asked him for a sign, but Jesus gave them only the sign of Jonah, broken and ravaged in the belly of the sea monster. Today, as the life-systems of the Earth are being similarly broken and ravaged, the sign speaks afresh. Each day it becomes more evident that the encompassing "sign of the times" for the present generation is the global ecosystemic crisis, and that response to it will demand of all human communities a literal regrounding of everything we do. Yet just as Jonah resisted his call, so do we. In this essay, which was originally written as an address to the annual meeting of the Society for the Study of Christian Spirituality, I propose that in such times those of us who study and teach Christian spirituality are called to place the Earth and its wounds at the center of our attention in very concrete ways. In doing so, I believe, we will be challenged to engage a prophetic element in our research, writing, and teaching. Prophets, to quote a short definition by Robert R. Wilson, are "intermediaries between the human and divine worlds."[1] In the crisis of our Earth community, the prophetic insight is that the divine world is not "somewhere else," but is crying out to us from the very heart of the Earth.

The wager I am making in this essay is that being prophetic does not have to mean abandoning scholarship for preaching. Rather, it means to have the courage to ground our critical thinking in a deep contemplative consciousness. What may be new in our time is the emerging awareness that this deep contemplative consciousness must itself be grounded, literally, in the life of the Earth.

In what follows, then, I will first explore what these times ask of us as scholars of spirituality, then examine a progressive series of avenues to understanding and enacting the kind of spiritual change that genuine "conversion to the Earth" requires.

WHAT DO THE TIMES ASK OF US AS SCHOLARS OF SPIRITUALITY?

The Call to "Third-Order" Change

My original choice of the title "Under the Sign of Jonah" as the title for my lecture had to do with an intuition that the global ecosystemic crisis presents us with a dilemma something like the one Jonah faced when he was called to preach to the Ninevites. Like Jonah, the human community today faces a crisis requiring the complete restructuring of its life in relation to a reality transcendent to itself. In Jonah's case, the call to prophesy came directly in the form of "the word of the Lord" telling him to go and preach to the Ninevites. In our situation, the immediacy of the call comes from the Earth, through a crescendo of disturbing information about global warming, species extinction, resource depletion, toxic pollution, and the worldwide breakdown of ecosystemic self-healing systems. To take just one example, let us listen to what a National Wildlife Federation report says about the ecosystem that sustains me as I write this essay:

> There is widespread agreement that the Great Lakes presently are exhibiting symptoms of extreme stress from a combination of sources that include toxic contaminants, invasive species, nutrient loading, shoreline and upland land use changes, and hydrologic modifications. Many of these sources of stress and others have been impacting the lakes

for over a century. These adverse impacts have appeared gradually over time....

In large areas of the lakes, historical sources of stress have combined with new ones to reach a tipping point, the point at which ecosystem-level changes occur rapidly and unexpectedly, confounding the traditional relationships between sources of stress and the expected ecosystem response. There is compelling evidence that in many parts of the Great Lakes we are at or beyond this tipping point. Certain areas of the Great Lakes are increasingly experiencing ecosystem breakdown, where intensifying levels of stress from a combination of sources have overwhelmed the natural processes that normally stabilize and buffer the system from permanent change.[2]

What is most unprecedented about our time is that this kind of ecosystemic stress and breakdown is global as well as local. The wounded earth-systems cry out everywhere, without respect for human divisions of nation, race, class, religion, or culture.

Jonah, as we know, ran away from his call, heading for Tarshish instead of Nineveh. Another way of putting it, though, is to say that he concluded that if he had to change, he would do it on his own terms, not God's. Jonah did not want to believe that in God's view the Ninevites, who in his time and culture bore the iconic status of the ultimate evil enemy, were worthy of being invited and empowered to change their sinful ways—and that God had elected him (Jonah) to serve them in that process! To accept this complete change of worldview was as hard for Jonah as dying; he had to pass through the belly of the sea monster before he could do it. Likewise, the initial impulse of most segments of the human community in relation to the present massive ecosystemic crisis is resistance to its more profound implications. It requires a kind of death to shift from the belief that we can deal with this crisis on our own, intrinsically anthropocentric, terms, to the recognition that it is a call to be turned inside out for the sake of servant-membership in the global ecosystemic web of life.

The insights of the anthropologist and philosopher Gregory Bateson may help us to reflect on what is going on here. In *Steps to an*

Ecology of Mind, Bateson identified four increasingly comprehensive levels of human change, which he termed Learning I, Learning II, Learning III, and Learning IV.[3] Most of his discussion focused on the first three, which can be correlated with the way an alcoholic typically reacts to the problems created by his or her addiction to alcohol.[4] At the stage of Learning I or "first-order change," alcoholics try to control their use of alcohol without changing anything else in their life. When that leads to repeated disastrous crises, they may eventually move to Learning II or "second-order change," accepting a new paradigm—that of being an alcoholic who must enact specific behavioral changes guided by those who have a professional understanding of alcoholic psychology. The problem of alcohol addiction is not fully surmounted, however, unless the alcoholic arrives at Learning III or "third-order change." Third-order change is a deep, systemic change of consciousness that involves opening oneself to the reality of profound interdependence with what Alcoholics Anonymous terms a "Higher Power." Bateson calls this "an involuntary change in deep unconscious epistemology, a spiritual experience."[5] Most alcoholics have to undergo one or several experiences of catastrophic "hitting bottom" before they are open even to second-order change, let alone to the far more profound re-founding of consciousness that is third order change.

A central tenet of Bateson's schema is that purposive consciousness is only one part of the larger cybernetic whole of the human capacity for knowledge. As long as we human beings rely on solving problems by using our ability to consciously understand and manipulate parts of the world, we are doomed to create even worse problems despite the best of intentions. As Bateson puts it:

> The cybernetic nature of self and the world tends to be imperceptible to consciousness, insofar as the contents of the "screen" of consciousness are determined by considerations of purpose. The argument of purpose tends to take the form "D is desirable; B leads to C; C leads to D; so D can be achieved by way of B and C." But, if the total mind and outer world do not have this lineal structure, then by forcing this structure upon them, we become blind to the cybernetic circularities of the self and the external world. Our con-

scious sampling of data will not disclose whole circuits but only arcs of circuits, cut off from their matrix by our selective [purposive] attention. Specifically, the attempt to achieve a change in a given variable, located either in self or environment, is likely to be undertaken without comprehension of the homeostatic network surrounding that variable.[6]

This quotation illustrates why the comparison of the human contribution to the crisis of the global ecosystem to an addiction is so apt. The case of substance addiction may appear extreme, but as Gerald May detailed in *Addiction and Grace*, it is also a paradigm for the spiritual struggle of every human being.[7] Addiction involves an inability to change a pattern of behavior that gives real rewards at the same time that, within the larger picture of one's life, it creates worse problems. We modern humans are addicted to the technological "fixing" of our environment—a pattern of behavior that is hugely rewarding for the presently well-off, but unspeakably damaging to the poor and to future generations. What may be new about our situation today is that all over the globe, human communities appear to be heading into a "hitting bottom" period in which these catastrophic effects of our addiction to destructive anthropocentric ways of operating are more widely experienced as intolerable.

As the ecosystemic crisis comes to consciousness, the first response is typically to try various kinds of first-order and second-order changes. A first-order approach tries to control the crisis without having to change anything fundamental; for example, by turning the oil-powered heat down a couple of degrees or by making oil-driven cars more efficient. A second-order approach recognizes the need for a significantly different paradigm but still aims at a technological fix; for example, switching to renewable sources of energy may be a second-order change if it is done with a new paradigm of ecosystemic sustainability in mind. These responses obviously have merit, but they do not directly address the more fundamental issue of human membership in the complex homeostatic web of the global ecosystem. Ultimately, ecosystemic balance is unlikely to be recovered unless humans come to know themselves as fundamentally members of the family of creation, integrally making choices that participate in the good of the whole. Thus, the times demand what Bateson calls the "third-order change" of "deep unconscious epistemology" that will re-found human consciousness in participative availability to the creative, self-healing potential of creation itself.

Third-Order Change, Contemplation, and Critical Thinking

As specialists in the study and teaching of spirituality, what is our responsibility in such a moment? First, I believe we have the responsibility to ask the more fundamental questions, such as: Exactly what is the character of the spiritual change of consciousness that is necessary if human communities are going to rediscover how to be responsible participants in local and global ecosystems? What wisdom is available from historical or emerging spiritual traditions that can guide us, individually and communally, through such a change? How is that spiritual wisdom to be coordinated with the other kinds of knowledge and skill that are needed to return balance to the life of ecosystems?[8]

But if it is true that the crisis that faces us today will not be met without a third- (or even fourth-) order change of consciousness, the challenge in all our investigations of such questions will be to go beyond the level of simply introducing new paradigms (that is, second-order change) to a level that can constructively critique and re-found all paradigms (that is, third-order change). The insufficiency of only second-order change can be illustrated by recalling the fact that an ecocentric paradigm was actually promoted by many powerful figures in the German National Socialist (Nazi) movement during the 1930s. Here is a quotation from a 1934 book by Nazi supporter and botany professor Ernst Lehmann:

> We recognize that separating humanity from nature, from the whole of life, leads to humankind's own destruction and to the death of nations. Only through a reintegration of humanity into the whole of nature can our people be made stronger....Humankind alone is no longer the focus of thought, but rather life as a whole....This striving toward connectedness with the totality of life, with nature itself, a

> nature into which we are born, this is the deepest meaning
> and the true essence of National Socialist thought.[9]

Peter Staudenmaier notes that integral themes in Nazi ideology included "the agrarian mystique, the health of the Volk [people of the land], closeness to and respect for nature,...maintaining nature's precarious balance, and the earthy powers of the soil and its creatures."[10] Several key Nazi leaders argued fervently against anthropocentrism and were very forward-thinking in pressing for ecologically sensitive practices, at the same time that they were promoting fascism and genocide.

In an essay entitled "Third-Order Organizational Change and the Western Mystical Tradition," organizational change theorists Jean Bartunek and Michael Mach build on Bateson's works as they write about what is required to arrive at third-order change.

> The capability for third-order change requires greater
> awareness than that afforded simply by the experience of
> on-going second-order changes. This experience must be
> linked to an appreciation of the inability of any schema to
> capture the contingencies present in any given situation. To
> achieve this appreciation, a person must be aware of an
> experience that cannot be contained in or represented by any
> conceptual scheme, and must be exposed to a form of com-
> munication that is not simply analogical, but that exposes
> the person to a transconceptual reality that provides the
> ground for conceptual human understanding.[11]

The next section of the essay explores a progressive series of avenues to that kind of transconceptual knowing, which Bateson calls the "total mind." This section is integrally theological and spiritual, for the experience of transconceptual awareness is a form of knowledge that gives birth to theological expressions. These expressions, in turn, may become the catalysts for others' awakening.

AWAKENING TOTAL MIND

Touched by the Earth: A Personal Story

I begin with a personal story. Fifty years ago I was a small child in a good secular humanist family living in the Black Hills of South Dakota. One lovely fall Saturday we went picnicking deep in the Hills, to a remote lake that very few people knew how to find. Iron Creek Lake was a small, serene, gorgeous little lake surrounded by deep pine forests that seemed to breathe with an earthy and mysterious fragrance. I remember wading out into the cold water of the lake chest-high, and suddenly being overwhelmed by the awareness of holiness. I didn't have the word "holiness" in those days; in fact, I didn't have any words for what I felt and knew in that moment. Even today, there is more I can't tell you about that experience, than what I can tell you. But I remember this much as clear as day: the physicalness of the place, and that my soul trembled with awe and love.

So, fifty years later I stand here, still stammering, but trying to be faithful to that moment of being blessed by the Earth. Perhaps we could even say that in some sense I was anointed in that moment, for this moment, when I speak out for love of the Earth. But even if that is so, I do not take it to mean that I am special. We are all members of the family of the Earth, no more and no less. I suspect that many—maybe even all—children are thus anointed. What happens in such experiences is as if a great, clear space is opened up in the soul where God breathes forth goodness for the family of Earth-creatures. It is crucial that we name and claim those experiences, which are core moments of transconceptual awareness and ecocentric conversion. They are moments of grace that come upon us unbidden, yet change the contours of our souls.

Yet as we all know all too well, the child's story doesn't end there. The child goes on, and all sorts of debris gets tossed into that clear, empty space, and a complicated superstructure gets built over it, and God can hardly breathe there anymore. About fifteen years ago I went back to Iron Creek Lake. It wasn't the same. People had built vacation houses side by side all around its borders. The beach was crowded and noisy. There was trash on the ground and advertising by the side of the road. The forests no longer breathed with mystery and fragrance. They seemed empty, and probably were; the animals and even many of the plants had fled before the onslaught of humans. It was jarring to find that the place where the mystery of the Earth summoned my child soul looked so much like my jaded adult soul.

We each, it seems, have to learn the hard way that even though those deep convictional experiences of the divine in the Earth are so crucial, we cannot rest in a simplistic romanticism of Earth-connection. Earlier in this chapter, I reflected on the unsavory historical link between an ecological mystique and German fascism, not because I think such a connection is necessary, but rather to remind us that it is possible. Indeed, a realistic view of the natural world recognizes that violence and domination are as prevalent there as are harmony and balance. Returning to the story of Jonah for a moment, his passage through the belly of the sea monster is an apt image for this dark aspect of connection to the Earth. Swallowed by the sea monster, Jonah experienced, "up close and personal," the dark and horrifying reality that to be an Earth creature is to be the food of other Earth creatures. The wisdom that the Earth community needs in this time of crisis cannot be naive about the evil, futility, and death that confront us over and over again along our earthly journey. For too many of the Earth's creatures, human and otherwise, life on Earth is—in the poignant title of a Joseph Conrad story— the "Heart of Darkness."[12] The lamentation that this evokes is the beginning of prophecy. In Gregory Bateson's framework, it is comparable to the "hitting bottom" that has to happen before the alcoholic is ready to change. Yet more will be needed if we are move through lamentation to potentially revitalizing insight into the character of the third-order change that is involved in a true conversion to the Earth.

Into the Heart of the Earth: The Sign of Jonah

For this, I turn once again to the wisdom of stories. This time, however, it is not a personal story but a biblical one, deeply embedded in our religious and literary culture. In the story of Jonah, the prophet did not meet his end by being violently dismembered in the sea monster's belly but instead was saved when the creature vomited him up on the shore. He then went on to be such a powerful preacher that not only the

Ninevites, who in Jonah's context represented the most evil of human beings, but even the animals repented in sackcloth and ashes! The story thus announces the possibility that on the other side of catastrophe there can be a radical and all-encompassing change, not only of humans but of all creation.

Many centuries later, Matthew's Gospel took that story and opened it up in a new context. It is from this text that the original title phrase for this essay, "Under the Sign of Jonah," actually derives.

> Then some of the scribes and Pharisees said to [Jesus], "Teacher, we wish to see a sign from you." He said to them in reply, "An evil and unfaithful generation seeks a sign, but no sign will be given it except the sign of Jonah the prophet. Just as Jonah was in the belly of the whale three days and three nights, so will the Son of Humanity be in the heart of the earth three days and three nights." (Matt 12:38–40)

For Matthew, the aspect of Jonah's life that is a "sign" is exactly that dark, terrifying sojourn in the belly of the sea monster. With our ears tuned to the crisis of our times, it becomes especially significant to note that Matthew parallels that sojourn with the Son of Humanity's entry into "the heart of the earth." Early Christian tradition interpreted that image mythologically, elaborating the story of Christ's descent into hell to preach to those trapped there.[13] Using historical-critical methods, Scripture scholars today tell us that "the heart of the earth" refers to the Hebrew conception of Sheol or the nether world, which was pictured as a shadowy underground realm and the dwelling place of the dead. The focus of the text, then, is on Jesus' passage through death to resurrection. In the world of the text, "the sign of Jonah" is the harbinger of Jesus' resurrection from "the heart of the earth."[14]

An initial insight into the significance of Jesus' entry into "the heart of the earth" began to crystallize for me one day a few months ago when I chanced upon a History Channel program that traced the four and a half billion years of vast, wondrous, and often unbelievably violent change that has fashioned the Earth as it is today.[15] I saw in living color what it means to be an Earth creature who is, in the words of Psalm 139, "fashioned in the depths of the earth" (NAB). In an initial sense, then, "to go down into the heart of the earth" is simply to acknowledge with humility the truth of who we are as human beings. Every fiber of our beings is woven of over four billion years of Earth process. This was as true of the human Jesus as it is of every other Earth creature.

The world of the author of the Gospel of Matthew, of course, did not include the scientifically-delineated four and a half billion year history of the Earth, nor was the global human-caused ecosystemic crisis among his pastoral concerns. When we read his text with these as our context, however, something new emerges. With an ecocentric hermeneutic, Jesus' descent into the "heart of the earth" appears not only as the affirmation of his true biological humanity, but also as the expression of his complete and unflinching commitment to solidarity in the life of the Earth-community—even unto full participation in its terrifying rhythms of death, dismemberment, and being made into food for others. It is not by going "somewhere else" that Jesus revealed the transformed life that we call the resurrection, but rather by going into the very heart of the Earth, including those aspects that are a "heart of darkness."

Jesus, the prophet of prophets, reveals to us that although the Earth is not God, divinity truly dwells transformatively in the heart of the Earth. Perhaps it is Teilhard de Chardin who has best captured this insight into the divine at the heart of matter.

> [Oh,] The diaphany of the divine at the heart of a glowing universe, as I have experienced it through contact with the earth—the divine radiating from the depths of blazing matter.[16]

> Oh the beauty of spirit as it rises up adorned with all the riches of the earth! [Oh human one,] bathe yourself in the ocean of matter; plunge into it where it is deepest and most violent; struggle in its currents and drink of its waters. For it cradled you long ago in your preconscious existence; and it is that ocean that will raise you up to God.[17]

Creation Transformed: John of the Cross

Teilhard saw and articulated his own vision of a divinized Earth, but much work remains to be done in spelling out the relationship between this and the ecocentric vision needed today. For this, I suggest turning back five hundred years to the great Carmelite contemplative John of the Cross. On first perusal John may seem like an unlikely choice as a resource for an ecocentric spirituality, since he is best known for his emphasis on the necessity of letting go of every attachment to created things in order to be united with God. Yet the commentary he wrote on his poem "The Spiritual Canticle" offers a profound theology of creation and, I would suggest, a basis for a critical understanding of the "third-order change" needed for an ecocentric conversion.

In the "Canticle" commentary John describes three stages of the contemplative journey and how it changes a person's relationship to the created world. In the first stage, the soul observes the great beauty and diversity of the many creatures in the world and recognizes them as like "a trace of God's passing." Through them, John adds, the soul "can track down [God's] grandeur, might, wisdom, and other divine attributes," for it understands that every creature has been clothed in the beauty of God's Image—the Image that we know in its fullness in Jesus.[18] Yet with her gaze turned outward, the soul in this stage feels acutely that God is only dimly revealed in the created world. She hungers for more.

The turning point to the second stage, that of spiritual espousal, occurs when the soul suddenly knows the grace of God's eyes gazing on her. This inward awakening radically shifts her experience of creatures. John writes:

> Inasmuch as the soul in this case is united with God, she feels that all things are God, as St. John experienced when he said: *Quod factum est, in ipso vita erat* (That which was made, in him was life) [John 1:4]. It should not be thought that what the soul is said to feel here is comparable to seeing things by means of the light, or creatures by means of God; rather in this possession the soul feels that God is all things for her....This experience is nothing but a strong and overflowing communication and glimpse of what God is in

himself, in which the soul feels the goodness of [these] things.[19]

Discovering the truth of her own being as continually being created in God's loving gaze, the soul also discovers that all creation is with her in this infinitely dynamic process. Instead of gazing on the opaque outer face of creation, she is inside creation, and it has become "a revelation of the face of God"[20] for her.

Finally, in the stage of spiritual marriage the soul enters the inmost "wine cellar" and drinks so deeply of God that she passes completely beyond all ordinary knowing into a state of divine "unknowing." John writes:

> Particular knowledge, forms of things, imaginative acts, and any other apprehensions involving form and figure are all lost and ignored in that absorption of love....Transformation in God makes her so consonant with the simplicity and purity of God, in which there is no form or imaginative figure, that it leaves her clean, pure, and empty of all forms or figures, purged and radiant in simple contemplation.[21]

Paradoxically, John describes the soul's contemplation of the beauty of creation in this stage as "the night of the dark contemplation of this earth" and calls it a "knowing by unknowing" that does not involve any sensory perceptions, psychological images, or mental operations.[22] In describing this summit of contemplation as a "night," John links it to his well-known teachings on the "dark nights" that are transitional stages along the way. The "dark night of the senses" refers to the process of being denuded of attachment to all varieties of sensory and worldly pleasure, while the "dark night of the spirit" that follows involves an even more radical divestment that extirpates the very root of narcissism. In this final night of unknowing, John insists, "It should not be thought that because [the soul] remains in this unknowing she loses there her acquired knowledge of the sciences; rather, these habits are perfected by the more perfect habit of supernatural knowledge infused in her."[23] In John's schema the "night" functions as the ultimate critical principle, for it demands opening up to that transconceptual dimension that frees us from the limitations of all our intellectual categorizing.

In the culmination of this "serene night" of unitive contemplation, the soul is shown the living beauty of the Creator who "nurtures and gives being to all creatures rooted and living in him." In her joy she begs the Bridegroom to give her "the grace, wisdom, and beauty that every earthly and heavenly creature not only has from God but also manifests in its wise, well ordered, gracious, and harmonious relationship to other creatures." The final transformation, then, is to accepting the gift of oneself as a servant among servants in the company of God's wondrous cosmic ecosystem. In the words of a recent Dutch commentary:

> As mystical human beings we are no longer full of ourselves; in total self-forgetfulness we are now totally open to God. In us God can now utter his creative Word, the Word by which he calls all of reality into existence....Thus we bring to light how the earth was created to be transformed by us to be the face of God. This occurs when, living on the basis of our likeness to God, we cause God's image to blossom in creation.[24]

In short, what we discover in John's commentary on the "Spiritual Canticle" is that the positive fruit of the most profound contemplative "night" is a radical delight in and interconnection with the totality of the created world, such that one is transformed in its gracious harmony and becomes a prophetic conduit of that same transformation for the rest of creation.[25]

WHAT ARE WE TO DO?

After this exploration of the depth of the spiritual transformation that is needed to address the reality of ecosystemic crisis, the practical question arises. What does all this mean for those of us who teach spirituality and/or offer spiritual guidance? How can we at least begin to take halting steps toward this "third-order change" and its prophetic implications? In Albert Nolan's classic essay, "Spiritual Growth and the

Option for the Poor," he proposed that those who would commit themselves to the poor must pass through four stages, which he entitled "Compassion," "Structural Change," "Humility," and "Solidarity."[26] I find a close parallel in the stages through which those on the path to an ecocentric conversion must pass.

Compassion: Touching the Earth

Nolan said that in order to enter the first stage of "Compassion" for the poor, one must first be exposed to the poor. This means both having first hand experiences of the world of the poor, and learning at second hand about the realities of those whom one cannot personally encounter. The same is true for the Earth: the foundation of any shift toward ecocentricity is knowing the Earth's reality both at first hand and through study. In some spirituality courses one can give assignments that require students to spend time in the natural world, to learn about it, and to reflect together on what it teaches them. Another key element is to invite students to reflect deeply on their own past experiences of connection to specific Earth places. For example, I now start every course I teach with a short recollection of the local ecosystem and its stresses, and then have students introduce themselves with a few words about the ecosystem they come from. I then make a point of returning to that connection at other times during the course. When given a chance, almost every student articulates profound and poignant encounters with elements of the natural environment. It is not uncommon to hear powerful stories similar to the one I recounted earlier in this essay. For the most part our students do not need us to teach them connection with the Earth; rather, they need to have this experience honored and its significance brought to articulation so that it can be placed in dialogue with all their other learning.

Once this kind of reflection begins, it does not take long for students to arrive at a deep experience of lamentation over the destruction that is being wrought on the natural places they love. This is especially true when the class includes students from "Third World" settings where the destruction is often already beyond repair. Their lamentation and horror at the wrongness of what is happening in and to God's creation is the beginning of prophecy.

The practices named here are only examples of what may assist in this first stage of awakening to the Earth. This stage is foundational and absolutely essential; yet, in common with Bateson's "first-order change," it may result in comparatively superficial shifts in behavior.

Structural Change: The Science of Consciousness

Albert Nolan calls the second stage of option for the poor "Structural Change." Having come to know and feel compassion for the poor, one realizes that their lives will not change unless the economic and governmental structures that bind them change. Like Bateson's second-order change, this is a significant shift of paradigm, and it opens up a new range of actions that have the potential of much more impact. A similar shift takes place when people become active in ecojustice movements.

In relation to spirituality, however, the paradigm shift may also take quite a different tack. The new realization may be that only a more concerted dedication to the challenge of developing an Earth-centered consciousness will lead to significant change. A search begins for practices and techniques that can effect that change of consciousness. Often this leads to a fascination with alternative spiritualities, such as those of indigenous peoples and Asian monks. In fact, Thomas Berry once asserted that what is emerging today would require us to let go of the spirituality of the prophet in favor of that of the indigenous shaman.[27] The point he was making was that in the present circumstances it is crucial that those who seek wisdom learn from the Earth itself rather than searching only among ancient verbal traditions.

Indeed, one of the trends in recent studies of indigenous shamanism is to examine how its patterns derive from the inbuilt biological religious tendencies of the human species. Michael Winkelman, an anthropologist from the University of Arizona and a proponent of what he calls "neurotheology," summarizes:

> Cross-cultural studies establish the universality of shamanic principles in hunter-gatherer societies around the world and across time. These universal principles of shamanism reflect

underlying neurological processes and provide a basis for an evolutionary theology. The shamanic paradigm involves basic brain processes, neurognostic structures, and innate brain modules. This approach reveals that universals of shamanism such as animism, totemism, soul flight, animal spirits, and death-and-rebirth experiences reflect fundamental brain operations and structures of consciousness.[28]

Other scholars are making progress in the study of brain states during prayer, meditation, ritual drumming and dancing, and mystical experience.[29] Some familiarity with these studies of the biology of religious consciousness is essential insofar as it is another dimension of grounding our spirituality practice and study in the best of critical research, including that of the natural sciences. The risk, however, is that modern Westerners may be inclined to turn this knowledge into a set of techniques for inducing altered states of consciousness. Whatever may be the value of these technique-induced changes, they are not fully equivalent to the "third-order change" described at the beginning of the chapter and exemplified, for example, in John of the Cross and Teilhard de Chardin. This has to occur in another dimension, that of a contemplative differentiation of consciousness that engages with what Bartunek and Mach called "transconceptual awareness."

Humility: Guidance in the Dark

Nolan's third stage in the option for the poor is "Humility." This emerges, he says, when activism fails and the activist's ideals wither in the face of ugly realities. Some trail off in despair at this point. Only a thoroughgoing divestment of egotism can enable one to endure this time of profound loss and abandonment.

Bateson also wrote of humility. He said that it must emerge when the arrogance of the scientific mentality meets catastrophic failure and "there is the discovery that man [*sic*] is only a part of larger systems and that the part can never control the whole."[30] This discovery emerges first as a form of double-bind or impasse, in which there appears to be no way forward without relinquishing the very pillars upon which one's worldview has hitherto rested. It is related to the alcoholic's "hitting bottom," and on a yet more profound level, to John of the Cross's "dark night" of contemplative transformation.[31] It is the doorway to "third-order change." This is the transformation that humans resist most of all, and yet it is also the path to the fullness of life. In the context of the present ecosystemic crisis, it may be, very simply, the path to survival.

On this dark part of the journey, there is really no consoling technique or remedy that we can offer ourselves or one another. Yet being compassionately accompanied, as well as being offered a framework for understanding what is happening, does make a difference. One of the goals of the teaching of spirituality must be to prepare those who will be called upon to offer this kind of guidance.

Solidarity: The Gift of Unknowing

Nolan calls his fourth stage "Solidarity." Only in this final stage, he says, does one wholeheartedly experience oneself as a member of the community of the poor, working and struggling with them rather than for them. In Bateson's schema, this correlates with the "total mind" that does not rely solely on conscious skills of understanding and manipulation, but rather operates from an embedded sense of participation in the holistic processes of creation.

In previous work I have developed the idea that critical scholarship in spirituality requires the development of what Lonergan called "interiority."[32] The simplest statement of this notion of interiority is, "Know what you are doing when you are doing it." It involves becoming a kind of "artist of consciousness" who understands the capabilities and limitations of all the tools at his or her disposal, and deploys them both flexibly and with finesse. Lonergan's description of interiority shares considerable similarities with what Gregory Bateson said about Learning III. Both men wrote about a profound epistemological shift that progressively frees one to "learn how to learn" rather than remaining embedded in the narrowness of reified paradigms and theories.[33]

Both men, however, also pointed beyond this intellectual shift to another and even more determinative level that is spiritual and even cosmic. Bateson referred intriguingly to a stage of "Learning IV," and although he never clearly differentiated this from his third stage, in his later years he increasingly emphasized the necessity for human consciousness to let go into the totality beyond its grasp. Lonergan wrote of how "falling in love with God" re-grounds consciousness in a realm of transcendence that transposes all one's spontaneous responses and values.[34] More recently, some theologians have articulated what Jean-Luc Marion termed "the privilege of unknowing," identifying the incomprehensible matrix of human consciousness as the locus of true human dignity and ethical action.[35] Indeed, Mary-Jane Rubenstein even proposes that this is the undesired and yet crucial gift of our era. She writes:

> What if, through modernity, post-modernity, and post-post-modernity, we have undergone the most thorough divestment of conceptuality, so thorough that we cannot even remember we've undergone it in the name of God?…What if, having finally given up all claims to absolute knowledge, we might now be opened up to relationality? Could it be that now, at the height of aimlessness, in the depths of poverty, the unselfed self might receive itself back as much more than itself?[36]

What this essay suggests is that it is through such a radical "unselfing" that we may at last become responsible participants in the great communion of life that is going forward with vastly greater wisdom than our own. While this communion is cosmic, we must live it as Earth-creatures. The Buddha, at the moment of his enlightenment, touched the Earth. Jesus, in the hour of his glorification, went down into the heart of the Earth. We, too, are called to lose and find ourselves in the same earthly solidarity.

Of course, the kind of transformation described here is not "learned" in graduate school, or even in a lifetime of assiduous scholarship. How is it relevant, then, to the critical academic study of spirituality? A distinction must be made between the conscious operations of thought that are under a scholar's control, and the broader subconscious and/or superconscious framework within which one operates. Third- and fourth-order change, or "transconceptual awareness" in Bartunek and Mach's language, is about the latter. Whatever one's degree of scholarly knowledge and skill, scholarship is always exercised as an expression of a framework of meaning and motivation that is rooted at another level. That framework may be an egocentric drive for power, a sociocentric desire to have a recognized role in a group (for example, one's academic guild), or a theocentric passion, such as John of the Cross describes. While some aspects of scholarship remain the same no matter what the framework, others shift considerably. As Lonergan argued, fidelity to the exigencies of scholarship requires the ongoing conversion of the scholar.[37] This essay proposes that the urgency of the looming ecosystemic crisis constitutes a concrete call to seek a conversion through which the profound inner alignment of theocentricity and ecocentricity may manifest themselves in one's scholarly work.

CONCLUSION

In the Society for the Study of Christian Spirituality we have already had long debates over the question of "self-implication," but perhaps our next debate will need to be over being "cosmically implicated." To say that spirituality is a self-implicating discipline is to say that the scholar's own spiritual journey is intertwined with her scholarship in such a way that her transformation changes her scholarship and her scholarship changes her. To take the next step would be to shift the focus from the self to the larger systems of which we are members, and to say that the spiritual processes emerging in them must also be consciously intertwined with our scholarship.

While much of Western theology and spirituality has been premised on image of salvation as an ascent from Earth to heaven, it turns out that a humbler image bears more truth: salvation demands a descent into "the heart of the earth." That shift of imagery from ascent to descent has implications for our academic work, as well. It matters whether insight is imaged as an ascent to a "higher viewpoint" that commands power, or as a descent to the ground where one discovers the meaning of being a humble and responsible citizen of Earth-community. Over the last few years we scholars of spirituality have had conversations about our discipline as among those leading the way in a shift from a notion of knowledge as objective and distantiated, to claiming knowledge as engaged and transformative. My suggestion is that the global ecosystemic crisis should shock us into taking the next step in the trajectory of conversations. We are being called to bring our spirituality studies consciously "into the heart of the earth," and there to cultivate the contemplative interiority that provides the ultimate critical principle for prophetic participation in ecosystemic adaptation.

Notes

1. Robert R. Wilson, "Early Israelite Prophecy," *Interpretation* 32 (1978): 3–16.

2. National Wildlife Federation, "Prescription for Great Lakes Ecosystem Protection and Restoration," http://online.nwf.org/site/DocServer/prescriptionforgreatlakes_1_.pdf?docID=2621&JServSessionldr001=qa7d8v9av1.app44b (accessed October 3, 2008).

3. Gregory Bateson, "The Logical Categories of Learning and Communication," in *Steps to an Ecology of Mind* (Chicago: University of Chicago, 2000), 279–308.

4. Gregory Bateson, "The Cybernetics of 'Self': A Theory of Alcoholism," in *Steps to an Ecology of Mind*, 309–37. See also Bill Buker, "Spirituality and the Epistemology of Systems Theory," *Journal of Psychology and Theology* 31, no. 2 (2003): 143–53.

5. Bateson, "Logical Categories," 331.

6. Gregory Bateson, "The Effects of Conscious Purpose on Human Adaptation," in *Steps to an Ecology of Mind*, 450–1.

7. Gerald G. May, *Addiction and Grace* (San Francisco: Harper & Row, 1988).

8. A few representative anthologies that offer readers an introduction to many of the key ideas being discussed in this field include: Dieter T. Hessel and Rosemary Radford Ruether, eds., *Christianity and Ecology: Seeking the Well-Being of Earth and Humans* (Cambridge, MA: Harvard University, 2000); Roger S. Gottlieb, ed., *This Sacred Earth: Religion, Nature, Environment*, 2nd ed. (New York: Taylor & Francis, 2003); Laurel Kearns and Catherine Keller, eds., *Ecospirit: Religions and Philosophies for the Earth* (New York: Fordham University, 2007).

9. Ernst Lehmann, *Biologischer Wille: Wege und Ziele biologischer Arbeit im neuen Reich* (Munich: J. F. Lehmann, 1934), 10–11, quoted in Peter Staudenmaier, "Fascist Ideology: The 'Green Wing' of the Nazi Party and its

Historical Antecedents," http://www.spunk.org/texts/places/germany/sp001630/ecofasc.html (accessed October 26, 2008).

10. Staudenmaier, "Fascist Ideology."

11. Jean M. Bartunek and Michael K. Moch, "Third-Order Organizational Change and the Western Mystical Tradition," *Journal of Organizational Change Management* 7, no. 1 (1994): 27–28.

12. Joseph Conrad, *Heart of Darkness* (NY: Hesperus Press, 2002).

13. Philip S. Johnston, "The Underworld and the Dead in the Old Testament," *Tyndale Bulletin* 45, no. 2 (1995): 414–19; Daniel J. Harrington, "Sheol," in *The Collegeville Pastoral Dictionary of Biblical Theology*, ed. Carroll Sthulmueller et al. (Collegeville, MN: Liturgical Press, 1996), 904–5; Kilian McDonnell, "The Baptism of Jesus in the Jordan and the Descent into Hell," *Worship* 69, no. 2 (1995): 98–109.

14. Simon Chow, *The Sign of Jonah Reconsidered: A Study of Its Meaning in the Gospel Traditions* (Stockholm, Sweden: Almqvist & Wiksell, 1995).

15. The History Channel, "How the Earth was Made." An accessible textual presentation of this history can be found in J. D. Macdougall, *A Short History of Planet Earth: Mountains, Mammals, Fire, and Ice* (NY: John Wiley and Sons, 1996).

16. Pierre Teilhard de Chardin, *The Heart of Matter*, trans. Rene Hague (New York: Harcourt, 1978), 16.

17. Ibid., 72.

18. John of the Cross, "The Spiritual Canticle," in *The Collected Works of Saint John of the Cross*, revised ed., trans. Kieran Kavanaugh and Otilio Rodriguez (Washington, DC: Institute of Carmelite Studies, 1991), 5:3–4.

19. John of the Cross, "The Spiritual Canticle," 14:5.

20. Hein Blommestijn, Jos Huls, and Kees Waaijman, *The Footprints of Love: John of the Cross as a Guide in the Wilderness*, trans. John Vriend (Louvain: Peeters, 2000), 139.

21. John of the Cross, "The Spiritual Canticle," 26:17.

22. Ibid., 39:11–13.

23. Ibid., 26:16.

24. Blommestijn et al, *The Footprints of Love*, 144.

25. A similar point was developed in great depth in "Dark Passage to Prophecy," a lecture given at the 2007 Summer Seminar on Carmelite Spirituality at St. Mary's College, South Bend, Indiana by Constance FitzGerald, OCD.

26. Albert Nolan, "Spiritual Growth and the Option for the Poor," *Church* 1, no. 1 (1985): 45–48.

27. Thomas Berry, "An Ecologically Sensitive Spirituality," in *Minding*

the Spirit: The Study of Christian Spirituality, ed. Elizabeth A. Dreyer and Mark S. Burrows (Baltimore: Johns Hopkins University, 2005), 248. Originally published in *Christian Spirituality Bulletin* 5, no. 2 (Fall 1997), 1–6.

28. Michael Winkelman, "Shamanism as the Original Neurotheology" *Zygon* 39, no. 1 (2004): 193.

29. See; for example, Eugene d'Aquili and Andrew B. Newberg, *The Mystical Mind: Probing the Biology of Religious Experience* (Minneapolis: Fortress, 1999); Mario Beauregard and Denyse O'Leary, *The Spiritual Brain: A Neuroscientist's Case for the Existence of the Soul* (San Francisco: HarperCollins, 2007); Anne Runehov, *Sacred or Neural? The Potential of Neuroscience to Explain Religious Experience* (Göttingen: Vandenhoeck & Ruprecht, 2007).

30. Bateson, "The Logical Categories," 443.

31. See Constance FitzGerald, "Impasse and Dark Night," in JoAnn Wolski Conn, *Women's Spirituality: Resources for Christian Development* (Mahwah, NJ: Paulist, 1986), 287–311.

32. Mary Frohlich, "Spiritual Discipline, Discipline of Spirituality: Revisiting Questions of Definition and Method," *Spiritus* 1, no. 1 (2001): 65–68; reprinted in Dreyer and Burrows, *Minding the Spirit*, 65–78. Also Mary Frohlich, "Critical Interiority," *Spiritus* 7, no. 1 (2007): 77–81.

33. Bernard Lonergan, *Method in Theology* (London: Darton, Longman, & Todd, 1971), 101–24; Bateson, "The Logical Categories," 301–6.

34. Lonergan, *Method in Theology*, 105–6.

35. Jean-Luc Marion, "*Mihi magna quaestio factus sum*: The Privilege of Unknowing," *Journal of Religion* 85 (2005): 1–24.

36. Mary-Jane Rubenstein, "Unknow Thyself: Apophaticism, Deconstruction, and Theology after Ontotheology," *Modern Theology* 19, no. 3 (2003): 413.

37. Lonergan, *Method in Theology*, 130–2 and throughout.

13. Spirituality and the Body

Colleen M. Griffith

This chapter first appeared in *Bodies of Worship: Explorations in Theory and Practice*, ed. Bruce T. Morrill (Collegeville, MN: Liturgical, 1999).

The particular "liturgical body" addressed in this chapter is human physicality itself—flesh, bones, sinews, ligaments, tendons, a skeletal structure that bends and straightens, a heart which beats and contracts. "Oh, *that body*," the reader might respond with a twinge of discomfort, for we are not accustomed to focusing direct attention on our physical selves. Imagine raising this body up for theological consideration. Will reflection on it take us down an all-too-familiar and frequented road of individualism? Liturgy, after all, is a communal happening. Does turning to the physical body smack of a potential solipsism? And given present cultural obsession with body and body image, isn't discourse of this nature somewhat of a bourgeois fascination?

To these questions I respond with a resounding "no!" For I am convinced that honest reflection on human bodiliness, in all its vulnerability and limits, necessarily points us smack in the direction of other bodies. It moves us to reclaim the interdependence which is our hope, to recognize the ultimate Life through which we are created and sustained (however named), and to connect anew with the earth of which we are a part. Precisely this type of corporeal reflection is absent in the dominant strands of the historic Christian theological tradition.

THE MISSING BODY: A FABLE

It was there, buried in the deep recesses of Christian tradition. The mythic story of Creation affirmed its goodness. Incarnation gave it theological significance. Resurrection deemed it integral to human fullness of life. But where did it go? How long has it been missing? Why has the body disappeared?

The theologians have claimed innocence. Engaged in worthy conceptual pursuits, they have concerned themselves with the accuracy and adequacy of theological claims and have not seen a trace of the body in a long while. Nor have educators seen it. In their commendable efforts to develop the rational capacities of the human, they too have emerged bodiless.

Who, then, filed the missing body report? I am told that many people did: the aged man who lives at the bottom of the hill—the one slowly losing his ambulatory power, the single mother with AIDS, the dancer who experiences integrated selfhood through movement, the family of color that frequents the shelter in the village for their meals, and the contemplative that lives in the hermitage in the woods. The fifty-four-year-old woman with cancer from my street knew it was missing, but she was too sick and too tired to file a report. There were others too, whose stories I know not.

One wonders why someone would want to take the body away in the first place. It was sacred space, storied place, ordinary enough all right, but with extraordinary capacity to access deeper levels of being. I know that several folks resented the limits that it imposed; some women and men from the village used to laugh at this, finding in these limits the basis for their bonding. Others looked upon the body with distrust and thought it best subjugated, dominated, controlled. Then there were those minimally acquainted with it who had little opinion one way or the other.

Admittedly, the body was a peculiar character, obvious but elusive, bound neither by mechanistic physics nor by metaphysics. Society and culture fashioned it; individuals and communities interpreted it. And the body retained organic functions and rhythms of its own.

Who could have committed the crime? For over a thousand years, dominant figures in Western Christian history strove to distinguish "body" sharply from the higher and more desirable "soul." Then, in the seventeenth century, René Descartes tried conceptually to separate the body completely from the soul. That makes him a suspect, but the man has been dead for years. More recently, twentieth-century Pulitzer Prize–winner Ernst Becker lashed out at the body in print, calling it a material fleshy casing causing persons to be split tragically in two. Becker felt condemned by his finitude, but he does not seem like an abductor; like many, he was only looking for heroic transcendence in some immortality ideology. Some women from town came to resent the way in which persons overly associated them with the body, but this was not a motive for kidnapping. Finally one has to wonder about church authorities; they were always so suspicious of the body.

The search for the missing body has become more urgent. In the absence of clear and certain evidence, high-tech rationality has begun telling people that they do not need to worry about the body anymore; it can be transcended by technology. At the same time, consumerism is promoting an alternative body that it has produced, one that can be sold ever better looks, more vivaciousness, increased appeal and freshness.

Time is running short. People of diverse physicalities with clues to uncovering the missing body must step forward. No insight born of carnal remnants is too small or insignificant to matter. Meanwhile, the search continues.

A Possible "Clue"

This introductory fable serves to focus attention on the human body as a neglected area of theological reflection. Bodies, with their instincts, dispositions, proclivities, and perceptions, are the most obvious and unavoidable fact of our human existence. How we reckon with them, how we come to view their nature and function influences our daily choices, our attitudes, lifestyles, relations with others, and our experiences of God. Yet the matter of our matter continues to be undervalued in religious thought and practice.

Bodiliness is an overlooked component in descriptions of spirituality as well. One seldom finds specific reference to the fleshliness of our engagement with the world and our fleshly positioning within God. There is little mention of the body as the place where desire for God manifests itself, the body as the standpoint of relational exchange between the human, the world, and God, and the place where we come to know and receive the abundant giving of Godself. Though we proclaim that God has opted to "pitch God's tent" (see Lev 26:11–12) in body, we forget that this "tent pitching," realized completely in the person of Jesus, continues to unfold in bodies throughout history, making the mystery of incarnation an ongoing event.

A large clue to uncovering the "missing" body lies in our coming to a greater sense of *bodiliness as the location of our spirituality*. Such an acknowledgment could surely enrich our participation in liturgy, but it cannot be assumed. Rebecca Chopp explains: "Christian spirituality has often been understood to be at its highest point with various forms of detachment: from the body, from the earth, from the other,"[1] A survey of historical Christian classics serves to substantiate Chopp's claim. While such forms of detachment are seldom advised today, they have had a long "effective history";[2] they continue to exert limited but real influence on patterns of thought and practice.

It takes more than a change in mindset to acknowledge bodiliness as the location of spirituality. It takes courage. There is, after all, a rawness to being bodily—a vulnerability, a finitude to be dealt with, a relationality and interdependence imposed that at times is frightening. And life in the body is never "tidy"; it is always changing. One has the distinct sense of being forever in process and behind in the process. There are challenges to bodily life that cannot be romanticized, making it less comforting to claim that the body is the location of spirituality.

Some of the biggest stumbling blocks of all in moving toward a spirituality of the body are the ghosts of our religious and philosophical traditions that continue to haunt us. Two of the most shadowy phantoms and persistent ways of presenting bodiliness in the historic Christian West have been the hierarchical ordering of body and soul, and the dualistic rendering of them. The umbras from these notions of body present irrectifiable obstacles to a full embrace of bodiliness as the place of spirituality.

Two Historical Portrayals of the Body

The history of Western Christian thought on the body is remarkably complex. Throughout the tradition, diverse judgments have existed concerning the meaning of the body and its function. Bodies have been revered and held suspect, problematized and anathematized. The wide range of motivations, procedures, and goals present in historical Christian asceticism attest to this type of fluctuation in thought.[3]

Discrepancies exist often between the theoretical reflections of historic Christian authors regarding bodiliness and the pastoral practices advised by these same authors. One finds metaphysical affirmation of the body in texts coupled with denigration of it in practical guidelines for Christian life, especially in matters of sex and sexuality.[4] In general, historic Christian treatment of the body has been at best ambiguous.

The primary way that Christian religious and Western philosophical traditions have construed human bodily being has been in relation to a more desirable "soul." The hierarchical ordering of body and soul has been a consistent theme in dominant historical Christianity. The dualistic rendering of body and soul/mind emerges as a Western philosophical notion with strong Christian rootage. Both models continue to exert influence in stratas of contemporary culture.

Hierarchical Ordering

The hierarchical ordering of body and soul is an understanding of the human in which "body" and "soul" receive emphasis as constitutive dimensions of the person, but each element is given different rank. "Body" is perceived to be dependent upon the "soul" and is regarded, therefore, as inferior to the "soul." Examples of hierarchical ordering abound in the Christian tradition.

In the writings of Augustine (354–430), for example, one first notes a basic affirmation of the body as an essential aspect of personhood. Augustine writes: "A man's [*sic*] body is no mere adornment or external convenicnce; it belongs to his very nature as a man."[5] At the same time, body and soul do not receive the same valuation from Augustine. He continues: "The soul is not the whole man; it is the bet-

234 / Colleen M. Griffith

ter part of the man, and the body is not the whole man; it is the lower part of the man."⁶ Soul, according to Augustine and to many of the dominant figures of the historic Christian tradition is the body's greatest "good," because it is judged to have superior measure, form, and order. Speaking about the soul, Augustine explains: "Its nature is more excellent, and the blemishes of vice cannot make it inferior to the body—just as gold, even if dirty, is valued above silver and lead, however pure."⁷

In order for the two to be in right relationship according to the hierarchical ordering model, soul must rule the body. A relationship of domination ensues. At the end of part 1 of Catherine of Genoa's (1447–1510) *Spiritual Dialogue*, in which "Body" and "Soul" journey together in dialogue form, Soul addresses Body: "Now I will once more be in charge. If you wish to serve me, I will take care of all your needs; if not, I will still be mistress and be served. If need be, I will compel you to be my servant and that will put an end to our arguments."⁸ Soul obtains greater valuation than body in the dominant strands of historic Christian tradition because it is assumed that its perception far transcends that of the body. It is the soul, for example, that gets credited as the "placedness" which "receives" God, and it is the soul that then serves as the animating source of the body. Soul is described as having distinctly finer faculties. Thomas Aquinas (1225–74), writing in the thirteenth century, writes: "The human soul, by reason of its perfection, is not a form merged in matter or entirely embraced by matter."⁹ For Thomas, it is specifically the intellective power of the soul that stretches beyond the body organism.¹⁰

The Christian tradition affirms the body insofar as it is related to the soul, and hierarchically orders it, thereby assigning less value to it. The existential unity of body and soul described by key figures in the tradition never overpowers the essential separation through ranking established by these same authors. Far too often, the hierarchy endorsed in the tradition gets extended outward to the social order where male and female bodies get differentiated by means of a parallel association with soul and body and spiritual/intellectual nature is made to stand over and against corporeal nature. A whole division of creatures ensues. Thomas, for example, writes: "God rules corporeal creatures through spiritual creatures. Hence it is fitting that the spiritual nature should be established over the entire corporeal nature, as presiding over it."¹¹ Right ordering appears to reign supreme and it depends upon an unequal ranking in the possession of being. The hierarchical viewpoint in the historic Christian tradition overshadows a less dominant incarnational one. This has led to a very ambiguous and problematic valuation of human bodiliness.

Vestiges of the hierarchical ordering model remain today in Christian practices which ignore or negate the body, "spiritualities" which focus on transcending physicality, traditions that suggest that a celibate lifestyle is "higher" than the married state, and wherever relations of domination exist on the basis of particular physicalities. The hierarchical ordering model certainly deserves analysis from a historical perspective, but it also ought to be evaluated from a contemporary standpoint. A helpful guideline for doing this comes from theologian Francis Schüssler Fiorenza who writes:

> The justification and confirmation of a theory proceeds retroductively from a theory's fertility, that is, from its explanatory and pragmatic success....It has a present ability to illumine and it has a potential for further developments. Moreover, a theory is more warranted to the degree that it can guide praxis.[12]

Cognizant of the context in which this historical formulation of bodiliness arose, one must inquire into its validity for our time by considering its present warrants.

The key, it seems, is to bring the criteria of conceptual and moral adequacy to the task of evaluating its present warrants. Is the hierarchical ordering model conceptually adequate for understanding the body, given the consciousness of our time? Is it morally adequate considering the ethical responsibilities of this era? Does this way of construing bodiliness as inferior to soul have the potential to encourage and stimulate humanizing practices in people's lives? Is it in keeping with twentieth-century socioethical concerns? To these questions, we must respond negatively.

Dualism

In the seventeenth century, with the work of Christian philosopher Descartes (1596–1650), another historical portrayal of the body arises: the dualistic rendering of it in relation to soul/mind. The dualism of Descartes depended upon an initial hierarchicalization of body and soul, but it carried a further intention that distinguished it from hierarchical ordering strictly understood. In Cartesian dualism, the subjective "I" becomes associated with one part of the hierarchy, namely the soul/mind.

Descartes set out to establish a qualitative difference between body and soul/mind and to identify the essence of the human as soul/mind alone. His famous *cogito*, "I think, therefore I am" (thinking here being any mental activity of which one is consciously aware) serves as the cornerstone of his system. He establishes the consciously knowing subject as a first truth and then turns to the "I," the one doing the thinking, to examine it more closely. Believing that thought is the attribute for positing existence, Descartes jumps to the conclusion that the mind is essential to human identity in a way that the body is not. In *Meditation on First Philosophy* Descartes writes: "This single 'I,' the soul by which I am what I am—is entirely distinct from the body, and indeed it is easier to know than the body, and would not fail to be whatever it is, even if the body did not exist."[13] Being without a body in the strict sense in what Descartes believes to be his core essence, he seemingly has no need of "place." Feminist philosopher Susan Bordo comments: "[Descartes] can relate with absolute neutrality to the object he surveys unfettered by the perspectival nature of embodied vision. He has become quite literally 'objective.'"[14] Descartes presumes a false objectivity, one that purports to transcend bodiliness. Descartes takes flight into a realm of "pure" knowing, inviting others to aspire to a place of bodiless truth that is detached, impersonal, and notably above critique. Sadly for Descartes, and fortunately for us, truth of this sort does not exist. Limit and perspective are endemic to human thinking precisely because of the distinctive bodily experiences that serve as the condition of thought.

Like the hierarchical ordering model, the dualistic rendering of body in relation to soul/mind has had a life span well beyond Descartes, its primary architect. Contemporary philosopher Paul Churchland, author of *Matter and Consciousness*, writes:

> Dualism is not the most widely held view in the current philo-
> sophical and scientific community, but it is the most common
> theory of mind in the public at large. It is deeply entrenched
> in most of the world's popular religions and it has been the
> dominant theory of mind in most of Western history.[15]

Philosophers and psychologists frown upon dualism, yet it continues to
persist in the popular mind.

Dualism remains alive also in the very subsoil of our cultural terrain. We continue to educate minds while largely ignoring bodies. Our
consumerist mentality encourages a separation of body from self, treat-
ing the body as a thing with use-value and exchange value to be
improved upon with the help of products. Mechanistic treatment of body
parts separated from the whole self ensures the success of impersonalis-
tic medicine. The contemporary postmodernist body is frequently disembodied; what remains is socially constructed physicality only, a
privileging of culture over nature yet one more time. Finally, though the
body is seemingly flaunted everywhere in image and discourse today, it
is fading from view on the cybernet.

Hierarchical ordering and dualism construe bodiliness in ways
that are inadequate for our time. The understanding of the body inherent
in these models is neither credible enough nor substantive enough to
stand as the location point for spirituality. The body that serves as this
location point must be more than an appendage to something else or an
afterthought. It is imperative for lived faith and for our participation in
liturgy that we rethink the human body today in broader and more comprehensive terms than the dominant Christian West has envisioned it.

When we claim that bodiliness is the location of our spirituality,
and that this is what is to be engaged liturgically, what do we mean by
bodiliness?

BODILINESS: A PROPOSAL

The understanding of bodiliness I propose here is a threefold
notion of the body as *vital organism*, as *sociocultural site*, and as *product of consciousness and will*. This threefold description corresponds

with what is biologically given about the body, what is socially constructed, and what is personally chosen about human bodiliness. These interrelated facets of being bodily must be held together as a whole, as strands of a braid, in order to reflect adequately the contemporary experience of being bodily. While there is necessary overlap between the three dimensions, each highlights a significant aspect of the body that cannot be ignored if we are to live our corporeality with awareness and intentionality as the location of our spirituality.

The Body as Vital Organism

The body as *vital organism* refers to the many physiological aspects of the body that enable it to act at once as environment for and vehicle of representation of the self. There is an existential content to being bodily, a givenness to it. As living matter, the body has a particular physical and historical situatedness that is preconceptual. Human bodies actualize themselves in specific space and time according to inherent developmental principles of maturation. Undoubtedly this actualization is socioculturally influenced as well, and shaped by personal choice, but the basic biological ontogeny of the organism unfolds, resulting in an emanation of life stages, biological rhythms and cycles: as body selves we are born, we grow to maturity and persist for a time, we age and die.

The spatiality that the body as vital organism assumes becomes the elemental raw material of a *presence*, one that the French phenomenologist Maurice Merleau-Ponty referred to as "our general medium for having a world"[16] and "our point of view on the world."[17] This presence, the situatedness of the body, becomes a perspective and a living context for a self growing toward maturity. The vital organism suggests a self in process that is always in dynamic relation with the world.

At a most fundamental physiological level of existence, one not dependent upon our conscious knowing or naming of it, human beings are profoundly *relational*. Live bodies depend upon a dialectical exchange with the world that is ongoing. To breathe, for example, we must draw in oxygen from outside ourselves and push out carbon dioxide. In accordance with our metabolic system then, we look to the world outside ourselves for raw materials we don't have, and we excrete the waste products. Respiration and metabolism highlight our interdependence with the created order.

Further examples of the basic "givenness" of the vital organism include bodies having weight, color, texture, symmetry, interior ecologies, and exterior surfaces. There are also the dynamic strivings of the organism which are richly suggestive for a spirituality of the body. These include the body's consistent *favoring of wholeness* in its operations, and its *efforts to maintain balance*.

Every aspect of the body's framework, each tissue and organ, is made up of microscopically small units, the cells. The body is a giant community of cells, hundreds of billions of them, each with a specific way of developing and life of its own. The high level of cooperation between cells and the manner in which they cluster together, working for the body as a whole, point to a unity and soundness, a fundamental integrity to the vital organism. Cells act for the integrity of the tissue; tissues seek the integrity of the organs, and the organs work for the basic integrity of the whole organism suggesting an accord between parts.

The *conatus*[18] or leaning of the body then is toward lifefulness and maintenance of that life. The organism strives for *homeostasis*, a balancing of the body's inner workings that keeps its physiology intact. When that balance is disrupted the body begins at once the job of repairing itself. It is as though the body as vital organism recognizes the inner upkeeping required for a balanced physiology and is forever checking and adjusting its operations to keep close to this state.[19]

To pause before the body as vital organism is to join with the Psalmist's praise recognizing that we are indeed "fearfully and wonderfully made" (Ps 139:14). The body as vital organism points to the wisdom of God as Creator. And it underscores our particular connection with each other and with the earth.

The Body as Socio-Cultural Site

In addition to the physical givenness of the body, society and culture exert formative and transformative influence on it. The surface of the flesh is porous; bodies soak in distinct sociohistorical contexts. The cultural soul of a people and a time spreads over a body's parts, inscribing and shaping them.

The vital organism assumes its identity and lives in interaction with a social and cultural milieu. Society advises rituals, codes, and boundaries for persons' physical selves,[20] and human bodies become the carriers of society's mores. Society interprets the body and sustains itself by means of deliberate bodily investment.

Social theorist Michel Foucault has called attention to society's way of investing the body. He focuses on how the body functions as a material grounding for sociocultural power. According to Foucault, "Nothing is more material, physical, corporeal than the exercise of power."[21] He turns to the body for its revelations regarding social discourses and cultural commitments.

Undoubtedly many "isms" that hold sway in our day look to the body as their playing field. Consumerism, sexism, and technocentrism, so rampant in contemporary North American culture, for example, target the body, fastening themselves in seductive ways to flesh, influencing the desires of persons and causing them, through deliberate investment of their bodies, to support sociocultural positions. Consumerism, by means of strategic commercial intervention, successfully guides persons to long for alterations of their physical selves in accord with a body image presented by the media, which can be attained by means of products that promise to move one closer to this attainment. Sexism inscribes a "feminine ideal" for the postures, gaits, gestures, and bodily ways of women. Technocentrism leads people to suspend critical review of carcinogens, radiation, ozone depletion, and toxic chemical release for the sake of a reified technological advance, giving technology permission to enter persons' bodies at will. In all of this, the human body is more than a point of application. It becomes a participant in the ongoing perpetuation of sociocultural stances.

Bodies also serve as the vehicles/carriers of powerfully positive social discourses and cherished cultural commitments. They can be the producers and sustainers of life-generating religious values and traditions through community-influenced modes of bodily being. In his book *Landscapes of the Sacred*, Belden Lane recounts a story about Rabbi Schneur Zalman, founder of Lubavitcher Hasidism. Rabbi Zalman was reported to be a mystic and a person of intellect who could argue Talmud in unparalleled fashion. Once a man came from afar to learn from the tzaddik. The proud villagers of Ladi, realizing the visitor's desire, asked if he intended to listen to the great rabbi read Talmud first or hear him pray. "Neither," said the man. He wanted only "to watch him cut bread and tie his shoes." The villagers were mesmerized as the visitor simply observed the rabbi sitting and moving round in the light of the noon sun, and then went away inspired.[22] He had come to learn from the rabbi's bodily way. He left taught by the power of a rich spiritual tradition and the wisdom of a faith community that had been inscribed in this rabbi's body. It had lodged itself so deeply there that the rabbi's bodily presence was itself one of blessing, peace and truth.

To pause before the body as sociocultural site is to recognize that social and religious practices, discourses, and traditions all sculpt the body. When, for example, persons assemble for liturgy as communities of faith, the symbols and practices they gather around have enormous power to grip people in body, to attach themselves to bodies in effective and transformative ways. Initiation into and participation in a community of faith helps cultivate this kind of *bodily knowing*. Louis-Marie Chauvet writes, "To be initiated is not to have learned 'truths to believe' but to have received a tradition, in a way through all the pores of one's skin."[23] Liturgical theologian Bruce Morrill notes that tradition is not to be located exclusively "in the forms of the liturgy itself,"[24] as people sometimes suppose, but rather in the very bodies and bodily practices of the participants. Herein lies "living" tradition.

Not all religious or sociocultural constructions, of course, are equal. There have been negative and positive ways in which bodies have been inscribed. What seems imperative is that a community's spiritual practice of discernment be an ongoing reading of what has been written on the body, a conscious decision to resist ways that bodies have been invested for evil, and a choice for a fashioning of our bodies in a way of life that is respectful and caring of self and others.

The Body as Product of Consciousness and Will

What one thinks about the body, how one reflects upon it, integrates it, adjudicates amongst body concepts, and uses the body in tasks of everyday living are matters of conscious choice and will. To some extent, persons choose what bodies they will become, what incarnate identities they will assume, and how they will interpret their bodiliness in relation to self and world. Freedom, agency, and choice safeguard against biological or sociocultural determinism. It does ultimately matter whether or not we attend to the body, and whether or not we meaningfully interpret and creatively engage it. These factors influence our experience of bodiliness.

Persons cultivate body consciousness by: (1) deliberately attending to the body, (2) meaningfully interpreting it, and (3) creatively engaging it.

Attending to the Body: Bodiliness is an inescapable fact of human existence. One can attempt to ignore this multivalent space or consider it. Attending to the body involves focusing on it, listening, sensing the workings of the vital organism, and feeling one's body from within.

Proprioception is an umbrella term for persons' sense of their physical selves, something innate that can be finely tuned and developed. Proprioception enables people to feel the rightness of good physical functioning in bodily activity. It provides a sense of equilibrium and imbalance, alignment and misalignment. Proprioception makes it possible to connect with limbs and with breath, to experience movement and stillness, expansion and contraction.

Attending to the body means developing our sense of our physical selves. It implies having basic familiarity with "bodily felt sense,"[25] that excess of meaning and feeling carried in the body. And it urges that we incline our ear toward stress signals like back pain, neck pain, sweaty palms, and physical tension in order to free up emotions trapped in armored muscles and skin, and experience the energy release elicited in the process.

Interpreting the Body: Attending to the body leads to interpretations of it. The experience of bodiliness cannot be severed from the interpretive meanings with which persons appliqué it. There are determining dimensions to being bodily, but individuals and communities retain the freedom to ground these symbolically.

Interpretation highlights aspects of a body's significance. It is a conscious process that enables us to enter into the subjective formation of our physical selves. Frequently, the activity of interpreting includes envisioning an optimal mode of being for the body, one that provides direction and offers hope.

Persons depend upon symbolic, interpretive frameworks as they live their bodiliness, negotiating physical challenges, experiencing bodily limits and changes. A meaningful and evocative interpretation of the body encourages persons to tend to the body with dignity. It is an integral component of identity formation and self-esteem.

Engaging the Body: Interpretation influences actions. A rich understanding of and vision for the body stimulates praxis, which in turn helps persons locate and ground further meanings in the body. Activities in which we consciously engage serve to fashion our bodiliness.

We engage the body as women, men, Chinese, French, Africans, Jews, Muslims, pre-schoolers, seniors, Olympians, cancer patients, musicians, worshippers, students, paraplegics, and so on. Regardless of our specific bodily context, ways of engagement for all of us include acts of bodily maintenance and acts of bodily enhancement.

The first involves the upkeep and management of one's body. Corporeal life carries with it definite and uncompromising demands: persons must eat and sleep, wash and groom themselves, drink fluids and excrete waste, give and receive physical affection in order to avoid disease and disorder. How one specifically addresses these existentials of corporeal life, however, remains a matter of choice, except in situations of oppression where this basic right is wrongfully denied. Bodily maintenance is a universal imperative, but persons have their own distinctive styles and set of governing principles with respect to this.

The second way we engage the body is through acts of enhancement. Deliberate use of the body in acquiring a skill or sustaining an acquired skill is a prime example of an enhancement. Intentional participation in sensual or aesthetic experiences is yet another. By exposing ourselves to sensual and aesthetic experiences, it is possible to come to a way of knowing that is profoundly somatic, one closely affiliated with religious awareness.[26]

To pause before the body as product of consciousness and will is to realize that how we live bodily is, in large part, a conscious decision. We have much freedom with respect to the bodies we fashion. Cocreating our bodily selves is intentional activity, and persons reserve the right to face this formidable task with a larger or lesser degree of consciousness and will.

BODILINESS AS LOCATION OF SPIRITUALITY

The threefold understanding of bodiliness as *vital organism*, *socio-cultural site*, and *product of consciousness and will*, is reflective of a large spectrum of contemporary discourse on the body. It stands in sharp contrast with the notion of body advanced by proponents of hierarchical ordering and dualism. This is an account of incarnate subjectivity that is not devoid of historical and sociological content, one that remains attentive to the biological givens of organic life as well. Most importantly, this description of bodiliness enables us to grasp some of the breadth and depth of human bodily being as the location of spirituality, something grasped not as isolated individuals but as people in relationship. Communities of faith are able to glimpse the breadth and depth of human bodily being in the practice of liturgy.

The spirituality alive in physicality gets highlighted in a unique and expansive way when we are joined with other bodies in conscious relationship with God. In his book *Worship as Theology*, Don Saliers describes liturgy as "a common art of the people of God in which the community brings the depths of emotion of our lives to the ethos of God."[27] Depth of emotion is always bodily lodged. It is when we bring the full gambit of bodily emotions to the book, the font, the table that, in the words of Saliers, "the grace of God becomes audible, visible, palpable, kinetic."[28]

One can choose, of course, to leave real struggles in the body behind: countless folks attend liturgy this way. But to participate in liturgy without any sense of our bodies, without holding the challenges and graces of being bodily in two hands to be prayed, and without any attempt to integrate the bodily felt senses of longing, fear, or hope that we've known, is to deny ritual its power to attract and transform, and to remain indifferent to it. Truly participating in liturgy warrants our human bodiliness at full stretch.[29]

What is necessary is nothing less than the "full, conscious, and active participation" called for in paragraph 14 of the Constitution on the

Sacred Liturgy. But it is a specific dimension of that participation addressed here, namely bodily conscious participation, leading to a fuller experience of "Liturgy, Incorporated."

Liturgy, Inc.

Tracing back to the origins *incorporare, incorporatus*, "Liturgy, Incorporated" is liturgy that is embodied through and through. It means a communal glorifying of God from the standpoint of bodily selves in all their limits and neediness. It involves invoking the Spirit of God on the real struggles of aging, illness, disability, and infertility and celebrating that same Spirit in the joys of relational sexuality, physical attributes discovered, the exhilaration of good health, and new births. Incorporated liturgy beseeches God from a bodily standpoint that knows both the felt sense of divine presence and the felt sense of absence as well. It includes an interceding that remembers the bodies of others in their struggle, that faces abuses rendered against the body, and recommits to a "heart of flesh." Most especially, "Liturgy, Inc." recognizes the creative and restorative activity of God pulsing in what is most fleshly, material, and concrete. Liturgy must intentionally begin from a bodily standpoint and return to it anew.

In his axioms for the study of sacred place, Belden Lane states that sacred space is "ordinary place ritually made extraordinary."[30] On any given day, the *locus sacra* that is the human body may seem surprisingly unassuming. But when we bring that body consciously to our community worship and pause before it, we recognize the presence of God in this most relational and vulnerable aspect of ourselves.

Liturgy provides opportunities to delight in bodily lives as God's gift.

> *Blessed are you, Lord, God of all creation.*
> *Through your goodness we have these bodies to bring,*
> *which earth has nurtured and love has made.*

At the same time, liturgy gives us a context from which to speak the truth about being out of alignment with other bodies and in search of hope, forgiveness, and healing.

> *Come, Holy Spirit. Make these bodies whole. Make these*
> *bodily lives holy.*

As we come face to face with our incompleteness, felt profoundly in body, the words, gestures, music, and actions of liturgy speak to us of a God forever giving Godself, amazingly in and as body.

> *Take and eat.*
> *Lord, I am not worthy to receive you.*

In the receiving of Godself, mystery bears in on human bodies. We are drawn, repositioned, sent forth.

> *Filled with life and goodness, blessed and made holy.*
> *Go in peace to love, to serve.*

Thanks be to God.

Notes

1. Rebecca S. Chopp, *Saving Work: Feminist Practices of Theological Education* (Louisville: Westminster John Knox Press, 1995), 69.

2. "Effective history" is Hans-Georg Gadamer's term for the history of the influence of an idea. Persons inherit not only models but their effects. See *Truth and Method* (New York: Seabury Press, 1975), 267.

3. See Margaret Miles, *Practicing Christianity: Critical Perspectives for an Embodied Spirituality* (New York: Crossroad, 1988), chap. 5.

4. There is a tendency in dominant historic Christianity to associate body and its functions with evil. Bryan Turner comments: "The frailty and eventual decay of the human body and the inevitable physical finitude of human beings provided an obvious metaphor for original sin and natural depravity." Turner, *The Body and Society* (Oxford: Basil Blackwell Publishers, 1984), 67. Common also is the association of body with woman and woman with evil. Rosemary Radford Ruether notes: "Femaleness is both the symbol and expression of the corruptible bodiliness that one must flee in order to purify the soul for eternal life. Female life processes—pregnancy, birth, suckling, indeed female flesh as such—become vile and impure and carry with them the taint of decay

and death." Ruether, *Sexism and God-Talk: Towards a Feminist Theology* (Boston: Beacon Press, 1983), 245.

5. Augustine. *City of God*, ed. David Knowles, trans. Harry Bettenson (New York: Penguin Books, 1972), I.13:22.

6. Ibid., XII.24:541.

7. Ibid., XIV.9:354.

8. Catherine of Genoa, "The Spiritual Dialogue: Part One," *Catherine of Genoa: Purgatory and Purgation; The Spiritual Dialogue*, trans. Serge Hughes (New York: Paulist Press, 1979), 114.

9. Thomas Aquinas, *Summa Theologica*, trans. Fathers of the English Dominican Province (Westminster, MD: Benziger Bros., Inc., 1948), 1a, q.76, a.1 (372).

10. For Thomas, intelligence and will are faculties of the intellective part of the soul. About them he writes: "The powers of these operations are in the *soul* as their subject." Thomas Aquinas, *Summa Theologica*, 1a, q.77, a.5 (387). By contrast, Thomas claims that operations of the soul that rely on corporeal organs, operations such as sight and hearing, find their subject in the human composite, rather than the soul alone.

11. Ibid., q.102, a.2 (501).

12. Francis Schüssler Fiorenza, *Foundational Theology: Jesus and the Church* (New York: Crossroad, 1984), 307.

13. René Descartes, *Discourse on the Method* in *The Philosophical Writings of Descartes*, vol. I, trans. John Cottingham, Robert Stoothoff, and Dugald Murdoch (Cambridge, UK: Cambridge University Press, 1984), 127.

14. Susan R. Bordo, *The Flight to Objectivity: Essays on Cartesianism and Culture* (Albany, NY: State University of New York Press, 1987), 95.

15. Paul M. Churchland, *Matter and Consciousness* (Cambridge, MA: MIT Press, 1984), 7.

16. Maurice Merleau-Ponty, *Phenomenology of Perception*, trans. Colin Smith (London: Routledge and Kegan Paul, 1962), 146.

17. Maurice Merleau-Ponty, *The Primacy of Perception*, ed. James M. Edie (Evanston, IL: Northwestern University Press, 1964), 5.

18. For a detailed analysis of the origins and meaning of *conatus* and *conation*, see Thomas H. Groome, *Sharing Faith* (San Francisco: HarperCollins, 1991), 26–32.

19. Examples of this include the body's efforts to maintain its temperature, to keep blood pressure stable, and to continue the process of cell replacement.

20. See Mary Douglas, *Purity and Danger: An Analysis of Concepts of Pollution and Taboo* (Harmondsworth, UK: Penguin Books, 1973).

21. Michel Foucault, *Power/Knowledge: Selected Interviews and Other Writings*, trans. and ed. Colin Gordon (New York: Pantheon Books, 1980), 57–58.

22. See Belden Lane, *Landscapes of the Sacred: Geography and Narrative in American Spirituality* (New York: Paulist Press, 1988), 40.

23. Louis-Marie Chauvet, "The Liturgy in its Symbolic Space," in *Liturgy and the Body: Concilium* 1995, ed. Louis-Marie Chauvet and Francois Kabasele Lumbala (Maryknoll, NY: Orbis Books, 1995), 31.

24. Bruce T. Morrill, "The Struggle for Tradition," in *Liturgy and the Moral Self*, ed. Byron Anderson and Bruce T. Morrill (Collegeville, MN: Liturgical Press, 1998), 68.

25. See Eugene Gendlin, "The Wider Role of Bodily Sense in Thought and Language," in *Giving the Body Its Due*, ed. Maxine Sheets-Johnstone (Albany, NY: State University of New York Press, 1992), 192–207.

26. See Margaret Miles, *Image as Insight: Visual Understandings in Western Christianity and Secular Culture* (Boston: Beacon Press, 1985), 3.

27. Don E. Saliers, *Worship as Theology: Foretaste of Glory Divine* (Nashville: Abingdon Press, 1994), 27.

28. Ibid., 28.

29. This is a nuancing of Don Saliers' reference to our "humanity at full stretch." See ibid., 28.

30. Lane, *Landscapes of the Sacred*, 15.

14. Spirituality and the Common Good

Ada María Isasi-Díaz

This chapter first appeared as "To Be Fully Alive Is to Work for the Common Good," in *Church & Society* 89 (September/October 1998).

In my apartment in New York City I have placed a small poster in a strategic place, and I stop to read it as often as it catches my eye. It says, "To be fully alive is to work for the common good." I have come to believe—and try to live out the fact—that if we do not work for the common good we are not alive. It is against this backdrop that I turn to the task of making the intrinsic connection between spirituality and the struggle for the common good.

SPIRITUALITY

I believe strongly that the ongoing revelation of God happens in our midst today and that, whether we like it or not, God has chosen the poor and the oppressed as a preferential site for revealing who God is and what God is like. So we turn first to their experience. Grassroots Latina women with whom I work talk about their faith and about *la lucha*, the struggle that is their day-to-day living. But I never hear them talk about spirituality. I certainly do not think it is because they have none, so I have tried to pay attention to the fact that they do not use the word: the word is simply not part of their world.

Traditionally, spirituality has had, as its starting point, doctrinal teaching and theoretical language: what the churches tell us God is like instead of what the experience of God of the common folk is. Books about spirituality tend to be directed to "churchy" people, to ministers and church leaders. Conversation about spirituality often seems to be individualistic, detached from social concerns and the communal dimensions that are intrinsic to the Christian life. Talk about spirituality tends to be otherworldly, suspicious toward present historical realities. This has led us to fabricate a separation of the spiritual and the material that obscures the mystery of the incarnation.

We need to insist on a holistic understanding of spirituality. We need to insist that prayer and action are two dimensions of the human person that must be held together. We have to bring together our faith and the way we live our lives. Spirituality and ethics are two sides of the same coin, different ways of looking at how we live. Our relationship with God—and that is the core of spirituality—is not apart from the continuing, lived experience of Christians, from our moral values and norms. On the other hand, our moral life is shaped and nurtured by our relationship with God.

This means that the authentic life of persons created in the image of a triune and personal God cannot ignore the needs and demands of other persons in the human community. A correct understanding of spirituality has to point out that Christian living is made possible by God's gracious presence and action in our communities and our world. For us Christians, our religious beliefs are the context in which we understand and talk about virtues, values, and decision making.

A correct understanding of spirituality recognizes that there can be no spiritual growth if there is no moral growth. Any spirituality that proposes a quick road to the heights of prayer without attention to moral conversion is inauthentic to the Christian tradition and alien to our experience.

A correct understanding of spirituality recognizes that the most fundamental human experience, which is the focus of both spirituality and the Christian moral life, is the drive to fullness of being. This fullness of being calls us to continue a conversion from self-centeredness to justice and love. It calls us from individualism to responsibility in the community. It calls us to delve ever more deeply into what it means to be made in the image and likeness of God, what it means to participate in the fullness of being attained by Jesus. Jesus attained his fullness of being by fulfilling his mission. He becomes the Christ because he fulfills his mission and vocation.

The specifics of our mission and vocation as Christians vary greatly. Essentially they are feeding the hungry, giving shelter to the homeless, clothing the naked, comforting those who grieve. Nowhere in Scripture do we see better the fact that seeking justice and spirituality go hand in hand than in that well-known verse from Micah. To the question, "What is good and what does God require?" the answer is, "Do justice, and…love kindness, and…walk humbly with your God" (Mic 6:8). You cannot have a spiritual life, you cannot walk with your God, if you do not do justice and love kindness.

The Common Good

When we Christians talk about the common good we are referring to the conditions that are necessary for fullness of life. The common good refers to a common vision and to the means employed to achieve such a vision. It refers to shared objectives considered to be normative elements in a just society. Individualism is both unable to account for these elements in theory and likely to negate them in practice.

Local

The common good is not about a sense that the interests of the community are simply the sum of the interests of the members who compose it. The common good is a shared vision of justice and can never be exclusive of anyone or at the expense of anyone. So it has to take into consideration the members of this or that group, all those with whom we come in contact and all those whom we reach through our actions.

I tell my students that among the many things that we have to take into consideration when making a decision is its foreseeable effects. Invariably they do not like this. They do not want to have to think about themselves and those immediately around them as well as those who are not so immediate to them. I remind them that our Native American sisters and brothers tell us that we should care about the effects of our decisions and actions up to the seventh generation. That is the way we need to look at the common good.

The common good is the reason for the existence of civil authorities, for it requires guarantees for personal rights. But with our rights come duties and obligations, and our rights cannot be at the expense of others.

Global

As Christians today who prepare to usher in the twenty-first century, we need to think of the common good as an international common good. We have to accept the fact that a global common good requires the restructuring of the present order of the nation-states, including the United States. The common good has to do with how the world economic order works. The global common good calls us, for example, not to sacralize private property but to insist that all private property has a social mortgage. Intrinsic to our understanding of the common good has to be a deep commitment to sustainable economic development. We have reached a moment in the history of our world when development in one area of the world is usually at the expense of someone else or at the expense of our ecosystems. That is not development. That is exploitation because it is at the expense of someone else.

Within this understanding of the common good I talk about justice.

JUSTICE

Justice is intrinsic to God. Since through faith we participate in God, we live out God. Justice is a living out of what we understand God to be. To claim to have faith, to claim to have a spiritual life, is to commit oneself to do justice. If we are not just people we cannot think of ourselves as people with a spirituality. We cannot call ourselves people of faith.

When we talk about spirituality we are talking about our relationship with the Divine, and there is no real relationship possible without justice. Justice has to do with right relationships: relationships that respect, empower, promote, uphold, care for each of those held in them.

And when we talk about justice, we are talking not only of personal relationships but also of the web of multiple relationships that constitute and define society.

Because justice is living out God in our lives, it is a historical reality. This is why justice needs to have as its starting place the cries of the poor and the oppressed, the cries of those who suffer injustice. The starting place for justice is specific forms of injustice, not some abstract theory about what is due the other. A thorough analysis of oppression, of its multiple causes and expressions, is therefore the starting point for justice.

Global and Local Ethics

As people of faith, it is not our task to deal with justice in order to establish an overall theory and apply a very few premises to the whole of humanity. Instead, as people of faith, our accounts of justice have to deal with establishing justice in concrete relationships, in concrete situations, places, societies. Justice then is more than an understanding, it is a faith praxis: reflective action geared to radical change at both personal and societal levels, levels that cannot be separated. Because of the all-pervasive nature of injustice, we must concentrate on uncovering, understanding, and rejecting oppression. One definition of oppression is this: oppression refers to systemic constraints that are "embedded in unquestioned norms, habits, and symbols, in the assumptions underlying institutional rules and the collective consequences of following those rules."[1]

Oppression includes "the vast and deep injustices that some groups suffer as a consequence of often unconscious assumptions and reactions of well-meaning people in ordinary interactions, media and cultural stereotypes, and structural features of bureaucratic hierarchies and market mechanisms—in short, the normal processes of everyday life."[2]

Nevertheless, we cannot wash our hands and insist that, because these are unconscious assumptions and reactions of usually well-meaning people, they are not responsible. We have to take responsibility for what we believe and for the assumptions that undergird our lives. That is why we need to carefully study and understand oppression. What is oppression? How does it operate? Who does it benefit? There are different reasons or combinations of reasons for oppression, as well as different modes of oppression. No one mode of oppression—whether it is racism, ethnic prejudice, sexism, homophobia—is more oppressive than another.

Differentiating various modes of oppression, however, is important if we are to elaborate effective strategies to bring about justice. Here are five modes so that you can recognize, understand, and begin to devise effective means of working against them:

- Exploitation. This is when one person or organization appropriates the results of the labor of others.

- Marginalization. Marginalized people are not considered to be contributing anything worthwhile and therefore can be easily eliminated. For this reason, this is perhaps the most dangerous mode.

- Powerlessness. People who are powerless have no authority and have little opportunity to be self-defining or to assert their interest and values.

- Cultural imperialism. This is the basis for racism and ethnic prejudice.

- Systemic violence. This causes the oppressed to live in fear of random violence, which they suffer for no reason except that they are oppressed.[3]

Our understanding of justice has to be contextualized, for oppression is a concrete reality with specific characteristics. One of the reasons we don't like to be very specific about justice is that then we can dilly-dally about it, but if it is specific, then it forces us to make options concrete enough to play a central role in devising strategies for radical social change.

The General and the Specific

Our accounts of justice have to go beyond merely identifying and articulating values. Our understanding of justice has to focus on concrete projects. In Latin America they talk about *proyectos históricos*. What are our historical projects? What are we going to do this year to change this society's specifics? It has to focus on specific ways of implementing our vision of the common good.

I believe certain elements have to be present if justice is to flourish. I mention four:

1. Equal power in decision making: The oppressed must contribute to change the oppressive situation they suffer. They must contribute to what is normative in society. In other words, justice is not only about the rights of the oppressed but also about their responsibilities. They have to participate in creating the reality they hope to enjoy. Justice means recognizing the oppressed as moral agents capable of contributing to the common good—not only to the common good for themselves but to the whole common good.

2. Being committed, making room for ambiguity: Justice necessitates a changed understanding of differences from the one regularly used today. True plurality rejects placing groups and persons in mutually exclusive categories. Difference does not mean that there are not overlapping experiences or that there is nothing in common. Difference among groups and persons does not exclude some similarities and the potential sharing of some attributes, experiences, and goals. Differences have to be embraced and in order to be embraced they have to be understood as relational: as ambiguous, as shifting, without clear borders that keep us separate from each other.

   Embracing difference does not in any way mean accepting total relativism or an individualistic ideology. Embracing differences is only possible as part of an ideology of solidarity, a solid commitment to fullness of life for all. Only if we embrace differences will we realize that justice cannot be brought about at the expense of others or at the expense of the earth and other living creatures with whom humans share this world. Embracing differences requires interaction that cannot happen without honest dialog that, in turn, requires equalization of power among those in dialog.

3. Recognizing power dynamics: It is very important for us to realize issues of power when we talk about justice. Oppressive power uses force, coercion, and/or influence to control and limit self-determination and decision making in individual persons or groups of persons. Liberative power, on the other hand, transforms oppressive situations.

4. Living in history, being free from history's constraints: If the starting point for justice is the cries of the oppressed, then justice is a response to concrete reality in history. Nevertheless, although we have much to learn from history, justice has to be free from history. The future we strive for as people of faith, as justice people, is not simply dependent on the possibilities inherent in the past. As a matter of fact, this is precisely why we should privilege the vision of justice created by the oppressed. Since they have nothing to protect in the present structures that oppress them—since they don't gain anything from them—the poor and the oppressed are admirably capable of imagining a future radically different from the present, a future in which there may very well need to be more discontinuity from the past and from the present than many of us want to see.[4]

SOLIDARITY

So where shall we start? I propose that we analyze oppression in our own lives and in our own communities. I suggest that all those who participate in peacemaking programs commit themselves to see themselves most of the time as oppressors, and maybe at times also as oppressed, and commit themselves to stand in solidarity with the poor and the oppressed. I see solidarity as the keystone to justice. Solidarity is our way of living out the "love one another" of the gospel. Without solidarity, we can care for the poor but we will never be able to privilege their understandings of justice or to struggle for their participation as agents of change. Without solidarity we will never be able to put aside our fear of differences or to embrace differences. Without solidarity we will feel threatened and will not be willing to give up oppressive power or to work toward an equalization of power. And without the confidence solidarity gives us, we will not be able to welcome a vision of justice that recognizes the need for both historical continuity and historical discontinuity.[5]

These days there is little at times that gives hope. We have been called to struggle with each other. We have been called to rekindle our baptismal calling to holiness, to share in the life of our God. We have been called to be peacemakers, remembering that peace is not possible without justice, that peace is the fullness of being, the shalom that will be fully established when we are all family to each other.

Notes

1. Iris Marian Young, *Justice and the Politics of Difference* (Princeton, NJ: Princeton University Press, 1990), 41.

2. Ibid.

3. Ibid., chap. 2.

4. See Ada María Isasi-Díaz, *Mujerista Theology: A Theology for the 21st Century* (Maryknoll, NY: Orbis Books, 1996), chap. 6.

5. See ibid., chap. 5.

15. Spirituality and Ministerial Ethics

Lisa A. Fullam

A version of this chapter first appeared as "Ethics and Spiritual Guidance" in *Reflective Practice: Formation and Supervision in Ministry* 30 (2010).

Ask most people about ethics in spiritual guidance—defined broadly to include pastoral ministries, spiritual direction, and other forms of spiritual care—and you'll quickly find yourself in a discussion of two issues: boundaries and confidentiality.[1] If you push further and ask about accountability, often you'll get a response about financial transparency. Ask about responsibility, and perhaps they'll mention vulnerable people, especially children and others liable to sexual abuse or exploitation. All of these are important, even crucial, issues.

The problem starts when you then ask what should be done about these ethical problems. On boundaries, you might get a list of whom one may and may not date. On confidentiality, they will often respond with a list of who is a mandated reporter for what. Financial transparency? Have a pastoral council that provides budget oversight. Abuse? Have a window put in the door of your office. These are not bad ideas, but I will argue here that they miss a critical aspect of what it means to be a professional offering spiritual guidance: they miss questions about the character, the virtues, of the guide.[2] Further, skipping from ethical issues to practical suggestions obscures a dynamism intrinsic to spiritual guidance: the practice of spiritual guidance draws on and reflects in an essential way the guide's own spiritual practice.

In this essay, I aim to build a bridge between the ethics of spiritual guidance and the spirituality of the minister. First, I will explain this claim that the guide's own spirituality is an ethical resource and focus. Second, I will describe the renascent method of virtue ethics to show how this bridge might be constructed. Finally, I will explore the two ethical questions I offered at the beginning of this essay, accountability and responsibility, to demonstrate how a focus on virtue shifts the nature of ethical questions and engages the spiritual guide more holistically.

ETHICS AND THE SPIRITUALITY OF THE GUIDE

Consider this analogy. A person wishing to be a basketball coach will do well to learn as much about the game as she can. A better coach can employ this expertise in adaptable and flexible ways, given the situation on the court. Likewise, a good coach can read the strengths and weaknesses of another team and adapt her team's play likewise. These are what I will call the objective skills of coaching, and you cannot be a good coach unless you have some grasp of them.

But there's more to being a great coach than knowing the game. A great coach is involved not just in winning games but also in the development of the players. The cultural mythology about sports is built largely around its capacity to form players into better people overall; it is hoped that your alert and decisive point-guard will bring the same attentive self-confidence to her work as a trial lawyer. "The battle of Waterloo was won on the playing fields of Eton," the saying goes, and we regard cheating not merely as a violation of arbitrary rules of a game, but also as a reflection of a deeper lack of integrity of the players and, by extension, their coaches.

Spiritual guidance, of course, aims more at this second, formative level. While there are important skills and knowledge involved, it would be absurd to think of a minister hoping that his parishioners will become really expert at a particular spiritual practice as an end in itself. "Well, Janet might be a liar, a gossip, and a pilferer, but gosh she's always there for adoration, and she's inexhaustible when she leads the Rosary—and she gets it done quickly, too!" Such a statement might be an accurate statement about Janet's actual state of spiritual development but few would regard that as a satisfactory goal or end-point for one's faith life. The practices of spiritual life are aimed at deepening our relationship with the divine, raising our sensitivity to the numinous in the universe and especially in others, and cultivating ethical lives of devotion to service and the cause of justice in the world. If they do not at least have the potential for that kind of deep formation, then we would be better off spending our time doing something constructive. And a minister or director fails if he or she cannot be a resource, at least imperfectly, for that process of facilitating the spiritual growth of those we serve. Spiritual guidance, then, is the business of formation of those in our care. That much is obvious.

There is a second level of formation in spiritual guidance. Again, to see it more clearly, let us return to the basketball team. The personality, priorities, attitude, and values—the character—of the coach is important to the success or failure of the personal formation of the members of the team, within limits. The coach is a formator not only in how she directly interacts with the players for their development, but also, more subtly, by example of her own attitude to the game and the players. This step involves asking about the life of coaching: coaches can grow obsessed with winning and lose track of their players' well-being and also their own. And while there is a reasonable boundary in keeping details of the coach's life private from the team, still the overall color of the coach's life will be evident. Coaches become formators for integrating life and sport, life and work, for the fundamental attitudes toward challenge, opportunity, and adversity that are formative in a less direct, but perhaps more profound, way than the other levels of one's approach to the game.[3]

Spiritual guides are formative in the same two ways that coaches transcend mere knowledge of the game and become formators: first, in the direct formation of one's clients, but second, in how their own lives reflect or fail to reflect the goals of relationship to the divine, the numinous, and the neighbor. Because of the nature and aims of spiritual practices, the connection between these two levels is far stronger in spiritual guidance than in other endeavors like sports coaching. There is a distance between playing and coaching that allows non-athletes to be good coaches, and for coaches with serious dysfunction in other areas of their lives to be able to coach. But in spiritual matters, the practice and the spirituality are known by their fruits: if a spiritual guide lives a life of snappish anger or inability to love, the guide's message is compromised, perhaps entirely. Like the coach, there are reasonable boundaries of privacy about the details of the spiritual guide's life. But since the spiritual guide is engaged in a formative business that promises growth in the peace, harmony, and devotion to God and world, the glimpses and gleanings of serious disharmony concern exactly the matter about which the spiritual guide is supposed to be expert.

So can only the perfect and saintly presume to be spiritual guides? Not at all. Here also the basketball analogy is helpful: it is often said that the greatest players do not always make great coaches. The mid-level or lower-level players, those who might have to figure out through diligent practice and attentiveness to detail about how to move their feet in guarding a player, are often better at cultivating other players, at finding the seeds of grace in their game and helping nourish them. So too in spiritual guidance, where it is not so much sanctity that is asked, but diligent attentiveness to the practices and processes of spiritual life. After all, we all remain both graced and sinning, but, we hope, we are also devoted enough to respond to Jesus' invitation to "be perfect, as your heavenly father is perfect." Perfection, here, is not a state or an achievement, but a process worked by the Spirit with the collaborative soul. Spiritual guides must be devotees of the process, even—and especially—where they struggle.

So we have three levels of questions, one of knowledge and two of formation. The need for knowledge of one's tradition of the particular skills of guidance is obvious, and is rightly a principal focus of the training of guides. The first level of formation involves using one's knowledge in the service of the human development of one's clients in a holistic way. The second formative level concerns the guide's own life as a formative influence on others. In spiritual guidance, as I've said, the second two questions are inextricable because of the nature of what we offer. Most work on the ethics of spiritual guidance focuses on the formation of the client. Here I want to consider the formation of the formator. And this is the task of virtue ethics.

WHY VIRTUE ETHICS?

A virtue ethics approach to spiritual guidance will focus on the formation of the guide. While this methodology often seems to lack the zippy clarity of aphoristic rules, it seems to hold special promise for the work of those providing spiritual guidance. How does it work?

Virtue ethics holds that the first concern of ethics is not actions ("can I date a parishioner?") but character and its development ("what are the virtues of a good minister?"). In the Aristotelian/Thomistic school of virtue ethics which I employ here, virtues are understood as perfections of natural human capacities. Just as we are born with muscles that may be strengthened by exercise, so we are born with the capacity for justice, prudence, and other virtues that are developed by attentive practice. "We become builders…by building, and we become harpists by playing the harp. Similarly, then, we become just by doing just actions, temperate by doing temperate actions, brave by doing brave actions."[4] While it is true that "the just man justices,"[5] it is also true that the just man becomes just by doing works of justice deliberately and with self-awareness.

According to Aristotle, virtues become second nature—stable habits or ways of responding to the challenges of life. Most of the time, our actions reveal (as well as form) our characters. Think of the kinds of stories we tell when toasting a bride or bridegroom at a wedding or the stories we tell at a wake—in an incident, we try to reveal something about the kind of person the spouse or the departed is. "Oh, yes, that's him!" is the aimed-for response. In virtue ethics, all our actions, both those we think through carefully and those we do by rote or by simpler decision-making processes, are significant insofar as they have the effect of underscoring or eroding the character we possess.

Virtues are matters of practical rationality: they are habits of knowing what to do in varied and changing circumstances. It is the virtue of prudence that guides the virtues to acts appropriate to the situation and to recognize the next step in growing in virtue. Prudence is sometimes misunderstood as cautious holding back from what we are considering doing. In fact, prudence can as often urge us to take chances or go forward when caution seems safe but not virtuous. For instance, a spiritual director who finds himself with a client who seems not to be engaging the process honestly or whole-hearted can let the waste of time continue (despite the director's mounting irritation), or, he might, after sufficient reflection, raise the matter with the client. Prudence here would counsel addressing the issue, both for the sake of the client and the director.

A virtue is a reasoned mean between an excess and a deficit, both of which are vices. This is easy to see in the case of courage. A person deficient in courage is a coward. But it is also true that a person can have too much of what looks like courage and rush stupidly into unreasonable danger. Prudence points to the reasonable response in a given circumstance, for a particular person. Humility is also a reasonable mean. In Christian tradition, we tend to think of a dichotomy of humility and pride, in which pride is a grievous sin and humility, conversely, can be misconstrued as self-abasement. But an ethics of virtue urges us also to be aware that if pride is a vice opposing humility, so is its opposite vice: groundless and unreasonable self-abasement. Some of the people we guide—and guides ourselves—may need to be warned against excessive pride, but others of us need to be encouraged to more self-assertion because we are inclined to excessive self-abasement, declaring ourselves somehow not worthy of attention, celebration, or effort.

Since acquiring virtue is a process of perfection, growth in virtue is always construed in personal terms. We begin with a certain state of a virtue (except prudence, which Aristotle and Thomas agree is entirely acquired by education and experience). Our path to perfection is shaped by our natural "baseline" of a virtue, the particularities of temperament, and other life circumstances. A naturally choleric person has farther to go to achieve patience than a less irritable person. Both are called to perfection, but the small steps that take us there are prudential estimations of the best the individual can do at that moment on the way to true virtue. Likewise, the form a given virtue takes varies with the situation of the individual. Both pastors and fighter pilots are called to be courageous, but in different ways. Not every person who is patient or courageous will manifest those virtues in the same ways. The fighter pilot will always seem to be more daring than the average pastor, even when both have acquired the courage that fits their callings. A virtue ethic makes us aware of the infinite variety of manifestations of human excellence, humble in our estimations of others, and kind to ourselves also as we strive to become more fully virtuous.

People, Not Ideas

The benchmarks for virtue are not ideas but people. We do not encounter virtues as pure concepts; rather we see them at work enlivening the lives of people around us. We learn justice by noticing Rosa Parks refusing to move to the back of the bus. We learn compassion from watching the nurse at the hospital. We learn patience watching a teacher work with a student who just does not get it. This goes back to the beginnings of virtue ethics: in a stark disagreement with his teacher Plato, Aristotle said that we cannot begin with abstract ideas, but "we ought to begin from things known to us."[6] Aristotle derived the hodgepodge group of virtues he describes in his *Nicomachean Ethics* inductively. He looked around at who seemed to be flourishing in Athens and took note of the virtues they seemed to possess.

This process had flaws. If we merely look around at who seems to be doing well in a particular setting, we are likely to wind up with a fairly biased image of what is virtuous. In grade school, it can look like the people who are the most successful are the bullies or the teachers' pets. In a consumer society, the rich appear best off. Aristotle has been criticized for presenting a set of virtues that reflect the character of free, wealthy Athenian men, not humanity generally. But the definition of virtue is about human nature: a virtue is a perfection of a human capacity. So the method itself has a built-in corrective factor. A virtue, as virtue, must reflect human nature, not merely the desires of a given group. Since human nature transcends individuals, groups, and cultures, it is possible to enter into a true dialogue about the good life in ways that challenge or affirm our cultural heritage.

Choosing Exemplars Carefully

It matters, then, who we take (or who we offer to others) as exemplars. Bad exemplars will form us in the ways of vice, not virtue. Good exemplars will help us grow in virtue. How do we tell the difference? Remember, virtues involve an assessment of human nature: What are the qualities of character that help us to be "fully alive," individually and communally? Virtues are not ascetical practices that lead to happiness, as though we will be rewarded with happiness if we are sufficiently kind or temperate. In this tradition, virtues are the content of human happiness: to live in accord with virtue is to live in accord with our created nature, which, all other things being equal, will be profoundly, humanly satisfying.[7] Sources for how we understand virtue are in the stories we tell of "profiles in courage," of little engines "that could," of people like Gandhi facing down the British empire with only a loincloth and a smile. They are the narratives of human flourishing, of the integrity of lives well-lived, of being people like those we find worthy of imitation.

In a Christian virtue ethics, norms for virtue can be found in the person of Jesus, the lives of the saints, and our hopes for the reign of God. Ethicist William Spohn points to the role of the analogical imagination in ethical reasoning. Far from a facile "what would Jesus do?," Spohn challenges us to ask whether a given value or course of action "rhymes with Jesus." What would a person who tries to embody the virtues of Jesus do in trying to respond well to this or that situation?[8] Likewise saints point to a vast array of virtuous and flawed responses to the call of Christ. Collectively, they are a motley collection of people trying to refract the light of Jesus through their own personalities and contexts. Saints are all over the place, too. They are not just in the stained glass windows in our churches, but they are the people around us who possess traits we find admirable, that speak to us of the presence of the Spirit and the coming of the kingdom. Jesus described the reign of God in terms that are practically useless as action guides—"the reign of God is like a mustard seed"—but in terms that invite us instead to employ all the resources of imagination and energy to cooperate with the coming of that Kingdom.

Reconfiguring Virtues

Virtue ethicist James F. Keenan offers a set of cardinal virtues reconfigured for our time.[9] The word "cardinal" means hinge; cardinal virtues are virtues that contain or embrace all the other virtues that we posit. Keenan suggests that we consider four cardinal virtues of justice, fidelity, self-care, and prudence in light of the ways in which we are relational: we are related to the whole of human society, our capacity for which is perfected by the virtue of justice. We are related specially to those to whom we are closely and individually united—life-partners, children, individual clients, and others—and our capacity to engage those relationships is perfected by fidelity. We are related uniquely to ourselves, and so self-care is a cardinal virtue. Finally, Keenan understands prudence in much the same way as Thomas Aquinas and Aristotle, as the virtue that helps the other virtues to their own ends in given situations for different people.

I would add as a cardinal virtue for spiritual guides, and for other professionals as well, the virtue of trustworthiness, which would include all the distinct professional capacities we should possess, ranging from the specifics of academic preparation to the kinds of skills we need to practice well, like active listening, understanding the limitations of our disciplines, and devotion to continuing education. Most or all of the matter of trustworthiness can be understood in light of the other virtues; I add trustworthiness as a cardinal virtue chiefly to emphasize that virtues in professions are not just the broad human ideals to which we are all called, but include a special category definitive of the profession itself.

THE VIRTUES IN SPIRITUAL GUIDANCE

What does virtue ethics have to offer people who are working in spiritual guidance? Space does not permit a discussion of the full array of virtues for spiritual guides here. Thus, I would like to examine this question in general, but with special attention to virtues that are related to the concerns of accountability and responsibility with which I opened this essay.

The first-order insights of virtue ethics will seem obvious to most people engaged in this kind of work: the key to being an effective spiritual guide is the focus on the spiritual growth and integration of the client, and that growth can aptly be expressed in terms of virtues. But virtue ethics asks of guides: "Who do YOU wish to become in and through your work as a spiritual mentor? How are you pursuing those goals?" According to virtue ethics, the cultivation of a guide's own spiritual life and especially a guide's good relationship to the work is a professional skill. The conscious engagement with our own ongoing formation in the virtues is apt material both for one's own spiritual direction and for consultation/supervision sessions with other formators. Who are those who exemplify what is best about the practice we share? What are the qualities of character that they reflect, and how do we manifest them or try to manifest them, in our own practice? And as Gordon Hilsman proposed, assessing one another's virtues could contribute to preventing errant behavior by professionals.[10]

Prudential Precepts

Once we leave the realm of the cardinal virtues and begin to explore the subsidiary virtues, we begin to see that there is a wide range of virtues appropriate to good spiritual guidance. Further, those subsidiary virtues give rise to a number of "prudential precepts" that are shorthand ways of approaching certain situations that are generally, but not always, consistent with virtue. Those prudential precepts include some of the rules I listed in the second paragraph of this essay, such as "don't date your parishioners." Those prudential precepts are nearly always true, and if a pastor elects to violate a prudential precept, the pastor should do so with caution and self-awareness.

Prudential precepts are not absolute: they hold if and insofar as they are consistent with a virtuous response to a given situation. If pastors could never date parishioners, then single pastors in small rural denominations would often be faced with a choice of violating an absolute, dating outside a tradition that is both personally and professionally important to them, or being forced into unwilling and unchosen celibacy. None of these are appealing options. But are they the only virtuous choices?

An Aristotelian/Thomistic virtue approach invites a closer look at the precept and asks why the prudential precept is usually true. Then the consideration might turn to thinking of the influence pastors have on their parishioners, especially when pastors are seen in light of their presumed connection to the mysterious Voice to which church people tend to be drawn. It is about pastoral power, but it is also about the relationship of pastors to parishioners and to the people they date and how those relationships differ. It is clear to most of us that a person dating the leader of their own church has no pastor—no one in that community, at least, who fills the unique role of pastor. The virtue of fidelity to the parishioner requires, at a minimum, that the pastor consider whether the relationship is so important and so promising that it is worth depriving a parishioner of a pastor.

The virtue of self-care requires, at a minimum, that the pastor seriously examine his or her social life more broadly: Is the pastor so connected to the job that the pastor has no substantive relationships outside the community? Is the pastor using a community member to fulfill true needs that could be better met elsewhere? The virtue of justice to the community requires, at a minimum, that both consider how the pastor's role might be seen to change if some parishioners are seen as dates, and how the pastor's relationship with the whole community might be colored—especially if the relationship ends, and the pastor begins to date another parishioner. And prudence helps the pastor begin to engage the kind of reflection that might help a decision be more mature, fit in better with the pastor's commitment to ministry and the service of the community, and the pastor's vocation generally.

Being Accountable and Responsible

Accountability and responsibility, in an ethics of virtue, can be seen to overlap substantially. Accountability can be seen to be an external force. We are accountable to those who may ask us to give an accounting for our actions or decisions that affect our clients and also for how those decisions reflect or fail to reflect the vision or tradition of service in which we are trained. Accountability may be seen to be an objective constraint on the limits of good practice. Responsibility, on the other hand, implies our own inner sense of the requisites of good practice. Responsible people hold themselves accountable to the standards of the practice. Taken more literally, to be responsible is to be able to respond to situations in ways that are fitting in light of the relationships involved,[11] the potential for growth or harm inherent in the decision, and the effects of those ongoing processes of formation for the guide, the client, the tradition in which they live, and broader society as well. Structures of accountability are like prudential precepts in that, by and large, they reflect the practices of prudent spiritual guides. The most extreme of them—for example, rules against violating the safety of a client—are virtually absolute, while others are less stringent.

In a virtue ethic of spiritual guidance, however, responsibility has much greater reach than accountability: we are responsible to our clients, clearly, in that relationship of fidelity that defines the discipline. Our professional skills, which are partly acquired by and contribute to our professional trustworthiness, serve the client's needs. But we are also responsible to our discipline. For some of us, this implies contribution to the academic resources of the profession or to training new practitioners. For all of us, it implies conducting ourselves with honesty and integrity, sub-virtues both of fidelity in the immediate relationship and justice to others with whom we share our discipline.

At the height of the sex-abuse crisis in the United States, for example, many Roman Catholic priests felt especially suspect because of the pathological behavior of a small percentage of their confreres. The cover-up of the abuses of the sick minority by many bishops contributed to the widespread distrust of Catholic clergy which hampered priests' ability to serve. "Solutions" like requiring that one counsel vulnerable people, especially minors, in a room with a window in the door ignore the real problem, which in this case is a systemic pattern of toleration of abuse and secrecy that eroded, perhaps permanently, the public perception of Catholic clergy. The root problem was vices afflicting leadership—secrecy, clericalism, aversion to real reform, and others—not doors without windows.

Justice, Self Care, and the Temptations of Power

The virtue of justice also raises larger questions about social justice, its role in the lives of those we serve, and how we conduct our professions so that all may benefit, not only an economic or other elite. We are responsible for—and accountable to—those we fail to serve due to social, economic, or other injustices that afflict our societies.

Self-care is a particular concern when thinking about the responsibilities and accountabilities of spiritual guides. If we are seeking an integrated life of virtue ourselves, we cannot fall prey to the failures of self-care that contribute, for example, to the nearly fifty percent burnout rate of new ministers. Often, people new to ministry misunderstand Jesus' command to "deny yourself, take up your cross daily, and follow me," to mean a 24/7 availability that undercuts reasonable self-care. But a workaholic is preaching a different God from the God of Jesus. The exhaustion, harried mien, and short temper of the workaholic speak volumes to the client.

Moreover, the roots of misdeeds by spiritual guides may often be found in bad self-care. Inappropriate relationships are easier to trip into if we are too enmeshed in those we deal with professionally. Boundary violations of all kinds can reflect a needy and unreflective guide more than a deliberate predator. An ethics of virtue invites special attention to the phenomenon of counter-transference, a normal part of counseling relationships. This is a place where attention to good self-care can help the counselor cope responsibly and in ways conducive not only to good professional service of the client, but also to the guide's own self-understanding.

Remember that virtues are prudential means between excess and deficit. Responsibility is no different. Many of the temptations faced by spiritual guides take the form of failure to care for the client enough—to behave irresponsibly. A pastoral minister who just cannot take another conversation with a difficult parishioner may be tempted to tell the parishioner "what I really think." A spiritual director might subtly enjoy being regarded by a directee as uniquely wise and be tempted to drift into self-satisfying over-direction. We hurt others, we sin, more often from power than from weakness. We harm those entrusted to us by failing to care for them rightly. Virtue ethics also opens our eyes to the flip side of this scenario; it is also vicious to feel excessively responsible for the other. In some cases, this leads us to trespass into the sacred ground where God cares best for the client, and our responsibility is, in part, to stay out of God's way. Or a guide might feel responsible for a client whose life spirals sadly into addiction, despair, or even indifference. When guides assume too great a sense of responsibility for such situations, they are unlikely to be able to continue to work without harming themselves and perhaps others in their personal or professional relationships. Like all vices, the vice of over-responsibility is a lie, leading us to believe we have failed, when, if we have done our professional best in light of devotion to the virtues of our practice, we will have done all we can.

CONCLUSION

I have offered a case for a virtue ethics for spiritual guides. Such an approach is especially apt for our work because the witness of our own lives represents the vision of spiritual life that we offer our clients as much, or more, than do our words or professional skills. Virtue ethics invites us to regard professional ethics as a matter of formation of the formator, not only the supervisee or the client. I described virtues as perfections of natural human capacities; to be virtuous is not to be superhuman, it is to be fully alive, thoroughly human in light of our created nature. The perfection of virtue is a process in which we acquire virtues by attentive and reflective practice. We look to moral exemplars to show us what virtues look like in real life, in a myriad of different incarnations. The important role of moral exemplars reminds us that any community's vision of the good life for human beings is liable to be incomplete. Virtue ethics invites us to look beyond our borders to engage the wisdom of other cultures and those we tend to overlook in our own milieu. Ultimately, Christians seek the reign of God, a realm that, in the words of U2 lead singer Bono, is "a place that must be believed to be seen."[12] The reign of God demands our imaginative pursuit of the good life for all.

Spiritual guidance is an arena for the practice of numerous virtues. Responsibility and accountability are reflected in the cultivation of the virtues such as trustworthiness, justice, fidelity, and self-care, all under the guidance of prudence. While accountability implies extrinsic constraints, responsibility is a virtue, a virtue that calls us to manifest the virtues of fidelity, justice, and self-care in particular ways. Considering responsibility as a virtue also opens our eyes to the possibility of "over-responsibility," a harmful assumption that we bear too much of the burden of the spiritual growth of our clients.

Ultimately, spiritual guides are blessed to work daily on holy ground, where the people we serve seek the God we worship. Our pursuit of the virtues of spiritual guides leads us to recall that the service of God is never a zero-sum game, never a benefit of the client at the expense of the guide or of the guide at the expense of the client. God desires and enables the diligent seeker to draw closer to the ground of all being, and in this basic call and response, the guide and the client are on the same path.

Notes

1. See, for example, Richard M. Gula, *Ethics in Pastoral Ministry* (New York: Paulist Press, 1995), in which the framework for theological and ethical decision-making is followed by a discussion of two issues, sexuality (a consideration of boundaries) and confidentiality. Prof. Gula has since written a new work on ministry focusing on questions of justice: *Just Ministry* (New York: Paulist Press, 2010).

2. For essays exploring virtue approaches to pastoral ministry, see James F. Keenan and Joseph Kotva Jr., ed., *Practice What You Preach: Virtues, Ethics and Power in the Lives of Pastoral Ministers and Their Congregations* (New York: Sheed and Ward, 1999). For a more in-depth introduction to virtue ethics as a method for Christian ethical reflection, see Joseph Kotva Jr., *The Christian Case for Virtue Ethics* (Washington, DC: Georgetown Univ. Press, 1997).

3. The importance of role models in education is well known. See, e.g., Plato's *Republic*. For contemporary analysis, see A. A. Bucher, "The Influence of Models in Forming Moral Identity," *International Journal of Educational Research* 27, no. 7 (1997): 619–27. For a summary, see Daniel Rose, "The Potential of Role-Model Education," *The Encyclopedia of Informal Education* Web site, (2004), http://www.infed.org/biblio/role_model_education.htm (accessed 18 March 2010).

4. Aristotle, *Nicomachean Ethics*, trans. Terence Irwin, 2nd ed. (Indianapolis, IN: Hackett Publishing Co., 1999), 1103a.

5. Gerard Manley Hopkins, "As Kingfishers Catch Fire, Dragonflies Draw Flame," *Poems of Gerard Manley Hopkins* (London: Humphrey Milford, 1918), line 9.

6. Aristotle *Nicomachean Ethics,* 1095b.

7. All other things are not always equal—virtuous people can experience random misfortune just like the vicious can, of course. However, according to Aristotle, virtues assist in dealing with misfortune when it strikes, allowing us to cope with as much dignity and good-heartedness as the circumstances allow. To be, for example, impoverished and virtuous is better than to be impoverished and vicious—the virtuous impoverished person will be happier. Poverty is bad, but virtue always helps.

8. See William C. Spohn, *Go and Do Likewise: Jesus and Ethics* (New York: Continuum, 2000).

9. James F. Keenan, "Proposing Cardinal Virtues," *Theological Studies* 56, no. 4 (1995): 709–29.

10. Gordon J. Hilsman, "Tandem Roles of Written Standards and Personal Virtue in Appraising Professional Practice," *Reflective Practice* 30 (2010): 54–57.

11. See, e.g., H. R. Niebuhr, *The Responsible Self* (Louisville, KY: Westminster John Knox Press, 1999).

12. U2, "Walk On*,"* on *All That You Can't Leave Behind*, Universal Import, 2001.

List of Contributors

The late Walter J. Burghardt was a long-time editor of *Theological Studies* and theologian in residence at Georgetown University.

Charles E. Curran is the Elizabeth Scurlock University Professor of Human Values at Southern Methodist University.

Mary Frohlich is associate professor of spirituality at the Chicago Catholic Union.

Lisa A. Fullam is associate professor of moral theology at the Jesuit School of Theology of Santa Clara University.

Colleen M. Griffith is associate professor of the practice of theology and Faculty Director of Spiritual Studies at the School of Theology and Ministry of Boston College.

Richard M. Gula is emeritus professor of moral theology at the Franciscan School of Theology.

Kenneth R. Himes is associate professor of moral theology at Boston College.

The late Ada María Isasi-Díaz was professor emerita of ethics and theology at Drew University.

James Keating is Director of Theological Formation in the Institute for Priestly Formation, Creighton University.

James F. Keenan is the Founder's Professor in Theology at Boston College.

Enda McDonagh is emeritus professor of moral theology at St. Patrick's Seminary, Maynooth, Ireland.

Mark O'Keefe is associate professor of moral theology and former president-rector of the St. Meinrad School of Theology and Seminary.

Donna L. Orsuto is the Co-Founder and Director of the Lay Center at Foyer Unitas in Rome, Italy.

Norbert J. Rigali is professor emeritus of theology and religious studies at the University of San Diego.

The late William C. Spohn was Augustine Cardinal Bea, SJ, Distinguished Professor of Theological Ethics at Santa Clara University.